Open access edition supported by the National Endowment for the Humanities /
Andrew W. Mellon Foundation Humanities Open Book Program.

© 2019 Johns Hopkins University Press
Published 2019

Johns Hopkins University Press
2715 North Charles Street
Baltimore, Maryland 21218-4363
www.press.jhu.edu

ISBN-13: 978-1-4214-3449-0 (open access)
ISBN-10: 1-4214-3449-0 (open access)

ISBN-13: 978-1-4214-3447-6 (pbk. : alk. paper)
ISBN-10: 1-4214-3447-4 (pbk. : alk. paper)

ISBN-13: 978-1-4214-3448-3 (electronic)
ISBN-10: 1-4214-3448-2 (electronic)

This page supersedes the copyright page included in the original publication of this work.

Rousseau's Venetian Story

by the same author

Julie or La Nouvelle Héloise:
A Synthesis of Rousseau's Thought (1749–1759)

Robert Charbonneau et la création romanesque
(Une étude de textes)

Saint-Denys Garneau: Art et réalisme

(in preparation)
Art and Truth in Rousseau's Confessions

ROUSSEAU'S
VENETIAN STORY

AN ESSAY UPON ART
AND TRUTH IN
LES CONFESSIONS

by *Madeleine B. Ellis*

The Johns Hopkins Press, Baltimore

To My Mother
Lilian Fitzmaurice Ellis

Preface

For more than two hundred years the Western world has kept its eyes fixed upon the image of Rousseau. We are strangely mesmerized by the gaze that meets our own across the centuries, and are moved by thoughts that stir with new life as we respond to them. This ardent contemplation and perpetual dialogue is not confined to the writer's professed admirers. Their fervor, intense as it is, is equaled and even exceeded by that of his detractors. If this were not the case, surely we would relegate him to the dust. Instead, generations of serious scholars spend precious years scrutinizing the minutest aspects of his work and biography. Men of every nation and creed, of the most divergent interests and opposing convictions, devote their lives to the study of Jean-Jacques Rousseau. The bibliography thus accumulated is the most imposing monument that could ever be erected to the memory of a man.

What singular fascination can account for this continuous meditative dialogue with the past? Which view of Rousseau's many-sided personality can explain it? Are we perturbed by the philosopher whose bold efforts to apprehend the truth and whose explorations in the realms of thought led him further than he dreamed in a reappraisal of things that finally shattered the old order and prepared the way for the new? Or are we roused by the moralist whose impassioned indictment of the senses sprang from a heart all too sensitive to their charms and whose tragic youth taught him at last the need for asceticism in man's eternal quest for happiness? For the author of *Emile* "had learned wisdom in the school of misfortune." Or is our imagination caught by the historical figure of one who was a witness of his time and whose testimony we can hardly resist pondering, whether we trust his literal veracity or not? Each of these facets of Rousseau's brooding spirit is a theme for the restless and ceaseless searches of thinkers, historians, and critics through the years, and any or every aspect he assumes could justify his phenomenal ascendancy today.

Yet this is not the whole story. Surely these multiple, particular profiles of the man do not entirely explain the universality and durability of his appeal for people who share or do not share his ideas, and who approve or do not approve of his morals. Above and beyond these controversial features is a power that encompasses them all and from which they derive their extraordinary effect. To be sure, Rousseau is a philosopher and a man of ideas. But he is also a great writer whose genius consists mainly in his mode of composition. Indeed felicity of form accounts to a very large extent for the prodigious vitality that saves him from oblivion, since ill-expressed ideas are soon forgotten, whether they are good or bad, but well-expressed ideas, whatever their value, are not so easily dismissed. Rousseau the writer enjoys that faculty whereby a man of rare personal endowments scrupulously renders his every impression, inclination, emotion, and idea as the pure and perfect likeness of himself and no one else, investing with new meaning even the most commonplace premise and uncertain conclusion, as well as all the wisdom or folly between them. Throughout his work expression is the ornament of doctrine and lends persuasion to thoughts and sentiments. By expression I mean not merely the words in which concepts are framed, but also the concrete form with which they are clothed, and especially the effective use of imagery. There are striking examples even in his most abstract works, like *Du Contrat social*, but the best are to be found in his other books such as *Emile*, *Les Confessions*, and *Julie*, the novel which I have already studied from this point of view. In *Emile* he says openly that we must clothe reason with a body if we would make it felt. In fact so consequential is the formal presentation of feeling and thought in all his writings that one might wonder whether the true extent of his meaning and historical position can be fully grasped without an understanding of his artistic technique, any more than life may be interpreted without some perception, however elementary, of the symbolism residing in figures and events, that is, of the relationship existing between the form of things and their content.

Someone will say, of course, that these reflections are rather obvious and unnecessary. Rousseau's art is, after all, his least controversial aspect and the object of universal approval. Indeed readers of all persuasions may protest that, whatever his weaknesses may be, they are hardly artistic, that his literary virtues are unquestionable, that his eloquence is indisputable, in fine that his reputation as an artist is sufficiently well established after two hundred years. This is clearly so by common consent. It would be as unrealistic to challenge his prestige as a writer as it would be to question his fame as a man of ideas. I do not propose to be so bold. But just as the thinker requires study and exposition, so does the writer. Yet, curiously enough, while the ideas of the one have kindled the most violent reactions throughout the world of space and time, the literary and artistic intentions of the other have been shrouded in almost unbroken silence. Conceivably this is because of the revolutionary character of opinions that reflect the agitated spirit of the period and distract us from all other considerations. Whatever the reason, there is still a sad dearth of studies on the writer's art. It has either been ignored or accepted uncritically, as though there were no need to understand the principles and methods underlying the formulation of thought and modifying, even determining, its very essence and its peculiar quality.

In the case of *Les Confessions*, however, Rousseau's art has not been entirely ignored. In the Pléiade edition of his complete works, currently being published, there is a general introduction to the subject containing seven pages devoted to the twelve books, valuable pages but all too few. They are signed by Messieurs Bernard Gagnebin and Marcel Raymond, who pose the real problem of the autobiography in the following terms:

> People have often considered Rousseau's memoirs with the eye of an examining magistrate who is bent upon convicting the author. For example, they have sought to know who presented a version of events closer to the truth, Jean-Jacques or Madame d'Epinay. A very legitimate preoccupation, an indispensable task. But *Les Confessions* is also a work of art.

Unfortunately all too often readers consider the book mainly as a piece of apologetics instead of the skillful narration it really is. If we treat it in this manner, then the lamentable passion for positivistic facts and equally positivistic judgments and the mania for determining the villain or victim of the piece and for indulging in personal moral speculation blinds us to the artistic merits upon which Rousseau's reputation is firmly founded and, worse still, deprives us of the aesthetic pleasure that fine writing always provides.

In our righteous or self-righteous indignation, we have forgotten that, if Rousseau is in effect the writer he is reputed to be, then he must fulfill the initial purpose of any work of art, which is to please those who are capable of responding. No other purpose, apologetic, political, religious, or moral can take precedence over this, for only after he has brought pleasure can he attain any other aim, or even win a hearing in the minds and hearts of men. He knew this as well as anyone when he wrote the following passage at the end of the fourth book of *Emile*, where the adolescent undertakes the study of aesthetics:

> The knowledge of what people may find pleasing or dis-
> pleasing is necessary not only to anyone who needs their
> help, but also to anyone who wishes to be of use to them;
> you must please them if you would do them service and the
> art of writing is no idle pursuit if it is used to make men
> hear the truth.

Since, after two centuries, Rousseau suffers no lack of
readers, it is incontestable that he achieves the objective
of every art form and succeeds in pleasing. But we urgently
need to know by what means he accomplishes this, especially because he does so whether his theme is controversial, ideological, or moral, whether it is in itself edifying, indecent, beautiful, monstrous, attractive, or repugnant. How
does he do it? And from our point of view, how can we
explain the fact that, if we possess taste and maturity of
literary judgment, we may delight in his creativeness and
derive aesthetic pleasure from his writing without sharing
his views—or airing our own—on ethics, religion, politics,
or other polemical issues, and without passing judgment
on the writer as a man or even as a thinker? To show
whence this pleasure proceeds and how the author fulfills
the essential requirement of any genuine work of art and
literature, we must probe the secrets of the man of letters.
This is an arduous but imperative task. Unfortunately it
has been neglected or ignored for the sake of preoccupations
of a juridical, ethical, or philosophical order.

The present study does not presume to make provision
for such a serious lacuna in the Rousseau bibliography. At
most it may perhaps serve to draw attention to the problem it poses and to stimulate interest and further inquiry
among critics. The value of its conclusions about the art of
Les Confessions and the role of truth therein will have to
be determined by the readers. Probably its significance is
to be sought in a shift of emphasis, or if I may quote a
correspondent, in the presentation of Rousseau "as an
artist who lived and thought, as opposed to the traditional

view of Rousseau as a thinker who incidentally was a creative writer."

The style of this essay may also have a certain significance. It is carefully adapted to the themes of art and truth, and is therefore variable. Passages of exposition presenting Rousseau's own texts strive to reflect his original tone and attitudes; others recording historical and factual investigations demand more objective expression; while still others registering literary implications and interpretations, which are hardly revealed in all their fullness to the dispassionate intellect alone, require to be cast in a more personal mold. These variations in style are among the most unconventional aspects of the study and will therefore encounter most resistance on the part of anyone accustomed to a more rigid and consistent scientific form. Yet in reality they correspond to the various aspects and diverse functions of literary criticism itself which, after all, is not of such an uncomplicated nature as to be forever content with one and the same monotonous, often colorless and insipid, pedantic style. Such a presentation not only fails to satisfy the real needs of criticism but it also repels all readers except highly trained specialists. One might therefore be justified in questioning whether the interests of creative erudition are best served when it is embalmed and entombed, so to speak, in that manner. In the light of sweeping changes now being wrought in all spheres of life, thought, and education, some new experiments in scholarly methods may be advisable. The present study is one such experiment. It is an attempt on the part of modern scholarship to emerge from the rarefied atmosphere of esoteric research and to dwell among us. It seeks to serve the manifold purposes of its genre and at the same time to make itself readily comprehensible not merely to professors and professionals, but to educated people in general who may not aspire to be either, but who are nevertheless genuinely interested in literary problems.

Madeleine B. Ellis

Acknowledgments

The author wishes to express her appreciation to the directors and staff of the following institutions: the University of Montréal Library, McGill University Library, the University of Toronto Library, the Library of Congress, the Bibliothèque Nationale, the Bibliothèque Publique et Universitaire de Genève, the personnel of the archives listed in the bibliography, and The Johns Hopkins Press, particularly the editors Mr. J. G. Goellner and Mrs. Elizabeth Brown, the latter for her scrupulous assistance in preparing the manuscript for printing.

She also wishes to acknowledge her indebtedness to Monsieur Bernard Gagnebin, Professor and Dean of the Faculty of Letters at the University of Geneva, for his kind offices in providing access to valuable material; to Dr. A. F. B. Clark, Professor Emeritus of French of the University of British Columbia, and Professor C. D. Rouillard, Chairman of the Department of French Literature, University College, University of Toronto, for their stimulating interest in the manuscript; to Professor Henri M. Peyre of Yale University, for his good advice and generous appreciation of the problems of authorship. In fine, she would record her lasting debt of gratitude to the late Dr. J. S. Will, Professor Emeritus of the University of Toronto, who understood the real nature of literature in its relations to art and beauty.

CONTENTS

Preface, vii

Introduction, 1

I.   Les Confessions:
     Prologue to the Story, 14

II. *The Venetian Story, 33*

III. *Confessions of the Epilogue, 152*

IV. *Conclusion, 172*

Selected Bibliography, 184

Index, 191

"L'art d'écrire n'est rien
moins qu'une étude oiseuse
quand on l'emploie à faire
écouter la vérité."

—Emile

"J'écris moins l'histoire de
ces évenemens en eux-mêmes
('les évenemens de ma vie')
que celle de l'état de mon âme
à mesure qu'ils sont arrivés."

—Ebauches des Confessions

"C'est l'histoire de mon âme
que j'ai promise. ... "

—Les Confessions

Introduction

Of all Rousseau's works, the one that owes most to the passions and prejudices of its author, and therefore suffers most from those of its readers, is *Les Confessions*. His other books, expounding unconventional political, religious, or moral ideas in an apparently impartial manner, have given rise to controversy. But this one, where the same ideas are implied in highly subjective attitudes that relate them to the writer's intimate life and character, has produced even harsher disputes. A clash of personalities is always more bitter than a difference of opinion. The conflict is all the greater in the case of readers of the autobiography since they are more numerous than those of Rousseau's other books. Besides, no one even tries to read this work unemotionally. Probably it is not meant to be so read, since it was not written dispassionately. Yet, if we are to understand and judge what we are reading, then it behooves us to make at least some effort to master our spontaneous reactions and grasp the writer's meaning, in somewhat the same way as he has undoubtedly disciplined himself to convey it.

A large number of readers think of the book as being mainly an inventory of past events, rather than a record of feelings, since they expect a biography, even an autobiography, to be based upon objective fact and therefore to have historical value in the scientific sense of the word. Critics invariably begin their analyses of *Les Confessions* by verifying the writer's statements and then they proceed

to evaluate him as a man, as an historian, and as a philosopher. This method has its advantages, for we can not be
indifferent to the relationship that his statements bear
to reality. But it also has grave dangers, for discrepancies
may be more apparent than real and less incriminating
than they appear. In spite of the dangers of the "verification" method, it presided at the conception of this essay
at a time when I was engaged in a vast collation of *Les
Confessions* and contemporary documents including the
correspondence. The collation resulted in an extensive
comparative study from which the present essay has been
detached and which can scarcely be satisfactorily concluded until we have an adequate scholarly edition of
Rousseau's complete correspondence. The continual process
of relating memoirs to original epistolary material and
vice versa brings to light many similarities between the
two bodies of writing, but there are also differences and it
is these that create problems for the scholar.

The question is: what is the nature of these discrepancies,
and to what motive on the writer's part may they be attributed? They fall into various categories, including factual,
ideological, and linguistic, and may be classified as voluntary or involuntary. The ideological and linguistic ones
are probably voluntary, while the factual or historical ones
may or may not be. The latter are at the origin of most
disputes, not if they are quite obviously due to uninten-
tional lapses of memory, but rather if they are apparently
deliberate. If they belong to this unhappy category, then
we traditionally, but erroneously, draw two conclusions
at once: we infer that the writer of *Les Confessions* has
willfully falsified the facts of actuality, and we deduce
that he has done so for the sake of an apologetic purpose,
to vindicate himself. It never even occurs to us that the
archives may be false, or incomplete, which amounts
to the same thing. Or if they are indeed as beyond reproach as we like to imagine, and if the autobiographer is
really responsible for the discrepancy, it never enters our

minds that he may have had some other reason for modifying, without falsifying, the facts of actuality in his narration. Why is this? What is the reason for our customary
confidence in archives and epistles, as opposed to literature
and art? And how are we to explain our eternal distrust of
artists? There is probably one answer to both questions.
Our dispositions spring from the conviction that artists
are sensitive, passionate creatures, dreamers and vision-
aries. This is no doubt true. Yet it is also true, to varying
degrees of course, not only of *littérateurs* and artists in
general, but of everyone, including archivists, letter writers,
reporters, and historians, who are hardly "scientific" even
if they pretend to be, but who reveal themselves much
more deviously than the writer of *Les Confessions*. This is
a fact, verifiable in the archives of Paris and Venice, and
we are wrong to overlook it in our evaluation of the book.
Sometimes the memorialist is actually "telling the truth,"
and the archivist or epistoler is a victim of passion, ignorance, weakness, or intrigue. There is much more to be said.
If the autobiographer has deliberately modified external
facts, he may not have done so for apologetic motives.
His modifications, which are not necessarily distortions,
are usually not of an historical or ideological order at all.
They are almost always literary and aesthetic. If we refuse
to admit this as a possibility, and if we insist upon some
other explanation for them, then we imply that there is no
real distinction between a writer and a recorder and we
intimate that the one is as much a slave of actuality as the
other. At the same time, we consciously ignore the real
presence of literary intentions and processes which are
brought to our notice in the memoirs by a comparison
with correspondence, and which alone can explain the
many differences between them. For the *littérateur*, these
peculiarly literary differences are the most important of
all. The discovery of them is the supreme advantage to be
gained from a serious work of collation. The autobiographer
has quite obviously imposed form upon existence in the

interests of order and harmony and, in doing so, has given uncommon relief to the message contained in his book.

In this comparative study I have attempted to elucidate some of Rousseau's artistic principles in *Les Confessions* and in particular their implications with respect to the truth of the work. I have done so by an analysis of the Venetian story, together with its prologue and epilogue, in the seventh book. This story was recently proposed by the editors of the Pléiade Library of Rousseau's complete works as a rich field of study for an appreciation of the memorialist's art.[1] The seventh book is also valuable for a study of the interrelations between art and truth, both because of its obvious intrinsic worth and the copious documentation available on the subject. Its brilliant presentation of a year in Venice is a precious source of light for the searcher groping his way through the darkness of the long, somber years between the sunny idyll of the Charmettes and the blaze of genius fully revealed. Telling the tale approximately twenty-five years after the event, Rousseau devotes vast space to it, giving it more detailed treatment than most comparable intervals in his career, as though he regarded it as one of the weightiest. Moreover, for the past sixty years or more historians have been exploring the circumstances of those twelve months and unraveling the sequence of events of 1743 to 1744. They have disclosed abundant objective biographical material and official archives, unmatched in any other period of the author's life, and have provided us with a record of facts which are vitally significant in his later development. This wealth of historical data, together with Rousseau's *Correspondance générale*, including the so-called *Venetian Letters*, supplemented by the recently published *Venetian Despatches*, and completed by the *Correspondance complète*

---

[1] Jean-Jacques Rousseau, *Oeuvres complètes*, Bibliothèque de la Pléiade, I (Paris: Gallimard, 1959), p. xlii. In subsequent notes the term "*O.C.*, Pléiade," with volume and page number but without further bibliographical information, refers to this edition.

now in the course of publication,[2] makes it possible to reconstruct and even resurrect the actuality of that momentous year. It also enables us to grasp realities which, through skillful methods, are transmuted into art in the Venetian story of *Les Confessions*.

After these pronouncements, is it necessary to warn the reader not to expect another biographical treatment of Rousseau's diplomatic experience in Venice? Previous critics who have reviewed that experience have, without exception, made a study not of the Venetian story of *Les Confessions* but of its historical sources in life. There are many fine histories of that kind and I refer the reader to them and to the primary sources upon which they are based. He will then see how indebted I am to the traditional interpretations which have their obvious place and value and from which any less conventional treatment must inevitably take its starting point even though its goal may be as different from theirs as art differs from life. The goal that I propose herein is to discover the relative importance of art and truth to Rousseau as a literary man, and especially to the writer of the Venetian story of *Les Confessions*. This is the first primarily literary study of the famous narrative.

The form I have chosen as suitable to illustrate the author's aesthetic principles and their relationship to truth is a juxtaposition of the story, as an integral and inseparable part of the seventh book of *Les Confessions*, with the evidence supplied by contemporary records. The latter include, in addition to the above-mentioned correspondence, all his personal letters and other writings dating from the years 1742 to 1749,[3] the period treated in

[2] R. A. Leigh (ed.), *Correspondance complète de Jean Jacques Rousseau*, Vols. I, II (Geneva: Institut et Musée Voltaire, 1965). In subsequent notes the term "C.C." with volume and page number refers to this edition of the correspondence. For the "Dépêches de Venise" see *O.C.*, Pléiade, III, 1043–1234.

[3] For the date 1742 see *O.C.*, Pléiade, I, 1377–1378 *n*6 (to p. 282). The writings of 1742 to 1749 include: *Epître à M. Parisot*; publication of *Epître à M. Bordes*; *Projet concernant de nouveaux signes pour la musique*; *Dissertation*

the seventh book. First I have tried to extract the quintessence of his narrative, remaining as faithful as possible to the spirit and attitudes of the original text. Then I have sought to derive the most pertinent substance from all related documents, but only the most pertinent, taking pains not to lose sight of the real links between art and history by indulging in a flood of meaningless detail of mere anecdotal interest. In a word, I have investigated and set forth all the known historical circumstances that inspired the famous story of the autobiography, recounting them in the chronological order in which they have slowly come to light, and fitting the odd fragments of evidence into a pattern in much the same way as one matches together the pieces of a picture puzzle. This dramatic disclosure of factual data has two advantages. It recaptures for the reader some of the researcher's suspense and excitement as each new discovery is recorded and added to the sum of available facts. It also serves to put both researcher and reader on guard against the false impressions and erroneous rash judgments to which incomplete knowledge has led in the past and may lead us still, for our historical puzzle inevitably remains incomplete. I have simply tried to sketch it as it has emerged so far, in order to relate it to the work of art, where alone completeness can be found in the end. In this way, I have made a comparison between the two, handling the material in sections that are naturally suggested by the literary and historical texts and do no violence to either. I have noted all the discrepancies and differences, similarities and points of contact. If Rousseau alters the facts, I say so; if he does not, I feel equally free to say so, not for the sake of making moral judgments, for that is not my business, nor even in the interests of truth

---

sur la musique moderne; retouching of *Narcisse*; *Les Muses galantes*; *Fragment d'une épître à M. Bordes*; work on *Les Fêtes de Ramire*; *Institutions chimiques*; *L'Allée de Sylvie*; *L'Engagement téméraire*; *Le Persifleur*; articles on music signed "S" in *Encyclopédie, ou Dictionnaire universel des arts et des sciences, traduit des Dictionnaires anglais de Chambers et de Harris, avec des additions.*

for that is not my purpose. I do so to follow the close
interweaving of art and truth in the memoirs, to trace the
intimate and intricate interrelations of the two and to
extricate a few fundamental ideas on the writer as a man
of letters.

At the same time I have sought to show how the author's
work, his life, and his thought are brought into new perspective by an examination of his artistic methods. For example,
a comprehension of the various modes of artistic procedure
employed in the seventh book brings with it a realization
that the experiences narrated therein, and mainly those of
1743 to 1744 in Venice, are prophetic of the tumultuous
outburst of the *Discours* in October, 1749, when the name
of Rousseau broke upon the world. The reader, conscious of
art forms, becomes aware of the explosive potentialities of
almost all the situations of those portentous years, so that
both *Discours* appear as the inevitable culmination of the
past rather than the effect of an apocalyptic vision.
Throughout the seventh book the artist is everywhere
pointing to the handwriting on the wall, which we may
read as easily as Daniel did if we are as familiar with our
writer as the prophet was with his. Nor is it necessary, as
some readers have supposed, to have recourse to any hypothetical reconstitution of states of soul in order to foresee
the violent eruption.[4] Art alone shows clearly, for example,
that the tears Rousseau sheds over the Venetian Zulietta
are the same tears he sheds in 1749 on the road to Vincennes, apparently under the stress of some quasi-religious
revelation.[5] In fact, the Zulietta scenes and others too
confirm indications contained in the correspondence and in
contemporary writings to prove what certain critics have
long suspected, namely that there was no real cleavage

---

[4] Referring to Rousseau as he appears in the concluding pages of Book VII,
the Pléiade editors write: " ... un mal sourd le travaille, une insatisfaction
profonde que nous sommes réduits à reconstituer en partie par hypothèse, mais
qui seule explique l'explosion d'octobre 1749" (*O.C.*, Pléiade, I, 1369).

[5] For references to Zulietta in this study see the index.

in his psychic and intellectual development in 1749, but that there was rather continuity with the past. The same scenes also prove what no one suspects, namely that Rousseau himself admits this continuity very subtly in *Les Confessions*. Nor does he do so in isolated or unrelated instances, but rather in the cumulative effect of a series of tableaux that lead us straight to that of Vincennes. Yet we see this only if we read the book as literature and pierce the symbols abounding in its pages. Thus aesthetic appreciation may deepen our insight into the author's ideas and personality, besides cultivating an awareness of his powers as a writer.

It is precisely to focus interest on the art of *Les Confessions* that I have selected the title *Rousseau's Venetian Story*, since his story is to be found only in that book. The title seeks to draw attention to artistic activity dating from 1769 rather than to the actuality of 1743 to 1744, or even 1742 to 1749, except in so far as actuality is one of the sources of aesthetic creativity. I propose a critical evaluation of literature, not an historical restatement of life except inasmuch as life provides the theme of literature and inasmuch as a comparison of the two helps to disengage and define the intangibles of art that serve to recompose and impart meaning to vital experience. *Rousseau's Venetian Story* is a study of literary methods that evolved through a lifetime of discipline and were perfected in the effective handling of great scenes in *Les Confessions*. In this way it seeks to shed light upon the extraordinary prestige of the memoirs as a piece of literature.

In analyzing the Venetian story of *Les Confessions* we are in fact defining some of the last repercussions of the Venetian episode in Rousseau's life and work. When he was composing the book at the age of fifty-seven and looking back over the years at himself as a young man of hardly more than thirty, he was clearly conscious of the breadth and grandeur of the theme. He knew that the course of his fate and the trend of his thought had been largely fashioned in Venice, for his sojourn in that city had already furnished him with the essence and much of the substance of numerous works in the past. A cursory glance can recreate the memorialist's point of view, to show that the influence of the Venetian experience was by no means confined to the inspiration of the famous story in the autobiography. In Rousseau's life, that experience was a source of heartache and tragedy. It may even have been the origin of his spiritual disquietude and persecution mania, the obsession that he was continually surrounded by spies.[6] Indeed, it is known that he was closely watched in Venice by secret inquisitorial agents who reported his movements to the powerful and dreaded Council of Three. Moreover it is possible and even probable that the strenuous journey to Italy occasioned the initial onslaught of a physical illness, a nephritic condition, which plagued him to the end of his days.[7]

But whatever the role of the Venetian period in his personal life, its pre-eminent position in the molding of his thought and art could scarcely be doubted. Indeed it appears as a wellhead from which many springs of inspiration flowing through his works took their source. There is hardly one of his books which does not call forth memories of Venice or owe to the Venetian days some germ of artistic or philosophic production. If it is true, as someone

[6] The Pléiade editors see traces of a persecution mania in the hero of the memoirs after his return from Venice to Paris, and particularly in his reaction to Rameau's antagonism; see *O.C.*, Pléiade, I, 1411 *n*3 (to p. 338).

[7] This statement has the support of Rousseau's own testimony in the eighth book of *Les Confessions* and in his correspondence: *ibid.*, p. 361, and *C.C.*, I, 194–195, letter from Rousseau to M. de Conzié, September 21, 1743 (when he wrote this letter he was very ill, but had recovered by October 5: *ibid.*, p. 198); see also *C.C.*, II, 377–378 (Appendix 123), letter (perhaps apocryphal) from Rousseau to Altuna, June 30, 1748; and cf. *ibid.*, pp. 108–109, letter from Rousseau to Mme de Warens, August 26, 1748. According to *Les Confessions* he also suffered a violent attack in the summer of 1749. His enemies identify the illness as venereal disease.

has said, that had Rousseau made a success of the diplomatic career in Venice, he might never have written his *Discours*, *Emile*, or *Du Contrat social*, it is equally true that, if he had not gone there, he would never have written these or any of his works exactly as we know them.[8] For instance his bitter disillusionment in the diplomatic service was an indispensable spiritual preparation for the two *Discours* in which this cultured man, devoted to literature and music, denounces the arts for fostering moral corruption in a highly developed society where prestige and privilege bear no clear relationship to natural inequalities. Fortunately he could denounce the arts for their supposed evil social effects without feeling bound to renounce them. And so his initiation into the delights of Italian music at Venice proved to be an equally indispensable artistic preparation, not merely for his violently derogatory *Lettre sur la musique française* almost a decade later, but also for his dictionary in praise of the melodies of Italy composed a quarter of a century afterwards.

At the height of his powers, *Julie*, *Emile*, and other publications illustrate the inestimable value of Venetian reminiscences for the writer. For example we are able to trace certain evocations of landscape and states of soul in the novel to his travels and to his contact with Italian writers like Petrarch, Tasso, Metastasio, and even Machiavelli.[9] We may also ask ourselves whether Julie, the name child of

[8] Most critics recognize the influence of Venice on the political ideas of the *Discours, Emile,* or *Du Contrat social*; see, for example, *O.C.*, Pléiade, I, 1389 n5 (to p. 297); cf. Roland Derche, "Autour du séjour de J.-J. Rousseau à Venise. La politique et le caractère du Comte de Montaigu, ambassadeur à Venise de 1743–1749," *Annales de l'Université de Grenoble* (Nouvelle Série) Section Lettres-Droit, I (1924). Rousseau says in the memoirs (IX) that he would have entered public life if Montaigu had been reasonable.

[9] The influence of his travels can be seen in *Julie*, letters XXI and XXIII of the first part. For Italian influences on Rousseau see Carlo Culcasi, *Gli influssi italiani nell'opera di G. G. Rousseau* (Rome: Dante Alighieri Society, [1907]), and Maurice Mignon, *Les Affinités intellectuelles de l'Italie et de la France* (Paris: Hachette, 1923).

the Venetian Zulietta, does not find in her a counterpart, just as Emile and Sophie find their counterparts in Lord John and Miss Lucy of the Venetian sojourn.[10] Moreover, in *Emile* there is a long and valuable exposition of political ideas that germinated in Venice.[11] In fact it is commonly known—and this is now confirmed by the newly published *Venetian Despatches*—that the city played a leading part in the genesis of Rousseau's political thought, mainly in *Du Contrat social* but also in lesser works such as his studies on the Abbé de Saint-Pierre[12] and *Les Considérations sur le gouvernement de Pologne*,[13] where he pays tribute to the enlightenment of Venetian statesmen. By his own admission it was in Venice that he conceived the original idea of his *Institutions politiques* from which he derived the treatise *Du Contrat social*.[14] In that dissertation he meditates profoundly on the peculiar combination of aristocratic and democratic elements which he perceived in the structure of the Venetian government. These meditations, like almost all his ideas, were inspired by personal involvement, since in Venice, for the one and only time in his career, he was actually engaged in affairs of state. Besides, there, as in his native Geneva to which he compares the Venetian re-

[10] J.-J. Rousseau, *Oeuvres complètes*, II (Paris: Hachette, 1885–1898), 443. Here, in the fifth book of *Emile*, Rousseau writes: "Il est temps de finir. Ramenons lord John à miss Lucy, c'est-à-dire Emile à Sophie." Hereafter, all references to the Hachette edition of Rousseau's complete works will be indicated by the term "*O.C.*, Hachette" followed by volume and page number. Since only three of the proposed five volumes of the Pléiade edition have appeared to date, it is necessary to supplement this edition by an older one.

[11] This is to be found in the fifth book of *Emile* in *O.C.*, Hachette, II, 429–439. The note in the fourth book on the doge, cited as an example of the value of ceremonial in public life (*ibid.*, p. 295 *n*1), is discussed below.

[12] These studies were made about 1754–1756. For references to Venice see *O.C.*, Pléiade, III, 623 (*Polysynodie*, Chapter V), 633 (*Polysynodie*, Chapter XI).

[13] *Ibid.*, p. 983 (Chapter VII of the work).

[14] *O.C.*, Pléiade, I, 404. There are several direct references to Venice in *Du Contrat social*: *ibid.*, III, 396 (Book III, Chapter I *n*1); 407 (Book III, Chapter V *n*2); 421 (Book III, Chapter X *n*1); 442–443 (Book IV, Chapter III); 453 (Book IV, Chapter IV); 454–455 (Book IV, Chapter V).

public, he lived in a city-state, and he always favored the
city-state as a political ideal. Obviously then the year
in Venice produced the most far-reaching vibrations in his
life and work. What wonder if, in his memoirs, he gave to
his sojourn in the city of the doges a place of prominence
out of all proportion to the actual time he spent there and
to the role he played, bringing into high relief the central
drama and turning point that shaped his future course. In
so doing he proved once again the signal importance of
that drama which could offer a rich vein of precious material
for the crowning masterpiece of his writings, the book of
Les Confessions.[15]

In this book culminating a long career, the Venetian
affair, instead of being merely a part of existence or furnishing stimuli for the formation of ideas and tastes, for
the creation of literary themes and characters, or for the
construction of a philosophy, is itself wholly transposed
into a new form. The entire experience, which contained
the essence of so many pages famous in literature and
thought, is ingeniously gathered into a synthesis, filled with
motifs reminiscent of many books yet different from them
all. In this synthesis the close interrelation of the parts and
the breadth of thought holding them together reveal the
value of the Venetian period, not merely for the writer of one
or other of a dozen works from the *Discours* to the memoirs,
but for the writer of them all who is the author of *Les
Confessions*. In the Venetian story we see before us the
thinker, the moralist, and the man, but especially the
artist. More than anything else, this story is undeniable
proof of Rousseau's mastery of style and imagery that
imparts distinction even to the most commonplace events
and ideas dispersed at random through insignificant
archives and epistles. It casts bright light upon the secret

[15] Previous critics, for example Lemaître and Derche, have believed that
Rousseau dwells at length upon the Venetian period in *Les Confessions* in
order to contrast it with his earlier vagabond life and to show his enemies that
he had once occupied an honorable place in society.

of his prestige, not merely in the realm of letters but in every sphere he touched. And so this essay, without ignoring Rousseau personally, morally, or ideologically, is primarily a study of the artist who, in an act of creation, has produced for our delight and enrichment a work of ordered beauty in which the world of the spirit finds perfect expression in the world of matter.

I

Les Confessions:
Prologue to the Story

Les Confessions is a work of ageless beauty made to stir the sensibilities of generations yet unborn. Enchased in this work is the image of a man, the writer himself, as fascinated by his own reflection as was Narcissus, the theme of his first literary work many years before.[1] The self-portrait finds a complement in a picture of mankind and of the world of men and implies a philosophy of life as well. These are the traditional themes of literature and art. In using them Rousseau has all the universe of spirit and of matter at his disposal, for it is the substance from which, like any artist, he creates his portrait of a man among men.

PROBLEMS OF ART AND TRUTH

Yet the autobiographer who wrote his book only ten years after he had pledged his life to what is true by taking as his device Juvenal's phrase, *vitam impendere vero*, could

[1] For *Narcisse* see *O.C.*, Pléiade, II, 977–1018. The comedy dates from some thirty years before *Les Confessions*. It therefore antedates the period dealt with in the seventh book of the memoirs where however it is thrice mentioned (*ibid.*, I, 282, 287, 341). It was performed in December, 1752, by the Comédie Française and then published in two editions the following year. For the genesis of the work see *ibid.*, II, 1858–1865. For references to *Narcisse* in this book see the index. The first literary work published by Rousseau was *Le Verger de Madame de Warens* of 1739 and his first publication was a song set to music and published in the *Mercure*, II (June, 1737), 1419.

hardly be expected to do violence to beauty by divorcing it from truth. Nor does he propose to do so. On the contrary, he would use the one to embody and enhance the other. His aesthetics, defined at the end of the fourth book of *Emile*, make this very clear. There he says that the art of writing is not an idle pursuit when it is used to tell the truth.[2] But the author of *Les Confessions* does not promise to tell us the whole truth, which is not even implied in the *verum* of his motto. Over and over again, in an early preamble to his work, in the definitive exordium and elsewhere in its pages, he makes one pledge and only one which is constantly renewed. It is contained in a phrase occurring at the beginning of the seventh book where he says, "It is the story of my soul that I have promised."[3] In spite of his repeated statements, critics have until very recently been deaf to his words. At last his meaning has been brought to the attention of readers by the Pléiade editors and by Professor Henri Peyre, the latter in a superbly penetrating and comprehensive chapter of his book *Literature and Sincerity*. The autobiographer's intention is to impart to us his discovery of the truth within himself, spiritual, psychological, and moral, and we must judge him according to this engagement and not some other of our own imagining. Although his book contains physical self-portraits, it is mainly the story of his soul, wherein he registers his own personal and intimate response to life. Yet his experience is so profound that it assumes significance for all mankind, even more than that of Montaigne, who wrote that "each man bears within himself the whole form of the human condition."[4] This is the case with

---

[2] See epigraph to this study and *O.C.*, Hachette, II, 315. In the seventh book of *Les Confessions*, referring to Altuna's studies, Rousseau speaks lightly of the arts divorced from knowledge (*O.C.*, Pléiade, I, 327). But he consistently places a high value upon the art of writing.

[3] *O.C.*, Pléiade, I, 278. Rousseau writes: "C'est l'histoire de mon âme que j'ai promise. ..." Cf. p. 1148 (preamble of *Les Confessions*, Neuchâtel manuscript), p. 5 (preamble of definitive version), p. 175 (end of fourth book).

[4] Montaigne, Book III, Chapter 2.

Rousseau in spite of his convictions about his uniqueness,[5] although these are well justified, for in presenting himself to us he goes beyond the eccentricities of the individual to discover the human being whose essence each one of us shares. The hero of his memoirs, imagining that he is no worse than the best of men, like Duhamel's Salavin fancying that he is no better than the worst, flatters himself, for he exemplifies human nature with remarkable effectiveness. If, as he says, no man may boast of being better than he, it is simply because none may boast of being essentially other than he. Indeed, Les Confessions owes its universal appeal in very large measure to its humanity as well as to its artistry. The memorialist, unveiling his spirit to posterity, bequeaths to us a fresh revelation of the human soul.

If we ask what becomes of the rest of reality in this complex, composite spiritual portrait, the answer is not hard to find. Let us take for example the transcendental truth of ideas. This is not to be sought in the portrait of a man, of Rousseau, or anyone else for that matter. Absolute truth has not made her abode in the human heart and soul. In his profession of faith in Emile, the writer says quite clearly that truth is to be found in things, not in the mind that judges them. In that case, the portraitist of Les Confessions may express opinions that are mere platitudes or even sophistries without marring the truth or beauty of the spiritual likeness. More than that, he must surely utter fallacies, for human nature is full of falsehood. Man's errors and follies are as much a part and parcel of his life as his strivings after truth and wisdom. They must therefore find a place in any valid semblance of the soul.

When this is said, what are we to conclude regarding the artist's interpretation of the world about him? The reply

---

[5] O.C., Pléiade, I, 5. Here, in the preamble of Les Confessions, Rousseau writes: "Je sens mon coeur et je connois les hommes. Je ne suis fait comme aucun de ceux que j'ai vus; j'ose croire n'être fait comme aucun de ceux qui existent."

must be obvious even to the most heedless reader. Can any one of us, least of all the introvert Rousseau, give an objective or "truthful" account of people and things? In *Emile* he says openly that he does not even expect such fidelity in history.[6] He cares little whether the facts it contains (by which he means the positivistic facts of actuality) are true or false, faithfully reported or not. More still, he resents the monopolization of historical criticism by fact-finders, however significant their work may be. He is satisfied if the historian respects moral and psychological values, truth of manners and of character. He professes to agree with people who are indifferent to facts that happened two thousand years ago, and he might have said two hundred. History, he decides, is nothing but a tissue of fables whose moral lesson is well adapted to the human heart. If such be the case with history, what is to be said of biography and especially autobiography? In *Emile* he has much to say about the former. He declares that it has the same object as history, namely to depict human nature, but it does so more convincingly since history usually sets forth only stirring events and public images and is often conjectural and biased. His favorite biographer was also Montaigne's choice, namely Plutarch, who was a source of inspiration in the autobiography, at least as much as that other great soul searcher, Montaigne himself. In the educa-

---

[6] See *O.C.*, Hachette, II, 128 *n*1, where Rousseau says in the second book of *Emile*:

Les anciens historiens sont remplis de vues dont on pourroit faire usage, quand même les faits qui les presentent seroient faux. Mais nous ne savons tirer aucun vrai parti de l'histoire; la critique d'érudition absorbe tout: comme s'il importoit beaucoup qu'un fait fût vrai, pourvu qu'on en pût tirer une instruction utile. Les hommes sensés doivent regarder l'histoire comme un tissu de fables dont la morale est très appropriée au coeur humain.

Cf. *ibid.*, p. 209, in the fourth book of *Emile*:

On me dira que la fidélité de l'histoire intéresse moins que la vérité des moeurs et des caractères; pourvu que le coeur humain soit bien peint, il importe peu que les événemens soient fidèlement rapportés; car, après tout, ajoute-t-on, que nous font des faits arrivés il y a deux mille ans? On a raison, si les portraits sont bien rendus d'après nature. . . .

For the discussion of Plutarch see *ibid.*, pp. 210–214.

tional treatise Rousseau explains that Plutarch is concerned with inner, rather than external, action. He admires the great biographer for recording well-chosen, familiar, even intimate details to portray great men in little things which perhaps violate decorum and dignity but instruct us about the contradictions of the human heart. The author of *Emile* concludes that such portraits teach us to compare contrasting traits, to love nature, and know man, that is, to know ourselves and "grow wise at the expense of the dead." We might say the same of his own portrait. He was to do for himself what Plutarch did for others. These views on biography and history lead to a better understanding of Rousseau's intentions in *Les Confessions* and further prepare us not to expect an inventory of historical events in the book.

In the autobiography the author confesses frankly that he does not offer an objective document reporting the facts of actuality. In the early preface, and also in the seventh book, he warns us that he does not undertake to render literally or to relate impassively the events of his existence. In that preface, in a passage reminiscent of Montaigne, he faces the objection that the life of a man who is not merely ordinary, as the aristocratic author of *Les Essais* also professed to be, but who springs from the common people too holds little or no interest for anyone else. Here is his reply: "I am registering not so much the events of my life in themselves, but rather the state of my soul as they happened." In the same vein Emile, in the sequel to the book of that name says that "this is not the story of the events of my life; it is the story of my passions, of my feelings, of my ideas." This is exactly what the autobiographer offers us.[7] In that case, external realities may be modified in the autobiography. Indeed they must be. This does not necessarily

---

[7] See preamble of Neuchâtel manuscript in *O.C.*, Pléiade, I, 1150: " ... j'écris moins l'histoire de ces éve [ne] mens en eux-mêmes ('les évenemens de ma vie') que celle de l'état de mon âme, à mesure qu'ils sont arrivés." Cf. *Emile et Sophie ou Les Solitaires* in *O.C.*, Hachette, III, 6; cf. p. 16.

mean that they are intentionally distorted or violated. On the contrary, Rousseau usually records them with remarkable lucidity and exactitude, and even when he does not he betrays an astonishing awareness of them and a more scrupulous respect for them than we are accustomed to imagine. But in a work of literature embodying primarily the truth of the writer's soul, the spiritual purpose obliges him to transcend actualities. In addition, the tyrannical demands of art force him to transfigure them. We must expect this of any artist possessed of genuine poetic vision, and more particularly if he is concerned mainly with the soul. His freedom (the term "poetic license" is surely a misnomer) to metamorphose life to suit his purpose implies not simply a legitimate right, but, paradoxically, a binding duty. If *Les Confessions* is indeed literature—and in the past it has hardly been treated as such—then it is subject to the laws of literature, which protect the writer's freedom to perform his appointed task. His book must conform with the nature of a work of art. As one who is engaged in creative activity with a view to self-expression he could not even be *expected* to offer a literal rendering of the commonplace world. That world, taken as it is, would hardly suit his artistic and spiritual object for many reasons, for want of concentration and form, for lack of verisimilitude, or because it is in fact only a very small part of experience. The creator must therefore take the pale, diffuse substance of life and give us an intense interpretation or presentation, carefully selecting the most vivid, characteristic, and meaningful events that bear a close relationship to inner reality. He must mold them to convey to us the truth he promises. He must arrange them in orderly progression to reveal most effectively his soul and its reactions and to give forceful relief to his new vision of life and character. Only by such means as these can he accomplish his purpose as a portraitist who gradually broadens and deepens his perception until it embraces the

whole of humanity, as he exploits to the full all the resources
of his art.

We need not conclude from the foregoing discussion that
Rousseau, while professing to respect the truth, violates it
in fact. Mr. J. H. Broome is one of the few Rousseauists to
realize that the "inaccuracies" of the composite portrait in
the memoirs result from a creative process and fall into the
category of "art" rather than that of "lies," as he says in
an illuminating page on the art of the book appended to his
study of the writer's thought. Those rare scholars who are
to any degree aware of the autobiographer's artful arrangement of his material are distrustful of it on the grounds that
it weakens our concern with objective truth while creating
an illusion of verisimilitude. They are suspicious of that
"construction of the mind" which intellectualizes an art
deeply rooted in the impassioned movements of the soul.[8]
But, as the Pléiade editors show, it is precisely such artistry
that inevitably releases the subjective and spiritual truth
of the work, which is avowedly the writer's main concern
and ought therefore to be ours. In their excellent introduction to the memorialist's art, they ask: "Can a work of art
lie? Even if he wants to, can the artist do so if his work
necessarily reveals a unique world and at the same time a
universal truth?"[9] These questions hint at what we must
look for in *Les Confessions* if it is indeed a work of art: a
unique world, not the one we all know so well or so ill.
Something essentially the same but substantially different,
a vessel cunningly contrived to hold a universal truth, the

[8] See *C.C.*, I, p. xvi. Cf. M. J. Temmer, "Art and love in the Confessions of
Jean-Jacques Rousseau," *PMLA*, LXXIII (June, 1958), 215–220. This
article deals with Rousseau's presentation of Mme de Warens in the first part
of *Les Confessions*. In his book, Mr. Broome does not touch upon the symbolism
in the autobiography, but he has a fine understanding of it as posing "a particularly interesting problem of facts, truth [which he distinguishes] and art."
He at least formulates the "problem of the artist" in Rousseau's work generally,
though this is not really his theme, and so he has just one page on the art of the
memoirs. See J. H. Broome, *Rousseau: A Study of his Thought* (*London*:
Edward Arnold Ltd., 1963).

[9] *O.C.*, Pléiade, I, p. xxxviii.

truth of the writer himself who becomes in the end humanity. We must remember that the visage of the soul is not
to be sought merely in an inventory of actuality. It is to be
sought and found in a genuine act of creation wherein the
creator betrays himself in every detail of his work, in its
form, in its shapes and patterns as well as in the language
employed. If this is true, as it undoubtedly is, and if *Les
Confessions* is the literary masterpiece it is reputed to be,
then Rousseau is bound to expose himself, whether he will
or not, and whatever he says or does, however he tries to
disguise himself and whatever alibis, repudiations, and excuses he advances. This is all the more true since, as he confesses in the discarded preface to the work, he refuses to
submit to a monotonously uniform style that would conceal the wealth of inner reality.[10] But his success in communicating with us does not depend exclusively upon him.
It depends upon us too. We must be aware, rather than
wary, of his artistry and respond to it in a way that every
creative work demands if we would discover the artist at
his task and see in his portrait the truth of a soul con-
substantial with our own.

The author explains his method at the beginning of the
seventh book. In order to relive the past a quarter of a
century afterwards, he does not rely upon documentation
which he does not possess and he warns us of this at once.
Nor does he rely upon the intellectual memory. Like
Proust, though in a less dramatic way, he uses sentimental
recollection to revive the reality of old emotions and to
feel them anew:

> I have but one faithful guide upon which I may rely: this is
> the chain of sentiments that have marked the succession of

---

[10] *Ibid.*, pp. xxxviii–xxxix. Cf. p. 1154 (preamble of Neuchâtel manuscript);
and J.-J. Rousseau, *Correspondance général*, VI (Paris: Armand Colin, 1926),
209, letter addressed by Rousseau to Dom Deschamps, September 12, 1761.
Hereafter "*C.G.*" with volume and page number refers to this edition of the
correspondence. Since only the first volumes of the proposed thirty volumes
of the new *Correspondance complète* have appeared to date, the old edition
must be used for all letters after June 9, 1754.

my existence and through these the chain of events which
have been their causes or effects . . . I may omit facts, transpose them and fall into errors of dates, but I cannot be mis-
taken about my sentiments and the acts they have prompted
me to do. . . .[11]

Events, and he might have said the same of personalities
and ideas too, are important only as the causes or effects of
emotions and profound impressions to which they are subordinate and which they serve to depict. Let us note
parenthetically that in thus defining his method, the
writer implies again what he has already said so often,
namely that he renders, instead of things and beings
in their objective reality, the movements of the soul they
have aroused. These stirrings he conveys, not simply in
the musical tonalities of language, but through a vision
of the world shaped by passion and pride and prejudice, a
vision wherein he molds figures and events to translate his
innermost being in all the situations of his existence. Once
more he reminds us of his object, at the same time dis-
claiming any other purpose of an apologetic nature: "It
is the story of my soul that I have promised."[12] And so the
persons, places, and circumstances he describes may or may
not be literally true, providing they are figuratively true,
that is, perfectly suited to their artistic function, which is
to clothe with imagery the inner man. His experiences with
others are intended to reveal no one but himself, and this
is a point that has been consistently ignored. He merely
uses men and external creation as a vehicle to reconstitute
his inner life in the past. Through them he progressively re-

[11] *O.C.*, Pléiade, I, 278:

Je n'ai qu'un guide fidelle sur lequel je puisse compter; c'est la chaîne des
sentimens qui ont marqué la succession de mon être, et par eux celle des
évenemens qui en ont été la cause ou l'effet. ... Je puis faire des omissions dans
les faits, des transpositions, des erreurs de dates; mais je ne puis me tromper
sur ce que j'ai senti, ni sur ce que mes sentimens m'ont fait faire.

[12] *Ibid.*: "L'objet propre de mes confessions est de faire connoître exacte-
ment mon interieur dans toutes les situations de ma vie. C'est l'histoire de
mon âme que j'ai promise. ..." He often disclaims an apologetic object:
cf. p. 359.

constructs that hidden truth as it evolved at different periods in time and not merely at the moment of composition when, as the opening pages show, the distraught writer, living in exile and a victim of persecution mania, was surrounded by spies, by walls that had ears and floors that had eyes.[13] These tortured pages betray the intrusion of the present upon a reconstitution of the past, but in general the author does not become confused with the hero of the autobiography. Nevertheless he warns us that his recreation of the past and especially of the world within is presented in pictures that are not necessarily agreeable or highly colored. They are simply designed to eternize in living memory "a man and his love of justice and truth."[14] These images, to which the Pléiade editors refer briefly in their survey of the art of *Les Confessions*, dealing mainly with musical devices of style, are strikingly adapted from the forms of actuality. The imagery and also the peculiar quality of the writer's memory impart the freshness of life to his story.

The reader will have observed that Rousseau, in discussing his method, constantly recalls his object. This is logical. The problems of truth and of method are intimately bound, and one can hardly discuss the latter without constant reference to the inquiry with which we began. The failure to consider both together can only lead to misunderstandings. It is now clear that what Rousseau offers in *Les Confessions*, and what we are intended to seek in the Venetian story of the seventh book, is an artistic rendering of psychological reality. If we ignore this fact and its implications, not only do we deprive ourselves of a valuable aesthetic experience, but we cannot grasp the truth of the autobiography, even if we know what kind of truth is

---

[13] *Ibid.*, pp. 278–279: Rousseau says he has a few letters to guide him in his memoirs of a later period but adds that they are too voluminous to be rescued from the vigilance of his enemies, for he is surrounded by spies, etc.

[14] *Ibid.*, p. 279. He promises to satisfy "le désir d'achever de connoitre un homme, et l'amour sincère de la justice et de la vérité."

intended. We might also deny that it had any. Some critics have almost come to this conclusion, precisely because they overlook the writer's explanation of his method. They point out—and they are quite right to do so—that Rousseau often equivocates, and that he always sees beings and events through his own passions and selfish interests. But since he warns us of this himself we have no choice but to heed his warning and to see in those very beings and events a symbolic expression of the passions and interests which it is his purpose to record. Then, whenever he takes refuge in others to avoid making a direct, forthright confession as he often does, either to express his idealism or the sordid actuality of his life or both, he can never escape us, though he can make our task a difficult one and force us to wrest the truth from the literary form that invests it. But at least the task will be easier if we once begin to read the book as literature instead of history, and if we search its pages for a concrete presentation of inner life rather than a literal statement of historical fact. I do not imply that he exhausts for us the truth he promises, either human truth or the truth about himself. One reason for his failure to do so is that both are inexhaustible, and equally so since they are essentially one and the same. Another reason is that his work is admittedly incomplete. As for what he does tell us, the reader can see for himself in the Venetian story how the author's literary principles and mode of procedure permit him to give us an almost plastic interpretation of the most elusive facts of consciousness and of subconscious and intuitive reality.

THE AUTOBIOGRAPHER'S PROLOGUE

Rousseau's artistic treatment of factual, ideological, and spiritual truth in the memoirs is abundantly illustrated throughout the seventh book, of which the Venetian story is a well-integrated and inseparable component. The seventh book is the first of six books in the second and last part.

Having evoked in the preceding part an earthly paradise of thirty youthful years in Geneva and Savoy, interspersed however with foreboding scenes of exile, poverty, and suffering, Rousseau turns in the central pages to the middle period after 1741, which was the meridian of his life when the work was completed in 1770, although the story is not traced beyond 1766. The autobiographer, like Dante too "in the midway of this our mortal life," sees a whole inferno lying before him. In the seventh book he relives a period of seven years, from 1742, rather than 1741 as he imagines, to 1749. Thus he spans the time from his farewell to Savoy and journey to Paris in search of fame and fortune, to the sudden flash of genius that led him like a column of flame to immortality in the realm of art and letters, immortality won at the cost of blood and tears. Aesthetic intentions are visible in the formal distribution of material in the book where time and place are sacrificed for the perfect expression of the spirit. In apparent disregard for proportion and balance, the year in Venice occupies half the book and, what is still more noteworthy, the central half. Preceding and subsequent events are compressed and subtly proportioned to their spiritual content. The journey to Paris from Chambéry and the Parisian debuts of 1742 to 1743, before the departure for Venice, are given almost the same value as the five somber years in Paris after the Venetian tragedy. This seemingly arbitrary treatment of the subject is not a flaw in the formal harmony of *Les Confessions* but rather an artistic device that serves to underline a spiritual truth. The composition is carefully balanced to prefigure the varying impact of vital experience upon the inner man.

Rousseau has conceived almost every situation in the seventh book to express a great longing for justice and truth, which he rarely finds in the world of actuality. The resulting tension both complicates and explains what he defines at the outset as the basic conflict of his life. This is the conflict between the dreamer's desire for solitude and the necessity to engage society, driving him to action. [15] The story of his social debuts in Paris is meant to show that the society which the young man is loath to face and from which he would gladly withdraw is bereft of both justice and truth since its values are not natural, or true. In those pages the writer draws an artistic antithesis between the proud pretensions of a richly endowed nature and the cruel humiliations of social subservience that undermine, and thereby degrade, the individual. This paradox is a constantly recurring leitmotiv in the narrative. It is at the very root of Rousseau's indignation against existing social institutions and civil injustice, a feeling that is registered in each scene in the book. The same paradox is at the origin of his dreams of a regenerate society and a perfect city where justice and truth sit enthroned. Of course the theme has repercussions in all human experience, but its presentation in *Les Confessions* is unique, that is, the imagery and artistry with which it is treated and to which everything else is subordinate, including ideas and the recital of events.

The narrator begins with the journey from Savoy to Paris and at once provides a good example of the effectiveness of his method to convey his message. His account is not at all circumstantial. It is clearly designed to suggest states of soul in the unwilling traveler as he faces an encounter with society, armed with nothing more substantial than his comedy *Narcisse* and his newly invented system of ciphered musical notation. His natural diffidence and disinclination to accept the challenge are imparted in the sadness with which he takes leave of "his castle in Spain" at the Charmettes and its chatelaine, the Baroness de Warens, his beloved "mamma," and then lingers nostalgically in nearby Lyons. The writer deliberately moderates the pace of the narrative to express a sense of reluctance, as he

---

[15] *Ibid.*, p. 277. Since this essay follows the order of Rousseau's narrative in the seventh book of *Les Confessions*, these notes will not contain further page references to that work unless a passage is discussed out of context.

adopts the tempo of an adagio to introduce a few Lyonese friends one by one. At last they urge the young man on his way to assert his claims to social recognition, commending him to illustrious Parisians. The psychological reactions portrayed in these scenes of *Les Confessions* are also the theme of an epistle addressed to Monsieur Parisot of Lyons and written by Rousseau during the same sojourn.[16] The letter, together with another to Monsieur Bordes, also of Lyons, composed by the author the previous year on a related theme,[17] is valuable for purposes of comparison with *Les Confessions*, to make the reader more conscious of that unique combination of beauty and inner truth that distinguishes the memoirs. Both epistles, although written in verse, are unpoetic and analytical. Especially in the one to Parisot, Rousseau theorizes and reflects abstractly upon his republican, stoic education, which, in spite of the lessons of the baroness and of the genteel society of Lyons, is no better preparation for life in Paris than his timid, frank, and independent nature. Like Molière's misanthrope Alceste, with whom Rousseau was later to identify himself, the epistoler recoils from the thought of winning his way by dancing attendance upon the world of rank and fashion. If, in the earlier letter, the new Alceste finds his austere virtues tempered by the refined pleasures of Lyons, in the second one he pleads again for his desert solitude to which he would willingly sacrifice the pursuit of glory in favor of the sentiments of the heart. All this discursive reasoning is presented by way of a synthesis in *Les Confessions*. It is embodied in living forms in the fine tableaux of the first six books where the "bliss of solitude" is passionately recalled. It is expressed again in the opening pages of the seventh book in regrets of "mamma" now left behind and in the hesitations of a journey into the uncertain future.

[16] *Ibid.*, II, 1136–1144.
[17] *Ibid.*, pp. 1130–1133.

The story of the Parisian debuts follows and it too illustrates the writer's use of events to bring out effective contrasts in mood. It contains an artistic transposition of the struggle between pride and humiliation, which is of far lesser magnitude than the one contained in the Venetian story but bespeaks the same thirst for justice and the same reactions to iniquity. Arriving in the French capital the hero makes extraordinary efforts to overcome natural indolence and win a place in distinguished society consistent with his inborn talents. He begins by forming a connection with the philosopher Diderot, whose friendship is also, significantly enough, the theme of the last scene in the same book, and who later made the aspiring musician aware of his literary vocation. The ardor of Rousseau's youthful aspirations is proved when, on August 22, 1742, he presents his new system of ciphered musical notation to the Academy of Sciences, and then, when it is indifferently received, offers it to the public in a book entitled *Dissertation sur la musique moderne*,[18] published at the beginning of the following year. Immediately afterwards he lapses into a state of languor and loneliness induced by the unsatisfying judgment of imposing academicians and by public indifference, rather than by Rameau's solid objection to his system. This objection, also made by the academy, in spite of the memorialist's statements to the contrary, is that the relative position of traditional notes on the musical staff calls forth a more immediate visual response than ciphers could possibly do. Rousseau's correspondence of February and March, 1743, contains letters to literary journals wherein he explains his method and defends it somewhat impatiently against misunderstanding and absurd and irrelevant criticism, but he ignores serious objections in his anxiety to win

[18] For the *Projet concernant de nouveaux signes pour la musique*, which was read to the academy August 22, 1742, and the *Disseration*, published in January, 1743, see *O.C.*, Hachette, VI, 253–321.

acceptance.[19] The weakness of his frustration in the face of rejection, whether the latter was justified or not, is best shown in *Les Confessions* where he renounces almost all society, with the notable exceptions of Diderot and Marivaux, the latter of whom complacently retouches *Narcisse*. He then retreats into the world of poetry and chess, encouraged by the recollection that, more than two thousand years before, Athenian captives, after the defeat of Nicias at Syracuse, had earned their livelihood by reciting the songs of Homer. The subtle irony with which the memorialist recalls rationalizing his passivity in a futile effort at self-deception draws attention to the theme of the seventh book, the ever-present disparity between individual worth and social judgments. The naïve young man tells himself that personal distinction must surely win prestige and fortune in the end, without need of devious intrigues and servile courtship of the great. He is made aware of the sophistry of this reasoning by the exhortations of a Jesuit friend who stirs him to action once more and sends him in quest of patronage to the salons of Mesdames de Beuzenwal and Dupin. The implication is that parasitism, not talent, is a condition of social success. The scene with the Baroness de Beuzenwal and her daughter, the Marchioness de Broglie, presents a modification of this idea. The baroness, ignorant of the respect due to culture, invites the visitor to dine with the servants, but he succeeds in winning her regard by reading aloud the unpublished epistle to Parisot,[20] thereby accomplishing a veritable *tour de force* since the poem sets forth the author's republican contempt for distinguished society. His reception in the Dupin mansion, instead of solving

[19] For the academicians' objection to the new method see *C.C.*, I, 168. Rousseau faced public criticism of the *Dissertation* in two letters, one published in the *Mercure de France* in February, 1743, containing a succinct account of the treatise, and the other published in the *Journal de Verdun* the following month, rectifying the fatuous remarks of some critic whose most serious objections the writer ignores (*C.C.*, I, 169–178). Incidentally, the same edition of the *Journal* also contained the *Epître à M. Bordes*, composed in 1741.

[20] The epistle was published in 1776.

the conflict between natural endowments and social position, only intensifies it. His whole association with the members of that household is deliberately shown to be little more than an exploitation of talent on their part and a prostitution of talent on his. His subjection to them is also the theme of contemporary letters, of April, 1743, addressed to both his patroness and her husband.[21] In these letters, after apologizing for a *faux pas* and observing characteristically that repentance is often better than innocence itself, he renounces his ambitions to place himself obsequiously at their disposal. However, his relationship with them is far more vividly portrayed in *Les Confessions*, from an initial indiscretion and misplaced act of homage addressed to Madame Dupin in person, to a brief service as tutor to the younger child, Dupin de Chenonceaux, and concluding with studies in chemistry undertaken as companion to the stepson Francueil.[22] In that book Rousseau finally realizes his abject and servile condition during an illness that detaches him from life and brings him to deplore his own "timidity, weakness, and indolence." We may infer, if we like, that these are defects bred and fostered in the individual by society. In a new effort to overcome them and to do justice to the "fire" with which he is "kindled," he conceives fresh desire to win renown as a musician, despite the failure of his method of transcription, by seeking an outlet for his energies in composition as he had done a few years earlier in a couple of abortive attempts. The heroic ballet, *Les Muses galantes*, one act of which he completes at this time, bids fair to win him recognition by combining his musical and poetic gifts in a single work. This challenge to his genius is soon abandoned for another of a different kind. Madame de Beuzenwal commends him to the court for the French diplomatic service and he is offered a post as secretary to the newly appointed French ambassador to

[21] *C.C.*, I, 182–186, letters of April 9 and 10, 1743.
[22] Dupin de Francueil was George Sand's ancestor.

Venice. At last the individual sees before him a promise of fulfillment for his latent powers. In all these situations the flux of life with its demands, its pledges, and its infidelities is used to reveal the alternating moods of the protagonist in his relations with the social milieu and to provide as it were the prologue of the Venetian story.

These pages of *Les Confessions* offer an example of what the writer proposes to do. The world of events appears as the cause or effect of his past impressions and therefore provides a chain of tableaux to exteriorize them and to symbolize a craving for what he calls justice and truth. The image sequence portrays a man looking naïvely to society for some form of sanctifying grace, to call into play the hidden springs of his nature and help him to become his highest self. But the reader is beginning to discern that society is not some cosmic power or some abstract anonymous principle as it is in *Du Contrat social*, where, as Emile observes, Rousseau builds his construction with pieces of wood instead of men. In the memoirs the opposite is true. Society is frail humanity with which the hero of the book engages in uncertain conflict, all the more uncertain as its weaknesses are in fact his own. Its defects therefore serve to reflect his through a device that has for him the additional advantage of suggesting that he is vitiated by the milieu. Society is a few academicians judging things foreign to them with pretensions that match those of the inventor of ciphered music himself; it is the vague, lethargic mass of men whose indifference is analogous to the central figure's indolence; it is Madame de Beuzenwal or Madame Dupin, whose ambitions and prejudices are of the same order as their protégé's pride. He despises the great more than they do him, but at the same time he entertains the paradoxical hope of finding a place in their esteem. His servility corresponds to their condescension and his snobbishness parallels theirs. The repercussions of life in the soul are embodied not merely in the self but in the world of things and beings which are known to us only in this subjective manner and are presented either by means of analogy or contrast. Theorizing could never impart so forcefully the ideas explicit in these forms which are living proof of Rousseau's skill in devising an artistic method admirably suited to his message. Art and psychology, in mutually complementary roles, are as intimately bound as body and soul. Not merely one of these, as some readers have believed, but the interplay of both is the distinguishing characteristic of *Les Confessions* and the real secret of its universality and lasting charm. This is true even though we have long been unaware of the fact. We testify thereby to Rousseau's discipline as a writer who deliberately conceals his artistry to make it the handmaid of moral truth in his work. This makes him one of the least "literary" of all *littérateurs* and therefore one of the most subtle.

II

The Venetian Story

The Venetian story is a concrete, even allegorical, portrayal of the thoughts and feelings that assailed the young Rousseau and determined his actions at one of the most decisive moments in his life. We become aware of this when we compare the text of *Les Confessions* with the actuality of the period 1743 to 1744. We may reconstruct events by probing archives and memoirs, official documents and secret reports as well as massive volumes of correspondence both public and private until we are nearly submerged beneath the weight of our research and have all but lost sight of human and literary values. On the other hand, by having recourse to the raw materials from which the autobiographer has taken his book, we can more easily grasp the means by which he has converted them into the transfigured reality of art to embody his youthful aspirations and frustrations. He shows us life and the world seen through his own temperament until they become modes of expression to reveal his soul and its rebellion during the critical Venetian experience.

THE ROUSSEAU-MONTAIGU ANTITHESIS

Although Rousseau's association with the French ambassador is the inspiration of some of the finest pages in *Les Confessions*, the writer gives us no description of the meeting of the two men in Paris. Nor does he give a physical portrait of either one. We are not even told that the ambassador is twenty years older than his prospective secretary and fifty-one years of age when they meet. But we are told at once that the Count de Montaigu is a former captain in the (Grenadier) Guards who won his diplomatic post by paying court to Barjac, valet de chambre to the Cardinal de Fleury, prime minister of Louis XV. The count offers the young man scarcely sufficient salary to maintain the external dignity considered essential for prestige. The latter rejects the post and then is persuaded by the chevalier, Montaigu's younger brother, who is in the suite of the dauphin, to accept a second offer when another secretary, called Follau and obtained through the Foreign Office, abandons the ambassador to his folly upon their arrival in Venice. This is all the author of *Les Confessions* says and all he really needs to say. There is nothing we can glean from other sources to add anything of real psychological value, for he has carefully selected the most eloquent details. Without oversimplifying for the sake of an antithesis and without reducing characters and events to mere abstractions, he subtly distills their essential meaning and gives it force by his very reticence and reserve. His few but well-chosen words are prophetic. They contain in germ the whole Venetian story, with its fund of artistry and inner truth, which grows out of the contrast here instituted between the principals. An abyss lies between the wealthy but parsimonious aristocrat and the impoverished but insatiably proud and ambitious young republican who was to be hailed as "the father of democracy."[1] A still greater abyss lies between the artist and the military man. We know that in actual fact Montaigu, after thirty-seven years' unrewarding service in the army,[2]

[1] His claim to this title is that he divests the prince of sovereignty and invests it in the general will of the people, formulated as law, to which all individuals including the prince must submit; see *Du Contrat social* in *O.C.*, Pléiade, III, 1477 *n*1 (to p. 404).

[2] For Montaigu's career see Prosper Faugère, "Jean-Jacques Rousseau à Venise," *Le Correspondant*, CLI (June 10, 1888), 816, 828 *n*1; Auguste de

did indeed owe his diplomatic mission to Fleury's valet, and, like many of his colleagues, was ill prepared for it.[3] We can judge his sense of values by the very modest salary he offered his secretary, while his own was thirty times as much.[4] Small wonder if Rousseau was little tempted. His hesitation is confirmed by history, which shows that he did indeed reject the offer at first, probably in the spring of 1743 and partly in the hope of completing *Les Muses galantes.* It is true that all details of *Les Confessions* are not similarly verifiable. For example, Follau, far from leaving Montaigu to his madness, as the writer alleges, was in fact dismissed by his employer at Chambéry for smuggling on their way to Italy. This modification of events in the memoirs is probably intended to give us a premonition of disaster without distorting the count's character as it evolves in the book. Other elements in the story are taken directly from life. Letters formerly in the Montaigu archives and now in the Bibliothèque Nationale prove that the young Rousseau had to be persuaded to accept a second offer, made at the end of June not merely by the count's brother, as the autobiographer says, but by his wife too, who did not join her husband in Venice for over a year. We also know from the same source that he did not leave

---

Montaigu, *Démêlés du comte de Montaigu, ambassadeur à Venise, et de son secrétaire, Jean-Jacques Rousseau* (Paris: Plon, 1904), pp. 4–6; and *O.C.,* Pléiade, I, 1387 *n*1 (to p. 295). He did not bear the titles "maréchal de camp" and "chevalier de Saint-Louis" but it is to be noted that captains in the French Guards had the rank of colonel.

[3] Several of Barjac's letters, addressed to the count, prove this; see *O.C.,* Pléiade, I, 1387 *n*2 (to p. 295). Mr. Leigh draws attention to letters of Fleury to show the cardinal's interest in Montaigu, but this interest was aroused by Barjac; see *C.C.,* I, 192 note *a* (to no. 57). These letters, like all the documents originally preserved in the Montaigu archives at La Bretesche and mentioned in this study, have now been transferred to the Bibliothèque Nationale in Paris.

[4] Rousseau received 1,000 francs a year and Montaigu 30,000: *O.C.,* Pléiade, I, 1398 *n*2 (to p. 312); 1404 *n*5 (to p. 326); and III, 1818–1819 *n*1 (to p. 1079). Some money was advanced for Rousseau's journey and the amount coincides with the sum stated in *Les Confessions: C.C.,* I, 190–192.

for Venice until July 10, 1743, only one day before the ambassador arrived there.[5] The situation is ominous. The two men were clearly ill matched, for the Montaigu of history was, strangely enough, not unlike his counterpart emerging from the text of *Les Confessions*, where he is gradually enlarged into an image of hostile society to serve as a foil to the writer's self-portrait. In the book as in life, the count is a man of action and the very reverse of the thinker and sensitive young artist who now wrests himself from his music and poetry, striving to overcome a brooding introspective nature and win his way in life by selling his talents.

The description in the memoirs of the departure for Venice and the journey there bears a fine symbolic relationship to spiritual responses. The young man's delay in leaving Paris is a sign of moral uncertainty and reluctance to face another engagement with society. His obvious doubts are reminiscent of those that preceded his first encounter. His misgivings are further conveyed in the story of his travels, which is treated as a phase in the story of the soul and is a perfect example of the writer's skill in adapting the experience of life to his artistic and spiritual purpose. Many critics have wondered and exclaimed at his reticence without realizing that it is imposed upon him by the nature of his book and that he does not use imagery for its own sake but rather for its psychological value. We know from contemporary documents that the voyage lasted almost two months, by contrast with Rousseau's earlier journey to Italy fifteen years before when he apparently traveled

---

[5] The second offer, made by the chevalier and Mme de Montaigu, is described in a letter from the former to his brother dated June 29, 1743: *C.C.*, I, 187–188. Montaigu was appointed January 1, 1743, but he did not reach his post until July 11 and did not officially assume his functions until August 26, when his presence was finally announced to the Venetian senate: *O.C.*, Pléiade, I, 1387 *n*1 (to p. 295); and *C.C.*, I, 191 note *b* (to no. 56). His wife joined him October 24, 1744; *ibid.*, I, 214 note *c* (to no. 71); *O.C.*, Pléiade, I, 1396 *n*2 (to p. 308).

from Annecy to Turin in less than three weeks.[6] In the
account of this new journey, as in the case of the one from
Savoy to Paris, the autobiographer gives literary form
only to what is meaningful to express the inborn temptation to abandon society forever and take refuge in some
desert hermitage. Such is the keynote of these travel
reminiscences. Everything that does not harmonize with
it is omitted altogether or transposed into other contexts
and utilized elsewhere. With what wistfulness the traveler
sets out, full of the desire to take the Mont Cenis road for
the sake of seeing his "poor mamma" in passing, but then
he is forced by the circumstances of war to take instead
the river route to the Mediterranean! Historical records
show that, whether he saw her or not, he did indeed visit
Chambéry.[7] Arriving at Lyons, heedless of all friends and
their generosity of the previous year, he went in haste to
the Charmettes like a man in pursuit of a dream and, only
after eight days' perhaps fruitless waiting for the absent
lady, combined with other business, finally returned to
Lyons for a three-day visit before continuing his travels.
What then is the meaning of those nostalgic words in
Les Confessions? They present no historical difficulty if
we understand all the circumstances of Rousseau's uncertain plans when he was preparing to set out for Italy.
The overland routes were the best, and he had a choice of

[6] July 10 to September 4, 1743. For details of his itinerary, see C.C., II,
275–278 (Appendix 54) and ibid., I, 194 note c (to no. 58), 197. The route was:
Paris, Chalon, Lyons, Chambéry, Lyons, Avignon, Marseilles, Toulon, Genoa,
Milan, Venice. The longest sojourns were eight days at Chambéry, three at
Lyons, five at Marseilles awaiting the felucca to cross the Mediterranean, and
eighteen to twenty-one days at Genoa. For the journey to Turin see O.C.,
Pléiade, I, 55, 58, and notes.

[7] For this visit to Chambéry see C.G., I, 237–238, where there is a note by
P.-P. Plan; also Noëlle Roger, "Jean-Jacques Rousseau et Madame de
Warens," Revue des Deux Mondes, XXIII (1924), 653; O.C., Pléiade, I, 1388 n9
(to p. 295); and C.C., I, 195. M. Plan and Mme Roger believe that Rousseau's
reticence about the visit is an attempt to defend the memory of "mamma,"
while the Pléiade editors and Mr. Leigh suggest that she was absent. The latter
are probably right.

two, of which he had made a study in 1739: the Mont Cenis
from Lyons to Turin via Chambéry and Savoy, and the
Mont Simplon through Switzerland, by which he later
returned to Paris. At the time of his departure for Venice
he thought of taking the Simplon road southwards, and
acquaintances in Paris believed that he actually did so.
At the last minute, however, he changed his mind and
decided to try to pass through Savoy and Piedmont in the
cherished hope of a reunion at Chambéry. The text of the
memoirs suggests that he would have waited there longer
if the events of the War of the Austrian Succession and the
imminent Spanish invasion of Piedmont had left him any
possibility of taking the Alpine road as Montaigu had done
such a short time before, instead of forcing him to take the
longer river route to the sea.[8] Obviously after he arrived at
Chambéry he learned at army headquarters, where the
Infant Don Philippe had established his administration,
that it was impossible to proceed. This must be so since
he expected his employer to pay the expenses of the trip
from Lyons to the Savoyard capital and later included
them in his financial account, evidently believing the claim
to be reasonable. All these explanations are omitted from
Les Confessions where the only motive recorded is the
psychologically meaningful one. It is imparted in a simple
but translucent phrase akin to a heavy sigh of the spirit, to

[8] Spain had declared war on Sardinia, Austria's ally in the War of the
Austrian Succession, and had occupied Savoy, and was preparing to invade
Piedmont. It is worth noting that just before he left Paris, Rousseau's itinerary
was uncertain. Even after he had left, the count's brother and banker both
thought he had gone through Switzerland (*C.C.*, I, 192–193). There is no
doubt that Montaigu took the Mont-Cenis road: he dismissed Rousseau's
predecessor, Follau, at Chambéry and dated his first dispatch from Turin on
July 3, 1743. See *O.C.*, Pléiade, I, 1387 *n*7 (to p. 295), and *C.C.*, I, 188, regarding Follau's discharge; for Montaigu's first dispatch see Faugère, "Jean-
Jacques Rousseau à Venise," pp. 824–825. Mme de Montaigu took the same
route the following year; see A. Monglond, "Rousseau, secrétaire de M. de
Montaigu, ambassadeur de France à Venise, documents inédits," *Annales de
la Société Jean-Jacques Rousseau*, XXVI (1935), 48. For Rousseau's study of
the two overland routes made in 1739 see *C.C.*, I, 96–97.

signify a longing for solitude as deeply rooted in the protagonist's nature as the self-distrust from which it springs.

The same longing is still more powerfully proclaimed in striking imagery in the story of his quarantine at Genoa, the only other theme of the autobiographer's comments upon the journey. Having said almost nothing of the six days' crossing from Marseilles in the heat of early August in an oar-drawn and vermin-infested boat, he dwells at length upon the detention to which all passengers are subjected upon arrival at the Italian seaport as a precaution against the plague raging in Sicily and Dalmatia. In this story, the austere nudity of a Genoese lazaret, where the young Rousseau alone chooses to be confined in preference to the ship, becomes a veritable image of his introspective soul. We see him in a spacious and windowless palace, furnished with scarcely more than his inkhorn and books, cleansing his body of vermin and purifying his mind in mysterious converse with his own thoughts for a fortnight of happy days, or seeking new horizons in nature by roaming about an adjacent cemetery with a view of the sea. The taste for solitude, austerity, and self-reliance manifests itself throughout this narrative of "the new Robinson Crusoe." It immediately identifies the writer of all the masterpieces that had flowed from the same pen. None of them expresses more eloquently than the lazaret incident the aspiration to purity and the need to withdraw from the filth and contagion of an unregenerate and degrading society. This symbolic presentation of character is the great virtue of *Les Confessions*, which of course has nothing to do with the virtue or vice of the character portrayed. By comparison other problems seem trivial, such as those posed by purely historical criticism. For example, does it really matter whether in actuality the quarantine lasted twelve, thirteen, or fourteen days;[9] and whether the French

---

[9] In *Les Confessions* Rousseau says fourteen days, but according to Montaigu's account of August 6, 1744, the quarantine lasted twelve days (*C.C.*, II, 275). Mr. Leigh says thirteen (*ibid.*, I, 197).

envoy to Genoa, who in life as in the book had Rousseau released and entertained him, also accommodated him in reality as he does in the story and as he certainly did years later, or whether Rousseau or merely his luggage or both were in actual fact lodged at an inn for the rest of the three weeks' sojourn to which he had been subjected?[10] These are matters of mere anecdotal interest. They are lacking in literary value and psychological significance. This can hardly be said of the memorialist's account of his travels, which in two brief themes deftly embodies the secret yearnings of his languid nature now sacrificed to the pursuit of prestige.

Rousseau's arrival in Venice is also a rich source of artistic and spiritual delineation in *Les Confessions*. Even his silence betrays him as much as his happiest phrases. For instance, the same writer who describes meticulously and exhaustively the empty lazaret of Genoa and spares us no detail, not even the vermin, is not at all inspired to recreate for us those enchanted isles, born of the sea like the goddess of beauty herself, with the delicate filigree of their pink marble palaces exquisitely set in an iridescent landscape. His restraint is all the more astonishing since he arrived in early September (September 4, to be exact) when the mellow glow of colors and the amber radiance of Venetian light are at their best. Those of us who would see in imagination the scenes of the writer's abode and fix his person in time and place must explore for ourselves the site of the former palace of France, in the poor Canareggio district near the present railway station and the Ghetto, remote from Saint Mark's Square and the suspi-

---

[10] In *Les Confessions*, Rousseau says he spent eight days with the French envoy, Jonville, but according to Montaigu's account of August 6, 1744 (*ibid.*, II, 275), he had his effects taken to a hotel and charged Montaigu for eight days' sojourn in Genoa. Whether or not he actually stayed in the hotel, he would still have incurred expenses for a week's sojourn. He cultivated Jonville some years later; see the tenth book of the memoirs in *O.C.*, Pléiade, I, 509–510.

cious Venetian government.[11] We must imagine for ourselves the ardent young man moving about the stuccoed rooms of the once noble Querini palace, a baroque mansion built in the early seventeenth century by Baldassare Longhena, the great architect of the Salute church. What does Rousseau's reticence mean? His lack of lyricism in this instance, puzzling to most readers, has been attributed to everything, from want of serenity and excessive preoccupation with work to "scandalous insensitivity."[12] More probably the secret of his reserve is to be sought in the nature of his book—the story of his soul. We can only conclude that descriptions of the Venetian scene are unsuitable substance for his art since they would not disclose what he has promised to tell. This must mean that Venice provides no reflection of his inner life and character.

The memorialist's silence is matched only by that of the young secretary in actual life. His correspondence contains no evocations of the city at all. Three of his personal letters, written during the first two months of his residence there, are extant. They are addressed to Madame de Warens, her friends or connections, and might have been sent from the bleak mountains of the moon. No one would ever suspect that the writer had just arrived in Venice. He pleads pathetically for news of "mamma," suffers anguish by her silence, and seizes the least pretext to speak of her to others.[13] These letters are filled only with his longing for her who had given the substance of reality to

[11] For the location of the palace which then belonged to the procurator Tommaso Querini see *C.C.*, I, 220. It is now Fondamenta delle Penitenti no. 968.

[12] See, for example, Jules Lemaître, *Jean-Jacques Rousseau* (Paris: Calmann-Lévy, n.d. [1907]), Chapter II; Maurice Montigny, "Jean-Jacques Rousseau secrétaire d'ambassade," *Revue des études historiques*, 95e année (January to March, 1929), pp. 419, 434; and Mongland, "Rousseau, secrétaire de M. de Montaigu," p. 76.

[13] *C.C.*, I, 194–195, 198–210, letters to M. de Conzié at the Charmettes, of September 21, 1743, and to Mme de Warens and the Comte de Lautrec, both presumably dated October 5, 1743.

his nostalgic dream of solitude. In each one the brilliant Venetian world is conspicuous only by its absence, as though it were alien to his nature. If so, it could hardly find a place in the self-portrait of the memoirs.

His relations with Montaigu furnish an even richer antithesis than that of the city and the soul. *Les Confessions* contains no account of their meeting at the embassy any more than in Paris. Rousseau merely recalls being impatiently expected by the ambassador. Then he plunges at once into memories of the tasks awaiting him without even interrupting his story for a moment to dwell more fully upon a formal introduction of the man who is to fill a central place in the annals of the soul and is dramatically revealed in the course of events. The new secretary, deciphering the accumulated dispatches, learns how simple are the ciphers that his employer is unable to master, and how tediously trivial the affairs entrusted to a man incapable of dictating fluently or writing legibly. This is the memorialist's boastful version of the situation.

Now if we turn from art to life and consult history, we learn that Montaigu, who delayed assuming his functions until August 26, only nine days before his secretary's arrival, used no ciphers at all before Rousseau's term of office or afterwards.[14] The truth is that the ciphers presented problems not merely for the man who used them but for the man who had to read them. For example, on November 19, six weeks after the secretary reached Venice, his dispatches were criticized by a short-sighted clerk in the Foreign Office for mistakes in ciphering, a complaint apparently directed against two in particular of October 26 and November 2, which contain the only extensive ciphering in the correspondence prior to the rebuke. However the same office admitted in a later communication intended for the embassy in Venice, but never sent and simply kept on file, that the complaint had been unjusti-

[14] This can be seen from the archives in Paris. The system of ciphering is explained in *O.C.*, Pléiade, III, pp. ccl–ccli.

fied. A study of the ciphers confirms this. Nevertheless Rousseau believed that he was guilty and says so in *Les Confessions* a little further on in the story where the supposed errors are attributed to haste and carelessness.[15] In reality the secretary handled the ciphers well, while the ambassador refrained from handling them at all. Quite apart from the matter of ciphers, it is verifiable that the autobiographer's charges about Montaigu's ineptitude for dictation and writing are founded in objective fact. Except when Rousseau was in charge of the secretariat, the embassy correspondence is vulgar and clumsy in style, even incorrect and incoherent, besides lacking in diplomatic expression in missives to the King of France and the Venetian senate.[16] The editor of the *Venetian Despatches*, Monsieur Jean-Daniel Candaux, frequently comments upon the count's muddled style in letters prepared when he was alone at the embassy, and even in parts of Rousseau's bulletins, for sometimes he insisted upon dictating word for word certain paragraphs dealing with matters of special importance. In these hybrid texts, says Monsieur Candaux, "the manner of the former captain of the guards . . . is often mingled with the style of the future author of the *Contrat social*." The Pléiade editor

[15] *Ibid.*, I, 304, 1393–1394; and especially III, 1825 *n*1 (to p. 1102).

[16] For the period before Rousseau's arrival see Montaigu's letters of July 13, August 3, 10, and 31, 1743, in Faugère, "Jean-Jacques Rousseau à Venise," pp. 824–831. On September 3, the Foreign Office (in particular Amelot, who was minister until April 26, 1744) reproved him for repetitiousness and lack of respect for His Majesty (*ibid.*); cf. Derche, "Autour du séjour de J.-J. Rousseau à Venise," pp. 156–158, and *O.C.*, Pléiade, III, 1811 *n*2 (to p. 1054). When Rousseau left, the embassy correspondence deteriorated. See, for example, Montaigu's awkward missive to the Venetian senate of August 15, 1744, in Joseph Souchon, *Correspondance diplomatique du Comte de Montaigu, ambassadeur à Venise* (Paris: Plon, 1915), p. 86; cf. Monglond's comments in "Rousseau, secrétaire de M. de Montaigu," pp. 46–47, and the note in *O.C.*, Pléiade, I, 1389–1390 *n*6 (to p. 297). Later, in 1745 and 1746, the Foreign Office (that is, d'Argenson, who succeeded the interim minister Du Theil on November 1, 1744) frequently criticized the form of memorials and dispatches; see A. de Montaigu, *Démêlés*, pp. 35, 38–40, 87–89; and Derche, "Autour du séjour de J.-J. Rousseau à Venise," p. 158.

assumes that it was during this dictation, while Montaigu
was, by his own admission, struggling in pursuit of elusive
words, that his secretary "habitually" took the employer's
chair, picked up a book, and looked at him pitifully.[17] Such
was the ambassador as he depicts himself in a letter written
the following year and as he appears in all his correspondence. As for the business of his mission, not only does it
seem for the most part trivial today, but it must have been
obviously so at the time. Otherwise when Rousseau was later
accused by the count of selling the embassy ciphers to the
Austrian Prince Pio, would he have dared to exonerate
himself by writing to the French Foreign Office, from which
alone he could expect redress, saying that it knew better
than anyone how important were the affairs entrusted to
the Count de Montaigu and that Prince Pio would not be
fool enough to give a penny piece for all the ciphers?[18]
Even if the letter is not contemporary, as has been suggested, Montaigu's instructions confirm its view of his
mission and state clearly that the residence of an ambassador in Venice had no more important object than to
flatter the republic.[19] In the almost unanimous opinion of
critics,[20] the historical personage reflected in all this documentation bears a rather pathetic resemblance to the figure
in *Les Confessions* who, though favored by birth and by
fortune, is incompetent and limited in vision and in scope.
He therefore lent himself perfectly to the part he assumes

---

[17] *C.C.*, II, 50–53, letter from Montaigu to the Abbé Alary, August 15, 1744.
This letter is discussed below. The detail about the dictation is frequently
referred to by critics, e.g. R. Grimsley and F. C. Green. For M. Candaux's
discussion see *O.C.*, Pléiade, III, pp. ccxlviii–ccxlix, cclii, 1811 *n*2 (to p. 1054),
1813 *n*1 (to p. 1057); cf. *ibid.*, I, 1389–1390 *n*6 (to p. 297).

[18] *C.C.*, II, 61–62. The letter is discussed below. Prince Ludovico Pio of
Savoy was the Austrian ambassador in Venice until December, 1743.

[19] *Ibid.*, I, 188. It is useless to discuss the matter further. Many critics have
expressed various opinions about it, the anti-Rousseauists like A. de Montaigu,
and Montigny emphasizing the significance of the embassy's activity, and the
others, like Derche and Monglond, taking the opposite view.

[20] The exceptions are A. de Montaigu and Montigny. The latter's whole
object is to vindicate the count's memory, against Rousseau.

in the book, which is to justify the young Rousseau's contempt for the great, glimpsed in the "Epistle to Parisot," and to crystallize further his conception of society and of himself and their mutual relations. Society is the count to whom he now sells the birthright of his genius for a mouthful of food which is not the bread of heaven as he would gladly think.

The autobiography shows how the hero's fond illusions are flattered as his employer confers upon him the office of secretary of the embassy, taking it away from the consul Le Blond,[21] who had been interim chargé d'affaires and the count's adviser in the period of his initiation, but of whom he had become jealous and resentful. Graced with this new dignity, the young man appears in the memoirs as the ambassador's envoy to the Venetian senate and as head of the palace of France, maintaining diplomatic privileges, preventing abuses, and countersigning permits for the importation of merchandise while Montaigu seeks vainly to share in the supplementary profits of the subordinate's office. In other words, the protagonist is clearly presented as secretary, not to the count personally, but to the legation, all too conscious of his position, fiercely proud of his duties no less than of his privileges, and extremely jealous of his rights.

These tableaux in *Les Confessions* are inspired by historical facts which modern erudition has analyzed repeatedly. Some critics refer to Rousseau simply as the ambassador's secretary; others point out that, since he performed the functions of secretary to the embassy, he was probably recognized and treated as such; still others conclude that he was so in reality, however he was called.[22]

[21] See *Les Confessions* in *O.C.*, Pléiade, I, 299, 301.

[22] See Victor Cérésole, *J.-J. Rousseau à Venise, 1743–1744 (Notes et documents recueillis par Victor Cérésole ... , publiés par Théodore de Saussure)* (Geneva and Paris, 1885), pp. 7–11, 21–22, 42–43; Faugère, "Jean-Jacques Rousseau à Venise," pp. 815, 817 n3, 1067 n1; Emile Faguet, *Vie de Rousseau* (Paris: Société française d'imprimerie et de Libraire, n.d.), p. 119; Eugène Ritter, "Jean-Jacques Rousseau. Notes et recherches," *Annales de la Société*

What is the fact of the matter? Abundant documentation is available. In contemporary correspondence he calls himself secretary to the embassy, envoy to the senate, and head of the palace of France. He does so, not merely in private letters to people like Madame de Warens, but in correspondence with the secretaries of French residents abroad, and even in writing to Madame de Montaigu, who remained in Paris the following year.[23] He assures the latter that he is at the head of her house in Venice by virtue of his eagerness and zeal still more than by his rank. He must surely have had the ambassador's authorization for making such a claim at the time even if Montaigu changed his mind later, as he apparently did. It is true that a note on the first memorial which Rousseau presented to the Venetian senate refers to him as the ambassador's secretary. However, on the previous memorial Le Blond is similarly designated although he was in truth royal secretary for the Italian language. As such he had acted as embassy secretary for years as well as during the six months prior to Montaigu's arrival, when he was in complete charge of affairs, and for this reason initiated both the ambassador and Rousseau in their functions.[24]

Jean-Jacques Rousseau, XI (1916–1917), 36; Ernest Seillière, *Jean-Jacques Rousseau* (Paris: Garnier, 1921), p. 43; L. J. Courtois, "Chronologie critique de la vie et des oeuvres de Jean-Jacques Rousseau," *Annales de la Société Jean-Jacques Rousseau*, XV (1923), 44 *n*3; Derche, "Autour du séjour de J.-J. Rousseau à Venise," pp. 134–135; Monglond, "Rousseau, secrétaire de M. de Montaigu," p. 51; Candaux in *O.C.*, Pléiade, III, pp. ccxlvii–ccxlviii, ccli, 1807, *n*1 (to p. 1048); Leigh in *C.C.*, I, 199–200.

[23] *C.C.*, I, 198, 212–213, and II, 39; letters to Mme de Warens, Mme de Montaigu, and M. de Vertmont, dated October 5 and November 23, 1743, and August 4, 1744. In a letter of May 12, 1745, addressed to Rousseau at the embassy after his departure, he is styled "embassy secretary" (*ibid.*, II, 82). Faugère ("Jean-Jacques Rousseau à Venise," p. 822) notes that the secretary was in fact head of the household.

[24] Le Blond was "secrétaire royal pour l'italien" and, in this capacity, performed the functions of secretary to the embassy under Montaigu's predecessor, the Comte de Froullay (November 28, 1733, to February 13, 1743), whom he also replaced during the ambassador's illness and after his departure: Derche, "Autour du séjour de J.-J. Rousseau à Venise," p. 146; and Monglond, "Rousseau, secrétaire de M. de Montaigu," p. 72 *n*67. For the two memorials see Cérésole, *J.-J. Rousseau à Venise*, pp. 10–11; cf. p. 21.

Since the count, grown distrustful of Le Blond,[25] displaced him as Italian secretary of the King's embassy in favor of the younger man, the latter must also have been recognized as such, even if he was engaged not by the French court but by Montaigu personally. Perhaps, as Monsieur Candaux suggests, he understandably confused that title with the not yet officialized one of embassy secretary, which was rarely used.[26] At this period secretaries of French embassies were, with very few exceptions, appointed not by the state but by the heads of diplomatic missions.[27] This may be why Rousseau says in the *Lettres écrites de la Montagne* that he had been First Secretary of the Ambassador of France. In any case the state archives in Paris and Venice prove incontestably that he performed the duties incumbent upon the secretary to the legation, such as the conduct of embassy correspondence, the delivery of memorials to the Venetian senate, or rather to the "College" or cabinet of ministers, and the countersigning of permits, one of which bearing his signature is reproduced in the new *Correspondance complète*. The correspondence also shows that he even provided the consul with permits and pre-

[25] For the relations between them see Derche, "Autour du séjour de J.-J. Rousseau à Venise," pp. 145–156. The ambassador, whose official instructions specifically referred him to the consul's guidance, resided with Le Blond for about a month after his arrival in Venice (*O.C.*, Pléiade, III, 1053, 1822 *n*2 [to p. 1094], 1810 *n*1 [to p. 1052]). But there was ill will between them as early as August 26, 1743, when the consul refused to transcribe the Venetian senate's oral reply to Montaigu's first memorial (*C.C.*, I, 203–204). Thereafter their hostility is obvious in the ambassador's letters of September 28 and December 7, 1743, and April 4, 1744, to the Foreign Office, where the consul is called ignorant and ill informed and is blamed for the unsatisfactory installation of the embassy household (*O.C.*, Pléiade, III, 1053, 1093–1094, 1096–1097). Thus Montaigu tried to discredit Le Blond at court, probably through jealousy as Rousseau says. He even tried to deprive him of his importation rights, with the result that the King himself had to intervene in the consul's favor. After all, Le Blond had long been established in Venice with his large family. In fact he had been consul for twenty-five years when Montaigu arrived and was to hold his post for over forty years.

[26] *Ibid.*, p. ccli.

[27] Mr. Leigh in *C.C.*, I, 199 note *h* (to no. 62) notes that there were some exceptions; e.g., there was one at Soleure (*ibid.*, II, 40).

pared them himself.[28] But it is debatable whether he could have borne the title of secretary to the French embassy, even if that title had been in general use at the time, since he was Swiss and therefore a foreigner, as he constantly reminds us in the memoirs.[29] On the other hand he could not be described as Montaigu's private secretary either since the duties of that office were discharged by the second secretary, the Abbé de Binis (or d'Ebenis), who handled the ambassador's personal correspondence during Rousseau's term of office and slightly longer. All these explanatory details, by their very aridity and dullness, their redundancy and failure to produce anything new, bring us to a fresh realization and appreciation of the autobiography. In that work we actually witness the birth of a new self-confidence in the young man's soul and an exasperated, even exasperating sense of his own intellectual superiority growing out of his contact with the count. These moral qualities take shape in the contrast—indisputably artistic if hardly modest—between the ambassador, whose character is no more extraordinary than his mind, and the subaltern, whose rich mind and character were to modify the course of occidental civilization. The opposition between the two men, which obviously has its source in actuality—and there can be no room for doubt on this point—is here used to externalize the strife within Rousseau himself between social prestige and individual merit. This inner strife is complicated by the contradiction between reality and appearance in his equivocal position as a Swiss national at the head of the palace of France. This paradox also corresponds to an essential inconsistency between his Swiss republicanism and his French "patriotism." The complexities of his situation in the suite of Montaigu are

[28] *Ibid.*, p. 202, letter from Rousseau to Le Blond, October 29, 1743. See opposite p. 232 for the permit with Rousseau's signature and cf. Cérésole, *J.-J. Rousseau à Venise*, pp. 22–23; A. de Montaigu, *Démêlés*, pp. 46–47; Derche, "Autour du séjour de J.-J. Rousseau à Venise," pp. 136–137.

[29] *O.C.*, Pléiade, I, 301, 325, referred to below.

eminently suited artistically to portray the vicissitudes of a youthful spirit. However unattractive the protagonist of the story may appear, the memorialist is unquestionably an artist.

Analyzing *Les Confessions* one is constantly reminded of Dr. Johnson's famous phrase reported by Boswell: "Pound St Paul's church into atoms and consider any single atom: it is to be sure good for nothing: but, put all these atoms together and you have St. Paul's." Our historical research does precisely this with Rousseau's masterpiece and the results are the same. In that work, synthesis rather than analysis is employed to translate into imagery the inmost recesses of mind and heart, and the drama enacted therein: a drama of inordinate pride suddenly prevailing over self-doubt and distrust as it seeks to find an outlet in life.

The following pages of the autobiography, containing a picture of diplomatic affairs at the embassy, are intended to show further the incongruity of Rousseau's subordination to the count by way of a cunning antithesis between the two men in the performance of their respective duties. The transparency of the symbolism leaves us no choice but to perceive natural genius exclusively on one side and arbitrary social distinction on the other. We see Montaigu commissioned to preserve Venetian neutrality with the collaboration of his Spanish colleague, the Marquis de Mari, whose friendship becomes a visible symbol of the bond between two crowns and their alliance against Austria in the War of the Austrian Succession. In the book the ambassador obeys instructions by giving the French court false and complacent assurances of success in spite of undeniable indications of the republic's sympathy for the common adversary. Moreover we are assured of his "ignorance," "stupidity," and "stubbornness" in all matters of correspondence in general. He forces his secretary, who must frame his dispatches from a few sparse notes, to cipher most of the tedious court missives, to answer letters that have not yet arrived, to redistribute all news to its sources, and then the would-be diplomat signs many of the communiqués without reading them. The secretary's absurd position is further illustrated by a vivid portrayal of the allegedly irreproachable integrity, courage, and talents that he lavishes upon his trivial tasks. We are persuaded that he does more than justice to his early training in Turin and Savoy,[30] serving well a foreign land to which he owes nothing and winning the esteem of everyone including the consul Le Blond whom he regretfully supplants in his office at the embassy. The opposition between rank and personal distinction was never more indignantly set forth than in these pages of *Les Confessions*, whatever relationship they may bear to the facts of actuality.

It is possible to compare this picture with historical records of the very occupations that moved the artist to paint it. His personal epistles furnish almost no evidence on the subject, but in the archives of Venice, Paris, and French embassies abroad, historians for eighty years or more have been spying upon Rousseau far more closely than the State Inquisitors ever did. They have brought to light much of the vast correspondence of the French embassy in Venice, which was a news center at the crossroads of Europe and the Orient. This correspondence contained weekly letters to the French court, both to the King and the Foreign Office, and to French embassies in Vienna and the large Italian cities (especially Naples, Bologna, Florence, Genoa, and Turin), along with less regular missives to the French Minister for the Navy and to diplomatic agents all over Europe including those at Frankfort, the Hague, Geneva, Constantinople, and St.

[30] *Ibid.*, p. 301. Again at the end of the Venetian story, p. 327, Rousseau recalls his early training in Turin and his studies at Les Charmettes between the autumn of 1735 and 1739. Regarding his studies see *C.C.*, I, 29–33, letter from Rousseau to his father at Nyon, presumably toward the end of 1735.

Petersburg.[31] It also comprised copies of all official letters, except court dispatches, written or received at the embassy and retranscribed for the French Foreign Office.[32] In addition it included memorials in Italian to the Venetian senate, the only means of communicating with the government of the republic except in special cases when a counselor was named for private discussion.[33] Copies and translations of these memorials and of the Venetian government's replies were also made for the French court. Nine of the memorials in translation have been included in the 130 recently published *Venetian Despatches*, most of which are addressed to the King and Foreign Office. Between September 14, 1743, ten days after he arrived in Venice, and July 25, 1744, almost a month before he left, this immense correspondence was with rare exceptions written by Rousseau and transcribed by his hand. The same may be said, judging by a few remaining fragments, of a fairly extensive memorial of late September, 1743, dealing with the local government and influential senators, drafted at the request of the French Foreign Office but torn from the archives in the last century and never recovered. A similar one of the following month, on the personality and character of members of the Venetian cabinet, is extant in the same hand and was, like the other, prepared so that the King would know the persons upon whom France could eventually rely in case of an emergency.[34] Scholars concur and

[31] See *O.C.*, Pléiade, I, 1391 *n*1 (to p. 300), where Montaigu's instructions are transcribed from the Archives of Foreign Affairs; cf. *ibid.*, p. 1394 *n*1 (to p. 306), where there is a note on the extent of the embassy correspondence; see also III, 1813 *n*3 (to p. 1057). The dispatches to the French court and Foreign Office were not supposed to be duplicates. In general, letters to the King summarize the main facts, while those to the minister give more detailed information about everything of interest from a practical, administrative standpoint.

[32] *Ibid.*, III, 1067.

[33] *C.C.*, II, 28–29, letter from Rousseau to M. Dupont, secretary to the French envoy at Genoa, July 25, 1744.

[34] *O.C.*, Pléiade, III, 1075–1077. The first memorial was sent on September 28, 1743. Fragments can be seen in Volume 205 of the political correspondence of Venice in the Foreign Office Archives in Paris between folios 114 and 115 (*ibid.*, pp. 1051–1052).

have proof that Rousseau did not simply transcribe these texts but played a major part in their composition. As a general rule Montaigu merely furnished brief indications of the points to be developed or else handed on news bulletins which came from local French residents and Italian informers, including priests, and were incorporated into the dispatches.[35] Sometimes of course he dictated passages himself, but these are easily identified by comparison with extant drafts and especially by their confused style, which stands out in stark contrast with Rousseau's clarity, precision, and occasional eloquence. This eloquence graces both French dispatches and Italian memorials alike and won the admiration of the Venetian senate and the King of France too, as the archives show.[36] However, apart from such rare glimpses of the future writer, we are hardly aware of his presence in this huge body of documentation, for he was engaged merely to give intelligible and tactful expression to the facts available to him. In this it must be admitted that he was as successful as the memorialist says he was in spite of a few peccadillos such as an odd mistake in date or some minor inattention hardly worth notice.

An examination of all these historical records leads to a better understanding of the art of *Les Confessions* and the role of circumstantial truth therein. Although the author magnifies the use of ciphers, which are limited, often arbitrarily, to about a dozen pages in all,[37] and although

[35] We have the ambassador's notes from which a dispatch was made and which are preserved in the Montaigu family collection in the Bibliothèque Nationale: *ibid.*, pp. 1081–1083, 1819 *n*1 (to p. 1083). We also have a news bulletin with an appended note from Montaigu to Rousseau, as well as the dispatch in which it was used: *ibid.*, pp. 1114–1115, 1827 *n*1 (to p. 1115); and *C.C.*, I, 211, 221.

[36] For these expressions of admiration see *O.C.*, Pléiade, III, 1129–1130, 1209, and especially 1211–1212. The editor remarks upon Rousseau's eloquence on pp. ccli, 1809 *n*2 (to p. 1050). Recovered drafts show Montaigu's awkwardness: *ibid.*, pp. ccxlviii–ccxlix.

[37] In the Pléiade edition of the *Venetian Despatches*, all ciphered passages are italicized. The use of ciphers is not always arbitrary; e.g., during "lista" discussions treated below, passages concerning Montaigu's counselor, Nicolò

he maliciously over-emphasizes Montaigu's peculiarity of redistributing news to its source, which is nevertheless exemplified on several occasions,[38] we cannot accuse him of inventing the idea that letters were answered before they arrived. In several missives to the Foreign Office the count himself admitted having adopted this practice. Sometimes the results are ludicrous. For example in one such letter, after expounding for the fifth time all the reasons that induced him to apply to the King for permission to request a Venetian counselor, he suddenly announced the arrival of the dispatch which he was in the midst of answering and which rendered his pleas superfluous by informing him categorically that he was not to have one at all. After five more pleas of a similar nature, the very opposite occurred: at the end of one of his missives hinting again at the value of a counselor, the face of things was abruptly changed by the delivery of a letter to which his own was supposed to be a reply and which contained news that the long sought permission had already been granted.[39] These absurdities on the part of the unfortunate ambassador contrast, even in the correspondence, with the secretary's undeniable intelligence in contending with the duties of his office. It is precisely this contrast that gives the texts their hybrid character and explains the dissimilarities in style previously observed.

Apart from peculiarities of method, the content of embassy communications yields even more valuable information for the reader of *Les Confessions*. From the welter of trivial matter two forms gradually emerge to complement each other, Montaigu and the city-state to which he was accredited. We see the ambassador obeying official instructions by allying himself with Mari to main-

(called Andrea) Erizzo, are sometimes understandably ciphered (*ibid.*, pp. 1194, 1195–1196, 1230). But other times similar passages are not, and for no apparent reason (p. 1225).

[38] *Ibid.*, p. 1150, and see 1834 *n*1 (to p. 1150); cf. p. ccxlix.

[39] *Ibid.*, p. 1114; cf. p. 1066. For Montaigu's admission see p. 1812 *n*1 (to p. 1056), and p. 1086; cf. p. ccxlix.

tain Venetian neutrality[40] and then giving the French court ungrounded assurances of his success. He does so in one-third of the *Venetian Despatches*. Since they also contain evidence of pro-Austrian and anti-French feeling in Venice, perhaps he meant that the republic, while favoring Austria, was too prudent to infringe its neutrality.[41] But the fact remains that it was not. Montaigu refused to admit this and even contradicted evidence supplied by French diplomatic agents in Vienna who, in spite of his repeated denials, convince us beyond a doubt that Venice was indeed secretly furnishing Austria with assistance.[42] His statements, challenged by the Foreign Office on several occasions, appear all the more incongruous since on January 2, 1744, he followed the lead of Mari and submitted a rather undiplomatic memorial to the Venetian government protesting its alleged partiality for Austria and warning that the French King was not indifferent to affairs in Italy.[43] In the senate's reply, and indeed in all its business with the embassy, we detect the pathetically degraded form of the oligarchic Venetian state in those last fateful years of the republic, a half century before Napoleon and, ironically

[40] Montaigu's instructions make it clear that he was to foster Mari's friendship: *ibid.*, 1805 *n*2 (to p. 1045); and *C.C.*, I, 199 note *d* (to no. 62). The dispatches confirm this: *O.C.*, Pléiade, III, 1045, 1047, 1059–1060, 1092, 1105, etc. His instructions also enjoined that he maintain Venetian neutrality since Austria was seeking to draw Venice into an alliance: *ibid.*, pp. 1809 *n*2 (to p. 1050), 1826 *n*1 (to p. 1108).

[41] For evidence of pro-Austrian feeling see *ibid.*, pp. 1052, 1053, 1061–1062 1195, 1227. But after Rousseau's departure the embassy correspondence contains much more evidence of this nature, especially from the moment that the Foreign Office questioned the assertions of Venetian neutrality as it did in letters to Montaigu dated December 8, 1744, and March 9 and 16, 1745 (A. de Montaigu, *Démêlés*, pp. 34–35; Derche, "Autour du séjour de J.-J. Rousseau à Venise," pp. 144–145). From that time on, allusions to anti-French sentiment become fairly frequent in Montaigu's dispatches to the French government (e.g., letters of January 9, April 14, June 12, 1745; January 2 and August 13, 1746). But in Rousseau's time, the French agents in Vienna make it clear that Venice was not as neutral as Montaigu declares in the same period.

[42] *O.C.*, Pléiade, III, 1830–1831 *n*1 (to p. 1128), 1843 *n*1 (to p. 1195), 1848 *n*1 (to p. 1226). Cf. Montaigu's denials on pp. 1046, 1048, 1104, 1105, 1106.

[43] *Ibid.*, pp. 1109–1110. For Mari's influence see p. 1111.

enough, the Austrians put an inglorious end to fourteen hundred years of glorious history. The government of the city answered the ambassador's memorial by humbly pledging friendship for France.[44] Yet it was moved by fear to court her rival, and in fact professed to seek the goodwill of all princes. At the same time it was aloof and distrustful of their envoys, forbidding its members to consort with them or even to exchange courtesies with them under pain of inquisitorial punishment, so great was its desire to spread a pall of mystery about its poverty and weakness.[45] This shadowy image of a cowering state to which Europe sent "the most inconsequential men as ambassadors"[46] is reminiscent of many a detail in *Les Confessions*. So is Montaigu's naïveté, which matches the pretentiousness of the Venetian government in all their relations with one another. For example, his aforesaid memorial to the senate, warning of the French King's interests in Italy, was unauthorized and therefore became a source of considerable anxiety to the French Foreign Office.[47] When he was finally able to supplement his memorials by conferring personally with a Venetian counselor, he committed worse blunders still. For instance, when the Foreign Office belied his affirmations of Venetian neutrality by forwarding a copy

[44] *Ibid.*, pp. 1827–1828 *n*2 (to p. 1117). This is a French translation of the reply. The senate answered memorials, not in writing, but by sending a Venetian secretary to read and even dictate the reply to the ambassador's secretary. Montaigu's counselor, in their first interviews together, conveyed similar assurances (pp. 1123–1124, 1128–1129).

[45] See *ibid.*, pp. 1815–1816 *n*1 (to p. 1067), and p. 1076, where it is recalled that a nobleman, suspected of consorting with foreign envoys, was once hanged, although his innocence was later recognized; cf. pp. 1098, 1129, where Montaigu reports that several nobles had been reprimanded for exchanging civilities with Mari.

[46] Philippe Monnier, *Venise au XVIIIᵉ siècle* (Paris: Perrin, 1908), p. 350; and Monglond, "Rousseau, secrétaire de M. de Montaigu," p. 40, where he quotes from the correspondence of the Cardinal de Bernis with M. Paris-du-Verney, published in London in 1790, I, 35.

[47] *O.C.*, Pléiade, III, 1833 *n*1 (to p. 1137); cf. 1140–1141; 1144–1145, 1834 *n*2 (to p. 1144).

of a dispatch from Vienna containing confidential information about the republic's collaboration with Austria, he at
once communicated its contents to his newly appointed
counselor, Nicolò Erizzo. The latter appreciated his
frankness much more than did the French minister to whom
the count artlessly reported his indiscretion without even
recognizing it as such.[48] But later, when the trusted
counselor took a less favorable view of certain abuses in
the administration of embassy affairs, he fell a victim to
what the critics call Montaigu's "rage," "lack of discernment," and "blindness."[49] These are precisely the qualities
which, even in the archives, contrast with the secretary's
competence and which the memorialist calls "ignorance,"
"stupidity," and "obstinacy." It is difficult not to see in
external reality an important source of his writing.

All these circumstances, scattered at random through
dispatches and letters, clearly represent the facts which,
like so many fragmentary pieces, are integrated into the
tableau of Rousseau's memoirs. But there ends the simi-
larity between archives and art. The work of art gives us
not a pallid reflection of life but an intense and composite
vision proceeding from the writer's nature, which assumes
consistency in figures and events. This is so even in the
pages on the ungrateful theme of the embassy functions.
Here we see the secretary's zeal and talents undaunted by
the tedious tasks entrusted to him or by the ambassador's
inadequacy. This inadequacy is, after all, that of society,
which we disclaim as alien to us much as the Greeks looked
upon their neighbors as barbarians, but its weaknesses are,

[48] *Ibid.*, pp. 1128, 1148–1149 show Montaigu's naïveté; Amelot's reply is
quoted on p. 1834 *n*1 (to p. 1149). Montaigu apologized later for his frankness
(p. 1184). The counselor, the chevalier Nicolò (Andrea) Erizzo, was later
named Venetian ambassador to Vienna and replaced as counselor by Count
Mocenigo. See Derche, "Autour du séjour de J.-J. Rousseau à Venise," p. 160;
Montigny, "Jean-Jacques Rousseau secrétaire d'ambassade," p. 432; *O.C.*,
Pléiade, III, 1825 *n*2 (to p. 1102); and especially *C.C.*, I, 239.

[49] *O.C.*, Pléiade, III, 1197–1198; 1843–1844 *n*1 (to p. 1198); cf. also 1216–
1217, 1220–1221, 1221–1223, 1225–1226.

in fact, our own. Without acknowledging this, the young Rousseau has the intoxicating illusion that he is strong enough to contend with them and to rise above them. For the moment the memorialist relives and espouses his blindness and intoxication, though later he admits that he knows better. He speaks a language whose accents we can understand, for they register faithfully and lucidly the pride and illusions of his soul, which resound in our own "to teach us to know ourselves and grow wise at the expense of the dead." To see this is not to approve or to disapprove of his nature or its affinity with ours, but simply to recognize the artist and the universality of his art, however pathetically fragile the flesh in which his gifts were lodged.

SCENES OF EXTROVERSION

After telling of the reportedly singular virtues expended upon Montaigu's absurd assignments, the writer of *Les Confessions* proceeds to relate a series of heroic actions which are momentous enough for him to allude to them again in the final pages of his last book recalling the "generous intrepidity" and "fermentation of heart" of Montaigu's secretary. The latter accomplishes these actions on his own initiative and on behalf of the French nation in Paris and abroad. The people are depicted as neglected and even ignored by their ambassador, who is completely absorbed in his friendship with Mari. These exploits are rendered the more astonishing by Rousseau's allusion to the isolation of embassy personnel, virtually debarred by the inquisitors from communicating with persons in authority such as Venetian nobles and members of the government. It is even impossible for the young hero to seek help from the consul who, born in Venice where he has a permanent residence with his family (like his father the consul before him and his son after him), feels obliged to show a certain deference to the Venetian authorities.

Nevertheless we see the energetic secretary obtaining the services of talented Italian dramatic artists for the Parisian theater; securing the release of a French merchant ship unjustly detained by the republic; intervening at his own expense to force a Venetian nobleman to repay a Parisian creditor; and finally saving the Bourbon realm of Naples from falling into the hands of the Austrians. These feats are the themes of a sequence of colorful scenes that are undeniably reflected in the Venetian dispatches and memorials and are therefore founded in actuality.[50] In *Les Confessions* they give visible form to some of the most complex states of soul recorded in the book, where they represent a supreme trial of strength on the part of the protagonist to prevail in a mighty struggle with the forces of society. Moreover, since in each case he appears as the instrument of the King of France's protection, all these situations betray the austere young republican's lasting affection for France, a country synonymous with the very social forces against which he is contending. This strange affection is also the theme of his little one act comedy, *Les Prisonniers de guerre*, begun in Paris about May, 1743, and later completed there, but largely inspired by his residence in Venice and significantly never published during his lifetime.[51] The playwright conveys his feelings through the character Dorante, a French prisoner in Hungary during the War of the Austrian Succession, who represents France in a foreign land much as the hero of the seventh book of *Les Confessions*. Dorante wins respect abroad for the civilizing role of France, native land of the human race, fostering knowledge and the fine arts even in the midst of war. Here the Swiss writer claims France as his own. Yet how much more intense and personal

[50] *Ibid.*, p. ccli, where M. Candaux points out that Rousseau's "services" are confirmed by the Venetian dispatches and memorials. For the above-mentioned allusion at the end of Book XII, see *ibid.*, I, 653.

[51] *Ibid.*, II, 1842. Rousseau mentions it sheepishly in a note toward the end of the seventh book of *Les Confessions*. Early in the fifth book, he speaks at length of his embarrassing love of France. Cf. *Lettre à Philopolis*.

is the feeling in the memoirs where he exults in deeds that
he himself performed at Venice in the service of the French
King! Little wonder if this affection caused the new Alceste
some embarrassment, for it was as paradoxical as the old
Alceste's love for Célimène, but as Molière wisely observes
reason does not govern love.

THE VERONESE THEME

The first scene manifests Rousseau's youthful enthusiasm
for the theater as well as a new delight in the dramatic moment and generous gesture. It is one of the few scenes in
which he visualizes himself in a typical eighteenth-century
Venetian setting, in the metropolis of pleasure and the
country of improbable adventures like those of Casanova.
We see him during carnival time, disguised in mask and
domino and accompanied by the ambassador's livery, as
he takes his gondola to the palace of the patrician impresario
Zustiniani where, being an alien, he might not normally
have access or expose himself to recognition. As a "siora
maschera," he is ushered into the presence of the noble
Venetian. Boldly unmasking, he claims the release of the
actor Veronese (and his daughter Coralline), who are currently appearing at Zustiniani's St. Samuel theater, although they are already under contract with the French
court to perform in Versailles and Paris. This action is the
young Rousseau's personal response to an urgent appeal
from the court chamberlain, whose orders are almost ignored by Montaigu and the consul as well. Finally, to ensure
success he sends a warning to Veronese himself, threatening
to have him arrested if he does not leave for France with
his two daughters, Coralline and Camille. Veronese departs
within a week and the secretary's triumph is complete in
these daring gestures on behalf of his adopted homeland.

This animated scene, which the Pléiade editors consider
particularly brilliant, has given rise to much historical
research. The scene is of course morally true, for it testifies

both to the secretary's paradoxical devotion to France and to his interest in the stage. This interest is also evident in the first memorial he presented to the local senate only five days after his arrival, requesting loges in four of the seven Venetian theaters.[52] But does the scene in the memoirs have any other links with life? Eighty years ago it was regarded by critics like Cérésole and Saussure as having no foundation at all in actuality since the correspondence then known contained no reference to it. Twenty years later Auguste de Montaigu, the ambassador's descendant, discovered in the family archives and then published a letter of December 7, 1743, addressed by Rousseau in the count's name to the court chamberlain, the Duke de Gesvres, proving that Montaigu had sent his secretary in carnival costume to deliver a note from the French court to a patrician impresario, Michele Grimani, proprietor of the St. Samuel theater.[53] The letter explains that the disguise was to circumvent the law forbidding communication between foreign ministers and Venetian nobility. It also gives a clue to the contents of the note which Grimani had not yet answered. The missive demanded seizure of the wages of a comedian Veronese, who was engaged with his daughter at the theater after he had ignored a contract with the French court and even collected part payment for his prospective services. Auguste de Montaigu also published at the same time and from the same source a brief Italian version of the court note prepared by Rousseau. Twenty years after the publication of these two pieces the duke's appeal to the embassy, dated November 6, 1743, which had accompanied his note for Grimani, came to light in the same archives and was published by Monsieur Joseph Souchon

---

[52] *Ibid.*, I, 1395–1396 *n*1 (to p. 308); cf. Cérésole, *J.-J. Rousseau à Venise*, pp. 11–13, 61. The memorial is dated September 9, 1743.

[53] For Cérésole's opinion see *J.-J. Rousseau à Venise*, p. 38, and cf. Saussure's on pp. 134–136. For the letter see A. de Montaigu, *Démêlés*, pp. 51–52; *O.C.*, Pléiade, III, 1098–1099, and *C. C.*, I, 216–217. Rousseau did not make any error in the name of the theater as had been supposed: *O.C.*, Pléiade, III, 1823 *n*4 (to p. 1097), correcting an error in Volume I.

in 1915. More recently, a draft of the note itself, also dated November 6 and no doubt identical with the original, which was probably destroyed by Grimani, was discovered in the archives of Foreign Affairs in Paris. It has now been reproduced in its entirety in Mr. Leigh's edition of the *Correspondance complète* together with Rousseau's brief Italian version already published by Montaigu's descendant.[54] It is well known that Coralline Veronese, the daughter in question, did not make her debut in Paris until May 6, 1744, exactly six months after the court appeal to the embassy.[55] This is all that can be positively said of the historical events that furnished the elements of the scene in the memoirs.

Yet more can be added with a fair degree of certainty, for some things are easily conjectured, and they do not essentially impugn the literal veracity of *Les Confessions*. For example, the court message of November 6 to Grimani must have been delivered by Montaigu's secretary on or about November 23, since at that time the Versailles dispatches took fifteen to twenty days to reach Venice.[56] This assumption is virtually confirmed by Rousseau's private letters, which help to clarify matters, although this point has been overlooked by the critics. On the same November 23 he wrote to Madame de Montaigu referring to the close bond between the houses of France and Spain which, in the eyes of the memorialist, so distracted the ambassador from his duties that the secretary was forced to take the initiative in embassy affairs such as the Veronese matter. A passage in the letter reads: "I have upset my

[54] Derche first drew attention to the draft of the court note in "Autour du séjour de J.-J. Rousseau à Venise," p. 135 *n*3. It was partly published in *O.C.*, Pléiade, III, 1822–1823 *n*2 (to p. 1097), and completely in *C.C.*, I, 204–205. For the duke's letter to Montaigu accompanying it see Souchon, *Correspondance diplomatique*, p. 366.

[55] See *O.C.*, Pléiade, I, 1392 *n*1 (to p. 302), and III, 1823 *n*4 (to p. 1097).

[56] If the court message was indeed delivered on November 23, it would be strange that it was not mentioned in dispatches of November 30, unless Montaigu waited in the hope of having something definite to report.

philosophy a little to dress like other people, with the result that I go about the square and the theatres in mask and domino as proudly as if I had spent my whole life in this attire."[57] The excitement and exultation in these lines remind us vaguely of the tone of the famous scene in the memoirs where alone the correspondence assumes meaning. If the event took place at the Grimani palace instead of the Zustiniani, this would not change matters in the least. The scene in *Les Confessions* would not be altered by a name or lose its literary or psychological value for such a trivial reason, especially since Grimani was also a patrician, as we have said, and in fact the doge of Venice at the time was Pietro Grimani.[58] The situation would therefore be essentially the same as the writer describes it. The editor of the *Venetian Despatches* also draws this conclusion, but he adds that Rousseau perhaps wrongly appropriates all the honor of the negotiation. This may be so. On the other hand, nothing prevents us from believing, as we read in the memoirs, that the bold and imaginative step was taken on the secretary's initiative, instead of Montaigu's, and that it was instigated by the ambassador's indifference and the consul's timidity. In fact the count's reluctance to intervene in the matter is visible in his reply to the court on December 7, where he concludes that he can really do nothing more about it except have Veronese arrested. Mysteriously enough he makes no further reference to the affair in the dispatches. If he had done anything else he would likely have mentioned it, since he loses no opportunity to recommend himself to the court. Where then does the denouement of the memorialist's story originate? I refer to the secretary's final and decisive action of threatening the

[57] *C.C.*, I, 212–213.

[58] Girolamo Grimani, a senator, made a memorial for the Council of Ten concerning the "lista" discussions, treated below. The name Zustiniani may have been in Rousseau's mind because it was the name of the senator who declined to take any action on Montaigu's memorial of August 31, 1744, against Rousseau; consult the index.

actor with arrest, which brings the affair to a happy conclusion and procures for the Italian comedy in Paris the
services of Coralline, one of that theater's most famous
actresses, whom Rousseau met personally a dozen years
later. Does the silence of the dispatches indicate that these
gestures were his own independent work, that the ambassador had no part in them, and that they were therefore
unauthorized and unworthy of recognition in the official
correspondence? Or should we suppose that the memorialist
invented them out of nothing? In either case the facts of
actuality are strangely inconclusive by comparison with
the text of *Les Confessions*, which was however obviously
inspired by them.

The truth is that even the conclusion of the Veronese
story in the memoirs may owe some debt to actuality. It
contains curious echoes of another entirely different affair,
discussed in more than a dozen of the *Venetian Despatches*
over a period of nearly three months, from January 25 to
April 18, 1744, but ignored in the memoirs to the surprise
of many scholars. This is the incredible affair of the renowned dancer, Barberina Campanini, who was in Venice
for the carnival, ignoring a contract with Frederick II
of Prussia similar to Veronese's engagement with the
French court.[59] The Prussian agent, Cattaneo, a Venetian
"gentleman" whom Rousseau frequented and whose
daughter he admired, appealed to Montaigu and Mari to
help him force Barberina to honor her commitment. The
count obliged by inviting her to dinner in the hope of
persuading her to respect the engagement, but the
capricious lady was more interested in another engagement
of a different sort with a young Scottish lord, James Stuart
Mackenzie, son of Sir George, who had followed her to
Venice from London and Paris and was said to be madly
in love with her. Whether Rousseau, who usually shared

[59] For references to the Barberina affair in the dispatches see *O.C.*, Pléiade, III, 1125, 1127, 1130, 1132–1133, 1135, 1138–1139, 1142, 1147, 1150, 1159, 1163, 1172, 1177, and notes on pp. 1829, 1833–1834.

the ambassador's table, was present at the dinner—at
least as Italian interpreter—we cannot tell. But there is
no doubt that it was he who, reporting upon the failure
of this expedient, wrote in a dispatch of February 1,
1744, to the King of France's minister that she had a
head as light as her feet.[60] Next Cattaneo made representations to the Venetian senate to intervene on behalf
of His Prussian Majesty, who, in case of refusal, was rep-
portedly planning to arrest the Venetian ambassador
traveling to London through Prussia to take up his post.
This threat stirred the senate to action, although Barberina,
as a native of Parma was subject not to Venice at all but to
Austria, which may have forced the republic's hand in
order to please the King of Prussia, as Rousseau's dispatches surmise. And so the dancer became a kind of pawn
in the War of the Austrian Succession. On February 15,
1744, when the distraught Cattaneo, as a last resort was
pleading with Montaigu and Mari to help him engage
"twelve or if necessary fifty men" to kidnap the ballerina
in the midst of the opera, the Venetian government suddenly ordered her to fulfill her engagement abroad, secured
her arrest the next day, kept her under detention for two
months, and finally in mid-April had her escorted to Berlin
where she arrived on May 8. There her Scottish lover
followed her but was promptly banished by the great
Frederick, who took the ballerina as his mistress. Such
is the story of Barberina, which we may trace through
Rousseau's Venetian dispatches.

Can it be that the writer of *Les Confessions*, ignoring
these events because he was not personally involved, was,
however, moved by them to invent the conclusion of the
Veronese story contained therein? I think not. But I do
think that the two affairs have a connection which critics
in the past have not suspected. It is very likely that the
greatly publicized events concerning Barberina inspired
and emboldened the young secretary to threaten the actor

[60] *Ibid.*, p. 1130.

with the dancer's fate and to frighten him into honoring his contract with France and leaving Italy within a week's time. In this case, he must have done so over three months after the carnival scene of November and about the time of Barberina's arrest in mid-February, thereby precipitating Veronese's departure and ensuring Coralline's Parisian debut of early May. In fact, if Veronese left Venice about February 22 and if he traveled at the same rate as Rousseau, he would have arrived in Paris in time for a debut about May 6. In the work of art events are telescoped, so to speak, and time is contracted in the story of the soul, or rather it does not exist. Exposition, climax, and denouement are brought into close proximity and interrelated so that the facts, which in themselves are unaltered, assume both coherent form and psychological significance.

But if the denouement of the Veronese story in the memoirs is, as we may now conclude, based upon the facts of actuality, why were these facts ignored in the correspondence? We have already proposed that there may have been good reason for this. Perhaps the secretary's zeal in issuing the summons was considered an act of insubordination, especially if, as *Les Confessions* implies, he failed to consult his superior. Is this how he alienated the latter in mid-February? His personal letters show that he did so sometime between February 7 and February 22, 1744. On February 7 he was clearly expecting to remain in Venice indefinitely since on that date he reiterated an earlier request for merchandise to be sent from Paris; but on February 22 he thought of returning to France, judging by a missive drafted at that time and supposedly intended for the Abbé Alary at the French court, through whom his appointment was originally proposed. In the latter draft he says that the air of Venice is bad for his health and that, in spite of Montaigu's goodness, he longs for Paris.[61] This letter, hinting that all was not well at the embassy, was

[61] *C.C.*, I, 229–230. Cf. p. 224, letter from Rousseau to Roguin, February 7, 1744. However, in a letter of February 8, Rousseau makes similar statements about his health (pp. 225–226).

written about the time Veronese would have left Venice if he was threatened at the moment of Barberina's arrest and if, as we are told in the memoirs, he left within a week of the threat. Of course the draft does not testify conclusively to the writer's estrangement from his employer and, even if it did, there is no internal evidence to connect the estrangement with Veronese, nothing but a coincidence in time. A similar coincidence is more persuasive in the case of another of Rousseau's letters containing definite proof that, approximately at this very period, the ambassador threatened to replace him in six weeks. On April 30, 1744, the secretary drafted a letter, probably for the Chevalier de Montaigu in Paris, alluding to some such threat made in February, asking whether he might expect a successor and rather naïvely trusting his correspondent to make good use of these confidences by following right sentiment and reason.[62] If it was the young man's zeal that aroused the count's hostility in actual life as well as in the pages of *Les Confessions*—for so we are told later in that book—then the dispatch of a menacing message to Veronese *may* have contributed to a rift in the embassy, especially if the count was ignored in the matter. In that case the failure of the correspondence to refer to it is comprehensible.

There is another possible interpretation of events, prompted by a collation of documents and memoirs. The secretary may have fallen from grace in February by taking some other independent and aggressive action connected with the same incident. For example he may have been moved by the Barberina affair to re-enact at the Zustiniani palace a scene that had taken place three months earlier at the Grimani house, since Veronese's second daughter, Camille, was engaged at the San Mosé theater, belonging to the Zustiniani family, and the comedian and Coralline could hardly have left without her. Besides,

[62] *Ibid.*, pp. 233–234.

Rousseau boasts of having obtained for France the services of both sisters. Mr. Leigh, in his edition of the correspondence, favors the possibility of two scenes, but without connecting either one with the Barberina affair or Montaigu's hostility. This hypothesis, though not easily defended, would have strong psychological support. Rousseau, who had parts of his ballet, *Les Muses galantes*, performed in another of Grimani's theaters, the St. John Chrysostom, would probably not have confused the name Grimani with any other, since he must have had permission for this privilege from the owner of the theater. Besides, would he really have forgotten a name which was also that of the doge? If the theory of two scenes were true—and it could hardly be proved conclusively—then both events and all accompanying circumstances would, in the work of art, be quite naturally translated into a single composite scene containing elements from both experiences. In any case, there are enough echoes of actuality in the Veronese story of *Les Confessions* to convince us that it is not a product of the author's creative imagination as everyone, even the best known critics, believed hardly more than sixty years ago.

Yet, quite apart from its literal veracity, it has great artistic and spiritual value, which a transcription or violation of actuality could neither make nor mar. This narrative furnishes not the least of all scenes in a work of art embodying the story of the writer's soul. It sets forth a new-found vigor and confidence born within the young Rousseau as a result of his contact with the Count de Montaigu. The memorialist, moved by an intuitive vision of himself, of his love for the theater, and his devotion to France, chooses imagery perfectly consonant with these states of mind and heart, even if they belie his professed convictions. Indeed it is precisely his infallible taste in selecting tableaux most appropriate to the psychological truth conveyed that gives conviction and distinction to the autobiography. The picturesque scene there immortalized does not lack historical verisimilitude either. Montaigu's secretary appears in carnival costume, worn six months of the year in eighteenth-century Venice, where a piece of black or white satin on the face and a black silk cape or "bauta" over the shoulders conferred the liberty to do or say anything and go anywhere with absolute impunity.[63] Arrayed in this manner and announcing himself as a "siora maschera," he is not posing as a woman as readers have supposed.[64] He is simply a mask and nothing more. The title he assumes, like the costume he wears, is the only one admitted for either sex during the carnival and is an open sesame that moves his imagination and fascinates his mind. Has the Queen of the Adriatic cast her spell upon the lonely hermit of the empty lazaret? Probably not. More likely the hermit has been drawn from his retreat by a consciousness of superior strength and by the demands of his post. Accordingly he is inspired with a love of grandiose gestures that infuses a fresh strain of lyrical romanticism into the art of the memorialist many years later, producing vivid pictures of his energetic grasp of embassy affairs rather than descriptions of landscape.

THE OLIVET THEME

The second of the heroic scenes in the seventh book of *Les Confessions* is almost as theatrical as the first. The secretary appears again in his gondola on the waters of the Venetian lagoon, playing an imposing role. This time we see

[63] Monnier, *Venise au XVIIIe siècle*, pp. 61–63. People went about masked from the first Sunday in October to Christmas; from Epiphany to Lent (the carnival proper); two weeks at the Ascension, on the feast of St. Mark (April 25) and other festive occasions. See also Charles Diehl, *Une République patricienne: Venise* (Paris: Flammarion, 1935), p. 297.

[64] *O.C.*, Pléiade, I, 1392 n5 (to p. 302); here "una siora maschera" is translated "une femme masquée." The title "Signora" is simply explained by the fact that "maschera" is feminine, even when referring to male persons. Similarly one says "Signora guardia" in addressing a police officer. "Une siora maschera" is therefore not "une femme masquée" but a mask in the sense of a masked person.

him far from the city, beyond the Lido at Poveglia,[65] alongside a French merchant vessel placed under an embargo as a result of a quarrel between the crew and some quarantined Slavonian sailors, engaged on a ship belonging to the republic. There, on the spot, he draws up an official report and while his companion, the Abbé Patizel, chancellor of the consulate and vice-consul, sits in utter silence, he alone, we are told, courageously questions the mariners to elicit replies favorable to the French ship in the hope of securing its release. He can hardly induce his companion to sign the report after him and, as in the previous scene, he is represented as acting independently, on account of the ambassador's indifference and the consul's reluctance to intervene. This grandiloquent gesture culminates a series of more conventional proceedings that throw it into artistic relief: notably, the presentation of a memorial to the Venetian senate on behalf of the French ship, and communication of the incident to the French government. His success earns for him the gratitude of Captain Olivet, the ship's master, and arouses new respect for the King's protection in the minds of all, including the Venetians.

This colorful scene has been the object of an enormous amount of research. Most of it is of an historical order and has cast suspicion upon the writer's veracity and upon the literal truth of *Les Confessions*. No one disbelieves that Captain Olivet's ship suffered the indignity described, inflicted by the Slavonian crew of a quarantined Venetian vessel. Nor does anyone doubt that, the following day, Montaigu's secretary submitted to the local senate a protest in the form of a memorial, the original of which, written in his own hand and dated July 7, 1744, is preserved in the state archives of Venice. No one doubts either that he communicated the matter to the French government. On the contrary, we know that copies of the memorial, in the hand of the second secretary de Binis, were forwarded to Paris,

[65] The name is not mentioned in *Les Confessions*. See *C.C.*, II, 17. In Venetian dialect it is called Poveggia.

to the Foreign Office, and the Ministry for the Navy respectively, and that the matter was mentioned in official dispatches of July 11, written by Rousseau to the same correspondents as well as to the King himself. It was also mentioned in Le Blond's dispatch to the Ministry, sent by the same courier. We know too that on that very day the Venetian senate replied to the memorial promising an examination of French claims for compensation.[66] The story in *Les Confessions* is therefore far from being entirely fictitious.

The only point that has been seriously questioned is precisely the dynamic decisive gesture in which Rousseau takes most obvious pleasure. Is this pleasure purely aesthetic? Or did he really take Patizel in his gondola to interrogate the ship's company? A copy of a report such as he describes, dated July 17, 1744, and recording a ship's side interrogation of July 14, was published in 1885 after being found in the chancery of the French Consulate in Venice, but it is not in Rousseau's hand, nor does it bear his signature or any reference to him at all.[67] It is signed by

[66] For Rousseau's memorial of July 7, see Cérésole, *J.-J. Rousseau à Venise*, pp. 26–27, and *C.C.*, II, 1–2. The copy made for the Foreign Office by de Binis and preserved in the archives in Paris was published by Faugère, "Jean-Jacques Rousseau à Venise," pp. 1062–1063, and in *O.C.*, Pléiade, III, 1218–1219. For de Binis' copy of Rousseau's memorial, made for the Ministry for the Navy, see *ibid.*, I, 1393 n3 (to p. 303). For the dispatches of July 11 (first published in the Cérésole book) see *ibid.*, III, 1220–1223, and *C.C.*, II, 7–9 (including Le Blond's on pp. 8–9). The senate's reply and Rousseau's French translation made for the Foreign Office and copied by de Binis were published in Cérésole, *J.-J. Rousseau à Venise*, pp. 128–134; cf. Faugère, "Jean-Jacques Rousseau à Venise," pp. 1061–1062. The complete Italian text and French translation are both reproduced in *C.C.*, II, 10–14.

[67] Cérésole, *J.-J. Rousseau à Venise*, pp. 26–36. The report confirms a declaration made by Olivet to the consulate on July 6 about an incident that had occurred the same day. During a violent storm a Venetian ship manned by Slavonians was thrown against the French vessel. A quarrel broke out between the two crews and finally a dozen Slavonians, armed with sabers, boarded the French ship, whose crew members either hid or threw themselves into the sea with the exception of one who was seriously wounded. The report contains the results of an interrogation of seven witnesses and participants who declared that the Slavonians had taken the initiative in the affair.

Patizel to whom the depositions are attributed. The same is true of other copies in the Foreign Office archives in Paris. One was forwarded by the embassy directly to that office, enclosed with a dispatch of July 18, which is extant but which does not even mention Rousseau although it contains an explanation of the enclosure and is written in his own hand. Other dispatches of the same date sent by the embassy and consulate to the Ministry for the Navy both ascribe the report to Patizel and show that Le Blond had undertaken to forward it to that department, presumably because commercial matters concerned the consul primarily.[68] He finally did so on July 25, specifying in an accompanying letter that the document had been prepared, at Montaigu's orders, by Patizel. It too is preserved in Paris and, like the one sent by the embassy to the Foreign Office, is copied and signed by the vice-consul. Eighty years ago the only logical conclusion of all this evidence seemed to be that Rousseau had no part in the report or in the inquiry upon which it was based. Such was the skeptical attitude of scholars like Cérésole and Saussure, supported by Auguste de Montaigu twenty years later, and still another twenty years afterward by Courtois.[69] The deduction might have been justified on the basis of the then known correspondence and records in Paris, since it seems strange that Montaigu, in writing to his superiors, would deliberately deprive the embassy of the honor of both the depositions and the report to assign them to the consulate, unless of course one were to suppose with Monsieur Monglond that his relations with his secretary were even more strained than with the consul and had moved him to eliminate the young man's signature in the communications

[68] For one copy of the report in Paris see *ibid.*, pp. 123–127. This research was done by Saussure, who published Cérésole's work. For the dispatches of July 18 to the Foreign Office and Ministry for the Navy see *O.C.*, Pléiade, III, 1226–1228, 1229.

[69] Cérésole, *J.-J. Rousseau à Venise*, pp. 27–28, 37–38, 127; A. de Montaigu, *Démêlés*, pp. 53–62; Courtois, "Chronologie critique," p. 46 *n*2.

with France.[70] Even if this were the case, historical research has done much to bring *Les Confessions* into disrepute.

However, many of its conclusions are unwarranted. The absence of Rousseau's signature on the copy of the report in the consulate archives of Venice proves nothing, for it may understandably have been removed by that office, which had jurisdiction in commercial affairs and ought therefore to have taken the initiative in the matter. That it failed to do so was made known forty years ago when a contemporary letter of July 15, 1744, came to light in the *Correspondance générale* to prove that the original report was indeed Rousseau's work and that the copies in existence are mere copies and nothing more. The letter is addressed by him to the count, who was on holiday in the country. He writes: "I must report to Your Excellency that yesterday I spent the day at Povveggia [*sic*] with M. Le Blond's chancellor and Captain Olivet, taking depositions from the crew and witnesses of the fact in question. If I can get the report ready to-day, I shall wait upon Your Excellency to-morrow morning, in accordance with your orders."[71] Here we see that the secretary was even then preparing the controversial document following the investigation and interrogation of the crew which he had made the previous day at Poveglia in the vice-consul's presence. With the discovery of this letter, Patizel's role was reduced to a signature. This has been confirmed today by more new evidence. Only recently have we learned that a year after the event— in a letter of September 18, 1745—Montaigu informed the Foreign Office, though belatedly, of his secretary's part in the affair but without explaining why the copy of the report, which he had forwarded at the time of the inquiry, attributed all negotiations to Patizel. The ambassador's letter was found in the Foreign Office archives by Monsieur Jean-Daniel Candaux, who published it in the *Venetian*

[70] Monglond, "Rousseau, secrétaire de M. de Montaigu," pp. 67–70.
[71] *C.G.*, I, 220–222, and *C.C.*, II, 81–82.

Despatches. Referring to the *procès verbal* embodied in the report, the count writes: "The consul stayed in the country so as not to incur the displeasure of the republic by making it himself which I was obliged to do through my secretary [J.-J. Rousseau] and the vice-consul."[72] Does this mean that the report was made under Montaigu's orders as his descendant declared years ago? The letter of July 15 makes this at least debatable. It shows that the count, no less than the consul, stayed in the country while the depositions were made and was represented by his secretary, as the consul was by Patizel, who ought to have assumed responsibility in a commercial matter but obviously did not do so, any more than did Montaigu. Although the ambassador may have been present at the embassy at the time of the memorial to the senate and left the city only when he received the rather indecisive reply, yet he did not wait for the matter to be definitively settled before going off to his villa, and in any case he had no hand in drawing up the report, nor did he ever pretend to have. The report was the secretary's work, even though all known extant versions bear the signature of another. Like the Veronese incident, the Olivet affair conceivably played a role in his disgrace, and in any case certainly coincides in time with his definitive withdrawal from the service of the legation. The Venetian government settled the matter in Olivet's favor on July 26, 1744, just ten days before Rousseau left the embassy,[73] although no reparation of any kind was made for the insult to the French flag. This is all we can learn from available documents. Once again historical study does little more than confirm piecemeal the isolated data from which the autobiographer was able to draw a scene considered by the editor of the *Venetian Despatches* as one of the most brilliant of all.

[72] *O.C.*, Pléiade, III, p. cclii.

[73] *Ibid.*, 1848 *n*1 (to p. 1225), and especially *C.C.*, II, 38. The connection of the Olivet affair and Rousseau's disgrace is discussed below.

But positivistic criticism does not and cannot solve the most vital matters which alone give point to the scene and justify its inclusion in the story of the soul. Was it the secretary's effort, springing from an irrational and all the more intense love for France, that moved the Venetian government to make compensation? Was it his memorial, based upon the captain's evidence and subsequently reinforced by the depositions and report, that effected the ship's release? Of course, even if it was not, the effort alone as recorded in the memoirs is eloquent of the writer's inner life. But it is far more so taken in conjunction with the repercussion of the affair in that book. I refer to the captain's gratitude toward the secretary, which makes the republic's concession in favor of the French vessel seem something more meaningful than a mere act of diplomacy. Olivet's acknowledgment, made in the famous dinner on board ship, the theme of one of the most memorable scenes in *Les Confessions*, which will be discussed later, must have some foundation in life. One can hardly assume that it is a figment of the writer's creative imagination. But if we accept it to be so, we can pay no greater tribute to his artistic sense, which is also admirable in the gondola scene at Poveglia. This fine conception not only has its origin in the circumstances of actuality, prosaically sketched in contemporary letters, in Rousseau's report, memorials, and dispatches, but it is resplendent with spiritual truth as well. The daring gesture is intended by the autobiographer to proclaim a new extroversion, a heart aflame with generosity, heroic devotion to duty, and an undying love for France, and is accordingly clothed in a dramatic form consistent with the boastful exuberance of these states of soul.

A MATTER OF JUSTICE

The third situation recounted in the memoirs shows the embassy secretary extending the King's protection far beyond the bounds of duty. Yet it is not in the least theatrical. On the contrary it is perfectly designed to give visible form to a simple love of justice. He undertakes to collect a debt from a Venetian patrician on behalf of a French hairdresser in Paris and is entrusted with the debtor's promissory note. Since the matter is a commercial one it concerns the consul, whose intervention is however ineffectual as usual. During the course of proceedings and in the confusion of the secretary's sudden departure from the legation, the note is lost and the Venetian refuses to pay the debt. Rousseau is obliged to settle it in its entirety at his own expense five years later, when he is finally compensated for his services to the ambassador. Such is the autobiographical account of an incident which is a source of distress and frustration to the author as much as it is to the young man he portrays.

This story is based upon an actual situation that may be partly reconstructed from correspondence published by Monsieur Joseph Souchon in 1915 and by Mr. Leigh in 1965. However all critics and editors without exception have failed to see the close relationship of the correspondence in question to the text of *Les Confessions*. Two letters in particular have a bearing on the problem of truth in that book.[74] Both are addressed at a later date to the Count de Montaigu. One is from the Parisian creditor and is dated April 17, 1745. The writer complains bitterly to the ambassador that he has tried unsuccessfully to collect a quarter of the debt from Rousseau in Paris and to convince him that the whole amount was even then deposited at the French consulate in Venice. Critics immediately hastened to point out that this letter belies *Les Confessions*. They accused the author of a double error, namely the two

[74] Souchon, *Correspondance diplomatique*, pp. 382, 418–419 (fragments) and *C.C.*, II, 81–82, 110–111. The most significant part of the first letter is quoted in *O.C.*, Pléiade, I, 1394 *n3* (to p. 305). For criticism see notes by both Souchon and Leigh, and also Monglond, "Rousseau, secrétaire de M. de Montaigu," p. 40 *n2*.

allegations that the debtor had refused to pay his debt, and that the creditor had insisted upon claiming the whole amount from the unfortunate arbiter. They concluded by convicting the autobiographer of boastfulness. What they failed to notice is that another letter, addressed to Montaigu by his brother, the chevalier, on October 21, 1748, relates to the same incident, and proves that Rousseau's whole text is based upon the truth. This letter is also far more informative than the hairdresser's and contains an account of the affair from 1744 to the end of 1748. From it we learn the following: that the creditor originally entrusted the promissory note to the Chevalier de Montaigu in Paris, who sent it to Venice in the autumn of 1743 by courtesy of the ambassador's French cook; that early in 1744 the embassy secretary used it effectively to present a claim before the senate which enjoined payment (although the said claim has not yet come to light any more than the senate's judgment); that, although the secretary later lost the note, the debtor was nevertheless eventually forced to remit but only after Rousseau's departure, when the sum was deposited at the consulate doubtless without his knowledge; and that the chevalier, who accompanied Madame de Montaigu to Venice in October, 1744, was upon that occasion unable to secure the money without Rousseau's consent, presumably because the latter could be held answerable for it. If the creditor's letter to Montaigu shows that the hairdresser tried unsuccessfully to collect a quarter of the debt from Rousseau in Paris in 1745, the chevalier's letter shows that in 1748 the same hairdresser successfully took the ambassador's brother to court for the whole amount by unscrupulously maintaining that the latter had taken the note to Venice himself and was therefore responsible for it. In his letter the distraught victim, forced to appeal the case, begs the count to send him proof of the senate's judgment and of the debtor's remittance, together with verification of the dates of these events and of his own visit to Venice. He also asks for Rousseau's address. This is all we know. If, as is most likely, the information was furnished, Rousseau in turn could have been indicted unless he paid the entire debt. He probably did so for that reason if for no other, but not until he received his salary from the ambassador the following year (1749). The writer of *Les Confessions* furnishes hardly any of these details. He imparts only the former secretary's unwillingness to submit to an obvious injustice. The latter's repugnance must have been aggravated by the thought that, if he had been remunerated when he should have been and had not been completely impoverished in 1745, he would have had to pay only a quarter of the sum. As for the money left at the consulate, which ought to have been forwarded to him or to the creditor, its fate is uncertain. The documentation remains fragmentary and obscure as usual. On the other hand, there is no lack of clarity in the story in the memoirs, where events are used to symbolize a love of justice which victimizes the hero and enriches others without winning gratitude or even gratification for himself. The youthful idealist does not always escape unscathed from the personal risks involved in the signal privilege of performing glorious or vainglorious deeds to bring the King of France's protection to his subjects. Years later, the writer's classical sobriety of style and simplicity of narration underline the contrast between his illusions and his disillusionment when he is brought to face the reality of life.

CLIMAX: WAR STORY

The fourth and last in the sequence of "heroic" scenes in the seventh book of *Les Confessions* is the most dramatic of all. The young Rousseau, whose work is all his study, is alone at the embassy going about the King's business while Montaigu, always impatient to be away on post days, that is Saturdays, is absent on vague errands. The War of the Austrian Succession is spreading through Italy. The

Austrian commander, Lobkowitz, is marching toward
Naples to wrest it from France's allies the Spanish
Bourbons, whose army has just effected a "memorable
retreat" under the Count de Gages. In this emergency,
news from Vienna reaches the embassy at Venice that a
spy in the service of Austria is on his way to Italy to arouse
the Neapolitans against their rulers as the Austrians ap-
proach. Rousseau forwards the message at once in a letter,
which he signs and dispatches himself, to the French ambassador at Naples, the Marquis de l'Hôpital. The kingdom is saved for the Bourbons and they "perhaps" owe this
grace to the service of Montaigu's secretary, who is warmly
commended by the marquis in a letter to his colleague.
But the hero only incurs his employer's resentment for his
distinguished role in these affairs and in others of lesser
consequence which are nevertheless the occasion of similar
expressions of approval from the King's ambassadors
abroad.

This story, the self-confident tone of which I have tried
to render as faithfully as possible, has been discredited ever
since *Les Confessions* was first published.[75] Its detractors
have sought to cast doubt upon its literal truth. Indeed the
whole incident was for a long time, and until about forty
years ago, regarded as entirely fictitious by all critics
unanimously.[76] Today we know that it is at least partially
true, in the narrowest sense of the word. We possess the
message from Vienna to Venice concerning the spy, dated
October 26, 1743. Although we do not have the letter from
the embassy to the marquis, we do have the latter's reply
of November 19 addressed to Montaigu. But Rousseau is
not even mentioned in the reply or in any other letters,
long preserved in the Montaigu archives or elsewhere, and
originating in French legations in Naples or abroad, whose

[75] Mme d'Epinay was the first to discredit it and this is recalled by Cérésole,
Faugère, and A. de Montaigu.

[76] This view is defended by Cérésole, Faugère, A. de Montaigu, and Montigny.

commendation the memorialist professes to have won.[77] Besides, the two missives from Vienna and Naples date from about four months before Lobkowitz's advance and de Gages' retreat that began the following March 7, 1744.[78] It was on June 16 to 18, more than three months after this military offensive, that the Austrians at Velletri surprised the King of Naples and the Duke of Modena, who were saved by an alarm from the Marquis de l'Hôpital and were thereby enabled to triumph over the enemy.[79] This is all that can be said with certainty about the circumstances in which the famous narrative evidently took its source. Modern scholars are therefore inclined to conclude that the writer of *Les Confessions* is guilty either of confusion or illusion. It is tempting to accept this explanation, so much so that even the editor of the *Venetian Despatches* adopts it.[80] In fact, he considers Rousseau's pretensions ridiculous, chiefly on the grounds that news of spy activities in Naples was peddled by all French embassies in Italy from the beginning of January to late March, 1744, and that the fate of Naples did not in any case depend upon such reports. He is surely right on both counts. But his conclusion is as dangerous as that of his predecessors.

The danger of such a dogmatic deduction resides in the lack of evidence to support it at the present time, even

[77] For letters from Naples, Genoa, and Constantinople formerly preserved in the Montaigu archives, see Souchon, *Correspondance diplomatique*, pp. 325–342. For the marquis' letter dated November 19, 1743, see *O.C.*, Pléiade, I, 1395 n4 (to p. 306). For the letter from M. Vincent, chargé d'affaires at Vienna, addressed to Montaigu, see *ibid.*, 1395 n5 (to p. 306), and III, 1816 n2 (to p. 1068).

[78] De Gages' retreat is often mentioned in Montaigu's official correspondence; see Souchon, *Correspondance diplomatique*, pp. 30–31, 60, and especially *Venetian Despatches* in *O.C.*, Pléiade, III, 1116–1117, 1132, 1139, 1147, 1157, 1159, 1175.

[79] The engagements at Velletri are discussed in the embassy correspondence; see Souchon, *Correspondance diplomatique*, pp. 75–76, 330–331, 343–344. See also the *Venetian Despatches* of June and July in *O.C.*, Pléiade, III; and cf. I, 1394–1395 n2 (to p. 306).

[80] *Ibid.*, III, pp. cclii–ccliii, 1835–1836 n1 (to p. 1160).

though it may perhaps be confirmed by future findings. We might be wiser to proceed more cautiously and to suspend judgment for the moment, especially if we recall that the memorialist's other statements, contradicted by well-known critics of the past, have gradually been authenticated, even if it took a century of research to confirm them. Thus we avoid giving grounds for Rousseau's contention in Book IV that "even when we meet with truth, we are subject to build our opinions on false principles." In Book IX he adds: "... how deceiving are judgments founded on appearances to which people give so much credit."

The reasoning that tempts us to doubt the memorialist's truthfulness in this particular case, while very compelling, is not entirely flawless and I think it is safer to admit it. For example, how can we form any opinion at all from the marquis' immediate reply to an early warning which he could hardly appreciate at its full value more than a month before Austria's ambitions in Italy became clear, four months before they were activated, and over seven months before they were finally thwarted? His letter of November 19 is not the acknowledgment to which Rousseau alludes in *Les Confessions*. It could not possibly be. The order of events in the book makes it quite clear that the acknowledgment mentioned dates from after the defense of the Kingdom of Naples when the marquis was in a position to estimate the value of Rousseau's "service to the common cause," as the writer phrases it. That service did not consist exclusively in the initial spy report, but in other bulletins as well, of which the memorialist says nothing but which were numerous in the ensuing months. In giving prominence to the first one he imparts concreteness to his narration. He also exercises the artist's right to use discrimination in selecting among the facts of experience the most striking and forceful circumstance for, as far as we know today, the warning forwarded by Montaigu's secretary in early November was the first intelligence Naples had of Austrian spy activities in the kingdom. All other warnings date from much later. The marquis may have realized this and acknowledged it after the issue at Velletri. But, whether he did or not, by that time he must have understood the value of other news bulletins which Rousseau sent to Naples to report on war developments every week throughout his term of office.[81] They surely constituted an essential part of his "service" to the Bourbons.

There are grounds for this broader interpretation of the work of art. Rousseau's weekly bulletins to Naples have not yet come to light and perhaps never will. However we can form a fair idea of their contents, for, like all the others sent to French ministers at home and abroad, they no doubt paralleled his weekly dispatches to Versailles and were based on the same material procured through Italian informers and French residents. Why is it ridiculous to assume that the communications with Naples won praise from the marquis, especially since the corresponding court dispatches were commended by the King of France, precisely for their fine reports upon the war in Italy? Let us look into the dispatches for a moment, beginning with the spy report, for of course it was also forwarded to Versailles.[82] In these letters Montaigu's secretary, after relaying to the King that first startling alert from Vienna, related other major events of 1743 to 1744 that were just as decisive in the history of Naples and even more so, such as Austria's designs upon the kingdom and Lobkowitz's intentions as these became clearer. In fact the usually well-phrased texts record step by step Austria's diplomatic entanglements with Sardinia and England, in her enterprises against the Bourbons of Spain and Naples supported by France. In particular the communiqués permit us to follow important troop movements in Romagna in the autumn of 1743 when the Austro-Sardinians under Lobkowitz and the Spaniards under de Gages faced one another there, biding their time for months while Franco-

[81] *Ibid.*, I, 1394 n1 (to p. 306).
[82] *Ibid.*, III, 1068, 1816 n2 (to p. 1068).

Spanish troops from the North slowly approached Sardinian Piedmont, with Austrian Lombardy and Tuscany separating them from their allies in the South. Suddenly, early in 1744, the Venetian dispatches warned the French court of imminent action in Romagna and Naples. On January 11 and more especially on February 1, a few weeks before Lobkowitz's offensive and de Gages' retreat began, the embassy in Venice informed the French king that the Austrian commander had assembled his troops on the Adriatic at Rimini and Cattolica, as if he were about to march against the Spaniards. Moreover he had publicly declared that he had designs upon the kingdom of Naples, in which case the Count de Gages was expected to retreat. On February 8, another dispatch from the embassy advised the King of France that Lobkowitz had definite orders from Vienna to attack the Spaniards and proceed with his plans.[83] It is inconceivable that all this news was not conveyed in the weekly bulletins to the marquis at Naples. It would have been of even greater value to him than the November warning about the Austrian conspiracy which, by the way, was confirmed by informers throughout Italy from January to March, 1744.

Even more urgent and crucial alarms are to be found in the Venetian dispatches of the ensuing critical months, from the eve of the offensive launched by Lobkowitz early in March to the beginning of summer when the danger was past. These dispatches to Versailles, which must have been practically duplicated in the lost Neapolitan ones, reported diligently and intelligently upon Austrian military tactics and de Gages' "memorable retreat" to the Abruzzi to join forces with Charles VII and the Neapolitans on the frontiers of the Bourbon realm. The communications verified information about the spreading Austrian conspiracy,

[83] *Ibid.*, 1135 and cf. *C.C.*, I, 248 note *f* (to no. 95). See also letters of January 11 and February 1 in *O.C.*, Pléiade, III, 1116–1117, 1131–1132. In fact, the fortunes and misfortunes of Lobkowitz can be traced throughout the *Venetian Despatches.*

forwarded news from Vienna,[84] and recorded all the movements of both armies down the Adriatic coast, until the
encounters at Velletri in the papal states on June 17 and 18,
1744, when Austrian progress toward Naples was definitively arrested, although the Austrians were not really
defeated until about three weeks later. These excellent
news bulletins, undoubtedly reproduced for the marquis
as they were for other ambassadors, were well received at
the French court and won praise, which Montaigu acknowledged in these terms on June 27, ten days after the engagement at Velletri: "I am very glad that the news I have been
giving to the King about the military affairs of the kingdom
of Naples pleased His Majesty even if it had no other merit
than that of being the only news to reach him."[85]

In the light of the memorialist's contention that the
secretary's zeal, evinced here and elsewhere too, caused
disputes in the embassy, a contention apparently supported by the Veronese and Olivet affairs, is it a coincidence
that on the same June 27, Rousseau, in despair over the
count's hostility, drafted a written appeal, presumably to
Mari, in the hope of restoring peace in the palace? Is it also
a coincidence that at this very time Montaigu located someone to replace him, as documents long kept in the family
archives prove?[86] Dissensions must have risen high if the
marquis was not less generous than the French court
in acknowledging similar bulletins at the same time, and
if, as we are told in *Les Confessions*, the secretary, having
signed some of them himself, was therefore specifically
designated. The memorialist's account *might* be true.
Montaigu, although careful to sign all dispatches to the

[84] E.g., *ibid.*, pp. 1169–1170. Regarding the spreading Austrian conspiracy
see pp. 1159–1160.

[85] *Ibid.*, pp. 1211–1212: "Je suis fort aise que les nouvelles que je donnois au
Roy des affaires militaires du Royaume de Naples aient été agréables à Sa
Majeste, quand elles n'auroient d'autre mérite que celui d'être arrivées seules."

[86] *C.C.*, I, 250, and Mr. Leigh's notes. See also A. de Montaigu, *Démêlés*, pp.
82–86.

French court and ministers in the French government,[87] was not scrupulous about signing letters to other ambassadors. This is proven by two very fine ones of June 16 and July 15, 1744, addressed to the Count de Castellane in Constantinople and signed by Rousseau in his employer's absence. They contain excellent reviews of the military situation and were recently found to confirm the text of *Les Confessions* and belie the critics who had doubted it for more than fifty years.[88] If Rousseau, left alone in charge of the embassy, performed this service for the Bourbons in Naples and won recognition for it, then his superior may conceivably have suspected him of excessive zeal and may even have destroyed some of the correspondence from the marquis, together with any other testimonials in the young man's favor, except the one from the King of France, who does not name him. Such an action would not be very surprising if we have some elementary understanding of human nature and reflect upon the bitter feeling that existed between the two men. Of course there is also the possibility that the missing letter of commendation from Naples may yet come to light. Even if it does not, there is really no serious discrepancy between the basic facts recorded in the correspondence and those incorporated into the autobiography.

This study of historical documents and the work of art,

[87] Rousseau's testimony in this matter (in *Les Confessions: O.C.*, Pléiade, I, 306) is confirmed by the archives.

[88] See, for example, Cérésole, *J.-J. Rousseau à Venise*, p. 211. One of the letters signed by Rousseau and dated July 15, 1744, was first published in its entirety by Monglond in 1935, together with three others to the same correspondent signed by Montaigu; see "Rousseau, secrétaire de M. de Montaigu," pp. 63–65. The other letter signed by Rousseau and dated June 16, 1744, was first published by Gagnebin; see Pierre-Paul Plan, *Table de la Correspondance générale de J.-J. Rousseau avec une introduction et des lettres inédites* (Geneva: E. Droz, 1953), p. xi. All these letters have been reproduced in the *Venetian Despatches*; see especially *O.C.*, Pléiade, III, 1207–1209, 1223–1225. The letter of June 16 has been reprinted in *C.C.*, I, 245–247. Castellane refers to it in a dispatch to the Foreign Office: *O.C.*, Pléiade, III, 1837–1838 *n*1 (to p. 1161). See also *ibid.*, I, 1395 *n*2 (to p. 307).

taken together, gives us new insight into their relationship. The comparison of texts ought to weaken considerably our traditional confidence in archives and epistles, as opposed to literature and art, an attitude fostered of course by scientific positivism. Without *Les Confessions* the correspondence or lack of it would often appear enigmatic and perplexing. Taken alone the letters are frequently hypothetical, allusive, and inconclusive. We have also seen that they can be as full of passion and prejudice as the memoirs. And yet, in letters as in life, when feelings are revealed at all and are not completely concealed, as they so often are, they are much more ambiguously and deviously conveyed, less fully and finely expressed, than in a literary work like Rousseau's masterpiece. The further we pursue our collation the more we are brought to realize that, while in the past the correspondence was used to test the "truth" of *Les Confessions*, on the contrary it is the autobiography that imparts truth and meaning to the letters.

Let the reader not misunderstand. The foregoing discussion merely shows that, if the war story in the memoirs cannot be proven literally true, it cannot be proven false either. Yet no one has to this day made such an admission. Suppose for a moment that the account is based upon objective facts, like the other stories preceding it, which scholars have gradually been forced to accept as inspired by actuality. If a whole succession of weekly warnings was sent to Naples, as it undoubtedly was, between the dramatic news of the now notorious spy from Vienna, which was relayed long before the Austrian conspiracy became common knowledge, and the final issue at Velletri almost eight months later, which proved the value of all bulletins from the first, it would be artistically permissible and even desirable for Rousseau in his narrative to epitomize and compress the diffuseness of actuality as he did in the Veronese case. He could quite legitimately juxtapose cause and effect, eliminate useless, repetitive detail, and reduce the story to its indispensable elements for the sake of greater force and concentration. To impart an idea of the most important and burdensome part of his work, namely the formulation of war bulletins, instead of speaking of them in general terms and thereby running the risk of redundance and vagueness, he could justifiably select the first concrete and impressive case of the spy. He could then lead the reader directly from this initial alert to the ultimate outcome, passing over in silence the many bulletins that followed, to reach the possible conclusion that the Bourbons may "perhaps" be indebted to Jean-Jacques as was their kinsman, the King of France, and as the ambassador to Naples allegedly professed to be. Rousseau makes no positive assertion about it. Their indebtedness would be owing to a warning about spy activity, issued long in advance of all other such warnings and followed for months by regular reports of military movements, which the memorialist ignores although the marquis could hardly have afforded to do likewise. In this case the only liberty the writer would have taken with material reality is the one he took in the Veronese case: he fails to mark clearly the passage of time. But this might be expected of an historian of the soul. An appreciation of his purpose in this capacity, and an understanding of his artistic procedure, undoubtedly foster a keener awareness of the writer's meaning.

Yet in whatever manner the memorialist handles the real events to which he refers, they are not the determining factor to assess the relative place of art and truth in his work and to judge of its value from the double point of view. The literal adherence of a scene to objective facts, or its deviations from them, cannot recommend or discredit it artistically or even psychologically. But it can draw attention to the writer's methods and throw into new perspective the spiritual qualities he seeks to embody in an artistic form. The war story in particular contains an unusually penetrating portrayal of Rousseau's character, as well as a fine example of his writing, aspects that have been overlooked by all critics without exception although they are the most important of all. The spy incident with which the story begins has the advantage of rendering the youthful excitement of the erstwhile introvert as he is now caught up in the events of a major European war. As for the part he assumes in the final issue, surely it is worth observing that he can scarcely contain his exultation as he contemplates himself as the savior of the Bourbons. Would he have been as pleased to be credited with having shaped the course of things to come, prepared the way for the revolution, and brought about the ultimate downfall of the monarchy in France? The paradox in his nature is here invested with figurative imagery and finds dramatic expression in these recollections of personal accomplishment in the service of France and her allies.

The importance that the author of *Les Confessions* attributes to this scene is indicated by its position in the narrative, which does not follow the chronological order of events. The writer is well aware that the Olivet report and the other commercial affair date from the time of the secretary's definitive disgrace and the last days in Venice, since he has already attributed the loss of the promissory note to the confusion of his departure and since later in the story of his resignation he reverts to the Olivet matter. Nevertheless the war story displaces the others and is given prominence as the climax of the seventh book and the highest point in the young man's life at the head of the palace of France. Since it represents the most substantial and responsible part of his task at the embassy, this is as it should be.

ANTI-CLIMAX

In the part he plays in these four scenes Rousseau seems suddenly unaware of the disparity between personal dignity and social distinction. The soul expresses itself no longer in a sequence of contrasts and conflicts but in a series of triumphs in which all its powers are challenged to fulfillment. The theme of the seventh book is almost reversed. The actual role assumed by the protagonist is great, exceeding the personal limitations of the indolent dreamer, and carries the individual outside himself and beyond himself. But the distinction he enjoys is hardly the kind he might have been expected to seek, for it violates his professed principles no less than his naturally introspective temperament. He whose republican birthright entitled him to share the supreme power as a member of the sovereign and to defend that noble privilege "with the heart of a hero and the virtues of a sage," as he says in the epistle to Parisot, is claiming his heritage in a compromising manner. Yet, for the moment, he seems insensitive to any inconsistency between his democratic convictions and his position as agent of the King of France, so gratifying is that position to his personal aspirations and to his sense of justice and social order too.

In the memoirs the secretary's situation is precarious, not because he is violating his nature and his creed but because his energy has aroused the count's suspicion. This is directly stated in the last of the four scenes. Reading *Les Confessions* in conjunction with correspondence and archives, we cannot help but observe that all the glorious or vainglorious deeds coincide perfectly in time with either Rousseau's discharge or his earlier letters of distress motivated by his employer's antagonism, as though his zeal were in very truth the cause of his disgrace. We are tempted to conclude from our collation that he fell from favor *because* he secured artists for the French court, freed a French ship for duty, and saved Naples for the Bourbons. In fact the autobiographer tells us openly that his dedication to his task instigated Montaigu's wrath and was the only complaint laid against him until the day of their separation.[89] We are intended to witness this devotion in the four scenes leading to the climax.

[89] *O.C.*, Pléiade, I, 307, 311.

The young man's hazardous paradoxical position inevitably determines the denouement of the story in *Les Confessions*. In the book his plight is subtly expressed in a series of implied antitheses, which have never before been brought to light. They underline the connection that the writer has already made between heroism and humiliation. The daring deeds, which are the source of complaints against him, find strangely ignoble counterparts in the mortifications of the sordid scenes that follow in the memoirs. There is a curious and very cunning parallelism between them. For example, the man who took pleasure in forcing a patrician impresario to release artists for the Parisian stage is himself publicly deprived of his loge in a Venetian theater by the ambassador's "gentleman," Domenico Vitali, a Mantuan bandit and pander engaged by the count and placed at the head of the palace.[90] Rousseau compels Vitali to make a public apology but thereafter is himself obliged to withdraw from a house where—we are assured—the discipline and dignity he has established give place to debauchery and licentiousness, and where even the ambassador's chamber is not very orderly. Vitali and an associate, who keeps a house of ill-fame at the Maltese Cross and is appointed to replace a good and long trusted servant of the embassy, make the palace of France intolerable for a well-mannered man. This sinister reversal of fortunes for the embassy secretary prepares us for the anti-climax of the Venetian story.

More vicissitudes lead to his resignation and correspond finely in the memoirs to other "heroic" gestures of brighter days. The champion of justice, who settles debts that are not his own, is himself the victim of injustice, defrauded

[90] Faugère, "Jean-Jacques Rousseau à Venise," p. 822, notes that the ambassador's household was composed of his secretary, two gentlemen or "maitres de chambre," four pages, six officers, two porters, twelve footmen, and twelve gondoliers. He quotes however from the "Relation manuscrite de l'entrée du marquis de Durfort," of November 28, 1759.

of compensation for his services to the legation. He lives
in the most abject poverty. The supper table, which is part
of his rightful payment, is ignoble, cheerless, and ill-lit,
nor is it graced by the ambassador's presence, for His
Excellency does not sup. Other privileges belonging to the
secretary are taken from him, such as his gondola and
liveried attendant. For a whole year—which is stretched
to five—his salary is withheld. The ambassador all the
while lives in luxury, leasing an extravagant holiday villa
on the Brenta Riviera and transforming it in the French
manner at enormous cost to himself. Even these frustrations
do not drive the young man from his post. What material
privation cannot do, anguish of spirit accomplishes. He
feels impelled to retire, we are told, only when he becomes
conscious of his employer's unmistakable intention to deny
him the honor due to faithful service. He discerns this
intention on two notable occasions. He, who acted to save
the realm of Naples for the Bourbons, is deemed unworthy
by birth to take his usual place at the ambassador's dinner
table in the event of a proposed visit from the Duke of
Modena. The duke, dispossessed of his estates by the
Austro-Sardinians, is temporarily staying in Venice with
his family. The fact that the dinner fails to take place does
not make the offense less hurtful. Greater mortification
still is in store for the secretary. He, who alone procured
the release of Captain Olivet's ship, is denied any recognition for his zeal. In the book the ambassador engages the
second secretary, who is also his private secretary, to
write an account of the affair for the Minister for the
Navy, divesting Rousseau of the honor of the depositions
and enclosing a duplicate of the report to attribute it to
Patizel. This is the last incident the memorialist confides
to us before confessing the circumstances of the secretary's
resignation. The latter relinquishes his post in spite of the
ambassador's desire to retain him, but not until he is as
convinced as the writer would like us to be that further

association with a man who has fallen into general dis-
esteem could never make but only mar his fortune.

Throughout the story of these vexations the reader cannot help but recall the epic scenes that prefigure them and
are now infamously inverted. It would be difficult to
believe that this clever parallelism or antithesis is not
deliberate. But whether it is or not, it is there just the
same and it performs a function, as we have already hinted.
It reinforces the connection that the writer has established,
and which the correspondence actually suggests, between
the secretary's almost exaggerated zeal and ensuing humiliations, as between cause and effect. The implication is
that the vainglorious deeds are the cause of his misfortunes,
as though his services were indeed considered crimes, as
the autobiographer says. Thus an artistic device casts
subtle light upon what is intended as a moral truth and
lends power to the closing episodes of the drama. At the
same time, the analogy of opposing scenes brings out once
more the leitmotiv of the seventh book, the discrepancy
between personal worth and social approval, which breeds
rebellion in the restless soul of the young Rousseau at a
critical moment in his brief public life.

Before analyzing historically these pages of the Venetian
story, I should forewarn the reader that, from this point,
we shall be considering largely the narration of an open
quarrel between the ambassador and his secretary. I do
not, for that reason, propose to change either my object
or my method. Rousseau is being treated not as an apologist
but as a writer who seeks to embody psychological truth
in an artistic form. I shall therefore continue to bring into
relief, not merely artistic devices, like the inverted parallelism discussed above with its moral implications, but
also the role of truth in the writer's art. I shall trace the
historical origins of these pages as I have all others, and
the elements of both circumstantial and psychological
truth contained therein, without hesitating to state the
facts as they are known to us, whether the author is or

is not the spokesman of the truth he promises, and whatever relation that truth bears to actuality. In stating
facts I seek neither to defend nor to attack, but merely to
pursue my literary purpose in order to learn to what extent
Rousseau pursues his.

The phase of the Venetian experience to which I have
been alluding, rich as it is in documents, archives, and
erudite research, is particularly valuable to determine the
relative place of the intuitive and romantic imagination
in the art of *Les Confessions.* Contemporary evidence is
sensational enough to show that the author probably had
material for memoirs in the manner of Casanova. This
evidence consists mainly of three spy reports, made for the
Venetian inquisitors on April 23, May 5, and May 10,
1744, and preserved in the state archives of Venice at the
Frari convent there. They contain the results of investigations on the neighborhood and household of the French
embassy at the time, and accentuate the classical discipline of Rousseau's narration.[91] He might have told us,
for example, as the spy does, that armed bandits, smugglers, thieves, and other criminals, living on embassy
territory, enjoyed the protection of diplomatic immunity
by paying tribute to Montaigu's "gentleman," who was
head of the "lista,"[92] and that one of them even frequented
the ambassador's court and rode in his gondola. The
memorialist might have related, as colorfully as the spy,
how "the Mantuan gentleman," as Vitali is called, as-
sociated only with thieves, swindlers, and panders, and
completely dominated the ambassador, together with an
associate, Carlo of the Maltese Cross, familiar to the

[91] These reports by the spy Falletti were published in Cérésole, *J.-J. Rousseau à Venise*, pp. 68–71; cf. p. 19. See also *O.C.*, Pléiade, III, 1822 *n*1 (to p.
1097).

[92] The "lista" is the territory occupied by the embassy and all adjoining
houses to which the rights and privileges of diplomatic immunity were extended (particularly exemption from customs duties), though sometimes a
distinction is made between "lista," as freedom of the palace, and "varij," as
freedom of the neighborhood.

reader of *Les Confessions*. Rousseau might even have added, as does the spy, that the ambassador himself was quite absorbed in revelry, courtesans, gaming, and the rest, but never thought of paying his debts.[93] He might have disclosed, finally, that these disorders provoked the Venetian police to intervene on embassy property, forcing Montaigu to protest to Nicolò Erizzo, his Venetian counselor, against such violations of diplomatic privileges, jealously guarded by the French government for over a hundred years. The seriousness of the ambassador's position may be judged by a contemporary report upon France's intransigent attitude in the matter of diplomatic immunity. The report was prepared on May 15, 1744, for the Venetian Council by the senator Girolamo Grimani and is preserved in the state archives of Venice. It contains a detailed history of innumerable disputes between French envoys and the local senate from 1639 to 1744 and was prompted by incidents that took place under Montaigu's jurisdiction.[94] Rousseau knew of these things, for he wrote numerous communications about them, not only to the French court,

[93] In his report of May 5, dealing mainly with Montaigu's household, Falletti writes:
On Sunday, after a conference with Erizzo, he [the ambassador] went to the Brenta with the Marquis Mari and Chichina ballerina. . . . These men continually go to amuse themselves in her house. The same evening at one o'clock he sent his Mantuan gentleman with the porter to the houses where wine was sold to stop the sale, except at the house of the widow Fera because the gentleman with Carlo of the Maltese Cross and G. B. Bozato and a certain Ruberti go to that house with prostitutes day and night. This gentleman frequents only thieves and swindlers and those who live on prostitution. . . . This gentleman, with Carlo of the Maltese Cross, leads the ambassador as he wishes and makes him do what he wishes. And indeed the ambassador himself is completely absorbed in revelry, courtesans, gaming, and so on, but he never thinks of paying his debts.
See Cérésole, *J.-J. Rousseau à Venise*, p. 70. In this connection, Monglond, "Rousseau, secrétaire de M. de Montaigu," p. 47, recalls one of the count's letters showing that he was in no hurry for his wife to join him (see Souchon, *Correspondance diplomatique*, p. 93). But it is also true that, one month after he arrived in Venice, Montaigu asked for permission to return to France to fetch his family, and on October 5 and November 30 he repeated the request; see *O.C.*, Pléiade, III, 1057, 1813 *n*1 (to p. 1057), 1093.

[94] Cérésole, *J.-J. Rousseau à Venise*, pp. 72–78.

but also to the Venetian government, whose inquiries brought the scandals to light. The autobiographer might have written a great deal more to win sympathy for the secretary against his superior, especially since he was not personally involved in the scandals. It is true that three years later, in a letter to the Foreign Office of June 17, 1747, Montaigu accused his "former secretary" of smuggling, but without naming anyone. It is also true that 150 years afterwards his descendant took up the accusation and applied it to Rousseau. But leading scholars have either exonerated him of all suspicion or else declared that it is impossible to prove anything.[95] In fact there is no evidence at all that he was in any way implicated. Besides, all spy reports and other disclosures prompted by diplomatic abuses date from after late February, when he lost his ascendancy at the embassy,[96] was estranged from his employer, and was even expecting to be replaced in a few weeks, judging by the draft of a letter dated February 22, to which we have referred, taken in conjunction with that of April 30, presumably intended for the count's brother in Paris. Rousseau cannot therefore be connected with the irregularities. Hence it is all the more noteworthy that the account of affairs in *Les Confessions* is strangely subdued by comparison with historical documents.

[95] A. de Montaigu, *Démêlés*, pp. 22–23, 46–47, 65–66. Théophile Dufour successfully exonerates Rousseau of all suspicion in his review of A. de Montaigu's book in *Annales de la Société Jean-Jacques Rousseau*, I (1905), 305–306, and is strongly supported by Derche, "Autour du séjour de J.-J. Rousseau à Venise," pp. 136–137, and by the editor of the *Venetian Despatches* in *O.C.*, Pléiade, III, 1844–1845 n1 (to p. 1201). As the latter points out, since smugglers used permit duplicates as permits by erasing the written (not printed) word "duplicate," Rousseau would have had to erase a word he had just finished writing himself. Strangely enough, Mr. Leigh (in *C.C.*, I, 239) reopens the case, alleging that Rousseau may perhaps have been guilty, although he admits that it cannot be proven. Perhaps it is better to consider a man innocent until he is proven guilty.

[96] On May 5 Falletti reports that the Mantuan gentleman and Carlo of the Maltese Cross enjoy primacy in the embassy, and on April 23 he refers to the Mantuan as "capo di lista." See above.

The memorialist's forbearance appears even more remarkable when we examine the *Venetian Despatches* in detail. They show beyond a doubt that, coinciding with the secretary's disgrace, there was a marked change in the ambassador's attitude toward rogues seeking refuge from justice under his protection. In the early dispatches, for example in the autumn of 1743, Montaigu zealously professed to rid the embassy, and the city too, of several scoundrels.[97] At that time he prided himself on adhering scrupulously to his instructions, which warned him specifically against abuses of this kind and enjoined upon him careful supervision of all embassy personnel. His explicit duty and expressed desire was to show Venice that the King of France did not seek to shelter criminals in the palace.[98] If even at the beginning of his term of office Montaigu occasionally encouraged adventurers, he did so in the hope of engaging them as spies to obtain secret information. It was in those first months that he dismissed Count Piati, the so-called "good and long trusted servant of the embassy" who was in fact found guilty of smuggling in December, 1743. Upon that occasion, Montaigu in writing to the Foreign Office blamed Le Blond for the unsatisfactory installation of the embassy household and choice of servants. His intention was to discredit the "ignorant and uninformed" consul in the eyes of the court. Yet it was because the ambassador ultimately replaced the smuggler by a rogue of another sort, and in the end retained notorious criminals in his service, that the Venetian police intervened.[99] When they first did so in February,

[97] *O.C.*, Pléiade, III, 1087.

[98] M. Pierre Duparc, *Recueil des instructions données aux ambassadeurs et ministres de France*, XXVI (*Venise*), (Paris: Editions du Centre Nationale de la Recherche Scientifique [Gap, impr. de L. Jean], 1958), p. 125.

[99] Regarding adventurers used as spies see *O.C.*, Pléiade, III, 1092, 1119. Regarding the dismissal of Piati for smuggling and Montaigu's attacks on Le Blond see pp. 1053, 1093–1094, 1096–1097, and *C.C.*, I, 218. The dispatches, which discuss Piati's activities and were written by Rousseau, show that he knew about them. Perhaps he felt that Piati was respectable by comparison with his successor. Montaigu certainly lacked discernment in the establish-

as the spy reports show, Montaigu made no allusion to the matter at all in his dispatches to Versailles. If, on March 22, he finally complained about such intervention in a meeting with his Venetian counselor, as the latter states in a report submitted to his government two days later, Montaigu's report to the French authorities on the same meeting indicates that the two men merely discussed the republic's neutrality and nothing else.[100] This sudden cautiousness is remote from his early naïveté, though less puzzling than the memorialist's discretion.

At last, in a dispatch of early April, the count artfully inquired of the French Foreign Office about the extent of diplomatic privileges, explaining that he had no reproach to fear but merely wished to know how to defend his rights in case of an emergency.[101] He fails to say that the emergency had already arisen, that the rights in question had been infringed two months before and that he could hardly wait any longer to vindicate them. He tried to defend them in a subsequent conference on May 8, necessitated by another incident of a few days earlier, but he failed in the endeavor and succeeded only in earning the contempt and derision of his counselor, who promptly reported the matter to the Venetian government and whose report, dated May 12, is extant.[102] Montaigu was less

---

ment of his household. His descendant held Le Blond responsible and Mr. Leigh accepts the idea (*C.C.*, I, 219). This is strange since the count alone was responsible for the state of affairs that forced the police to intervene, whatever ill advice he may have had in the beginning.

[100] See *O.C.*, Pléiade, III, 1163 (Letter to Amelot of March 28, 1744), and cf. p. 1843 n5 (to p. 1191) and see below, n102.

[101] *Ibid.*, pp. 1167–1168.

[102] *Ibid.*, p. 1843 n1 (to p. 1192). First on March 24 and then more especially on May 12, 1744, Erizzo reported to the Venetian senate on interviews with Montaigu concerning diplomatic immunity. In the second interview they discussed intervention by the Venetian police on embassy territory in February and May. During the discussion Montaigu claimed freedom of the palace and of the neighborhood too. As evidence of his good intentions to prevent abuses, he referred to his dismissal of an embassy gentleman for smuggling (presumably Piati, who was dismissed in December) and to his efforts to control the illegal use of permit duplicates used for importing merchandise on several occasions between April and June, 1744. For this report of May 12 now in the Venetian archives, see Cérésole, *J.-J. Rousseau à Venise*, pp. 79–84.

prompt to notify his superiors. Not until May 16 do the Venetian dispatches finally refer to the action of the police. Their intervention is represented however as having occurred only within the previous month, instead of three months before, and is attributed, not to disorders in the embassy, or to Le Blond's ill advice in the selection of the household, but to pro-Austrian and therefore anti-French tendencies in the republic, fomented by Montaigu's estranged counselor. In fact, the count uses the incidents to discredit Erizzo at Versailles in a malicious letter of May 30. In this incredible document he asks the King for permission to refrain from conferring again with the counselor, and even from applying for a new one. He requests the liberty to communicate with the senate exclusively by means of memorials, in order to undermine Erizzo's influence in the Venetian government and to show "how dangerous he is to the interests of the Bourbons with his haughty, supercilious air and indecent sneer." Here Montaigu displays what critics call his "lack of discernment," "rage," and "blindness."[103] Such were his violent reactions when his protests not only failed to stop the incidents but were ridiculed besides. The counselor's mockery is not incomprehensible. He must have wondered as we do, why, in a serious matter like this, the ambassador did not appeal to the senate if he was sure of his rights, since memorials were the usual expedients for negotiations of the kind, even though a counselor had been named.[104]

Documentation permits us to follow Montaigu's vagaries still further in this business with a view to comparing the flux of life with the story of *Les Confessions*. Only after waiting for months did he finally have recourse to official

[103] For the letter of May 16 see *O.C.*, Pléiade, III, 1191–1192, addressed to the Foreign Office. There Montaigu tells of complaining to his counselor, and in the next letter of May 23 he says that it was on that occasion that Erizzo showed his pro-Austrian sympathies; see p. 1194. The "incredible" letter is on pp. 1197–1198; it is entirely ciphered and is addressed to the Foreign Office. The words "lack of discernment," "rage," and "blindness," are Derche's words, adopted by Candaux: pp. 1843–1844 *n*1 (to p. 1198).

[104] *Ibid.*, p. 1828 *n*1 (to p. 1119); here Rousseau's translation of a message from the senate to Montaigu explains this.

channels and then he was careful not to let Versailles know about it. In an apparent effort to be tactful or perhaps to confuse the issue, he submitted to the senate two memorials almost at once, within three days of each other. In the first one, of June 5, he expressed his disapproval of contraband, urging the arrest of smugglers in the city who used embassy permits illegally. His object was presumably to ingratiate himself with the Venetian government and restore its confidence in him in order to prepare the way for the second memorial. Then at long last on June 8 he formally protested against police intervention on the *lista*, dating back over a period of almost four months.[105] The senate was not deceived. It ignored the protest memorial for six weeks but replied immediately on June 6 to the first innocuous one, which Montaigu forwarded to Versailles on June 13 together with the senate's answer and his regular weekly dispatch.[106] In the latter he explained his action against smuggling by saying that he merely wished the Venetian government to have no advantage over him in case of more essential matters. He refrained from enclosing or even referring to the memorial of June 8, probably to avoid divulging that there had been skirmishes with the police on embassy territory since February, and also perhaps to avoid giving the impression that the local authorities were justified. This impression arises from the combination of the two communications, the first of which, the denunciation of smugglers, was far too obviously intended to win a favorable reception for the second. The ambassador could not even mention the latter to Versailles without forwarding a copy at once, as he was supposed to do in any case. Meanwhile all his subterfuges were vain, for

[105] *Ibid.*, pp. 1203–1204. Cf. the memorial of June 5 on pp. 1200–1201 and in *C.C.*, I, 238.

[106] For the dispatch see *O.C.*, Pléiade, III, 1204–1205. For Rousseau's translation of the senate's reply see pp. 1845–1846 *n*3 (to p. 1204), and *C.C.*, I, 241–243, where Leigh gives the Italian text too. He also gives part of the dispatch on p. 243.

smuggling was not the only crime fostered at the embassy, and the police had to intervene again in July[107] before the republic was finally intimidated into giving satisfaction. It did so by an obsequious reply to the memorial of June 8 and by the arrest of its own officers. Only then was Versailles informed of the protest memorial, in letters of July 25, which were the last of Rousseau's official dispatches.[108] The secretary who handled all the correspondence must have understood the events it records, events of great seriousness in the eyes of the French Foreign Office, and the memorialist can hardly have forgotten them, yet he is noticeably restrained in his references to them.

This restraint is an aspect of Rousseau's writing that has psychological implications as well as artistic. If he refrains from regaling us with the lurid tales he must have known it is simply because he had no part in them and so they have no place in the self-portrait of *Les Confessions*. If he had been involved, he would conceivably have related them just as unabashedly and shamelessly as he does other lurid stories in which he was personally concerned. Yet the crimes encouraged by the embassy determined the course of his life, and he might therefore have been justified in dwelling upon them at length. Even so he desists with curious reticence. No doubt he felt that such incredible situations were an unsuitable theme for his art. Their lack of verisimilitude would only weaken his work, since they would distract attention from the story of the soul and overshadow psychological truth and the fruits of the intuitive imagination. In other words, material which would have been valuable to an apologist is willfully sacrificed in favor of the psychological object, or, as Rousseau would say, "in favor of nature and of truth,"

[107] *O.C.*, Pléiade, III, 1221–1223, letter to the Foreign Office, July 11, 1744.

[108] The letters are to the King and Foreign Office; see pp. 1229–1232. For the senate's reply of July 23 to the memorial of June 8 see pp. 1849–1850 n1 (to p. 1231). On August 15, Montaigu finally relented and asked for the release of the officers (Cérésole, *J.-J. Rousseau à Venise*, pp. 96ff.).

which amount to the same thing since he speaks the language of the classics. If *Les Confessions* in general, and the Venetian story in particular, is a failure as apologetics—and I think it is—the reason is partly to be sought in such sacrifices. But a more potent reason is the writer's frankness and success as a psychologist. He adhered too closely to Plutarch's classical ideal, and, by revealing his nature and its flaws too freely and too fully in his work, armed against him those whose sympathy he sought. But his art gains in sobriety and realism. He never allows these qualities to be obscured by sensationalism, even in the interests of self-justification and still less for the sake of self-glorification. Small wonder if the Venetian adventurer Casanova refused to call his own memoirs "confessions" upon the grounds that the Swiss writer had marred that fine title! The author of *Les Confessions* bridles his imagination and disciplines his mind and heart in order not to disfigure spiritual truth.

THE AMBASSADOR'S LETTER

In addition to the archives which tell us many things Rousseau does not say, we possess private correspondence containing references to all the situations that inspired his dismal picture of the last days in the ambassador's service: the desolation of life, the mean economies, the somber suppers, the public mortifications, the penury contrasting with Montaigu's extravagance, the affront occasioned by the Duke of Modena's proposed visit, and the unjust report of the Olivet affair leading to the crisis in the embassy. This correspondence is valuable since it shows more clearly still what happens to the circumstances of actuality when they are grafted into a work of art to express psychological truth. In particular there is a contemporary letter from the count to the Abbé Alary at the French court, written August 15, 1744.[109] It provides a

[109] *C.C.*, II, 50–53; cf. *O.C.*, Pléiade, I, 309–312.

strange commentary upon the whole denouement of the
Venetian story in *Les Confessions* and further underlines
the discreet realism of the writer's art. For this reason it is
worthy of study. In it, the ambassador, who confesses
that he has not paid his secretary for a year, raises the
question of the table which the two men normally shared.
Having said that they met only at dinner because the
younger man spent every evening gaming at the Venetian
casino[110] (and therefore presumably did not sup at the
embassy), he paradoxically complains of the secretary's
unreasonable demands for supper. A suppressed passage of
the original draft of the letter (for we have both versions)
is even more paradoxical, for there he says that he himself
does not sup. He must have seen that this detail invalidates
his previous explanation of why the two met only at
dinner. The explanation is weak in any case, since the
young man was penniless and could hardly have indulged in
such costly pastimes as gaming. Besides, the autobiographer, who confesses his most shameful sins to the world,
would surely have admitted the passion for gaming with
his usual immodesty, if he had been a victim of it, whereas
he professes in fact to have disliked games of chance.[111]
On the other hand, the inquisitors, who kept the ambassador under close scrutiny, testify, as we have seen, that
Montaigu was completely absorbed in these very amusements, like his colleague and constant companion, Mari.[112]
As he was wealthy, this would be a more credible reason
why he and his secretary did not meet at the embassy supper table. The detail is of no consequence in itself. But it

[110] The Ridotto in San Moise street near San Marco; it operated until 1774.
Of course there were other private casinos as well, since gambling was one
of the most popular Venetian amusements; see Diehl, *Une République patricienne: Venise*, p. 302.

[111] His dislike of gaming is mentioned in a letter written to M. de Saint
Germain, February 26, 1770, where he says that he played only once in his
life, at the Venetian Ridotto (*C.G.*, XIX, 240).

[112] We know that the ambassador of Spain gambled at the Ridotto; see
Montaigu's letter to the Foreign Office, written in Rousseau's hand, February
1, 1744, in *O.C.*, Pléiade, III, 1129.

serves to draw attention to the fact that the memorialist refrains from giving any explanation at all for His Excellency's alleged absence from supper. He makes a laconic reference to it and nothing more. This is another indication of artistic moderation in *Les Confessions*.

The count in his letter to the court furnishes abundant evidence of this nature for he himself is anything but moderate. He deals exhaustively with the most tediously trivial matters. He tells in great detail how he rejected his secretary's demand for a gondola a fortnight after the young man's arrival, and how he repeatedly ignored the plea even when it was made in writing two weeks later. He is careful not to state that he acceded to the "ridiculous" request in November, 1743, as we infer from his correspondence with his brother, which, incidentally, does not even suggest that the gondola was rented. He clearly implies to the court that the secretary never did have a gondola, and even ascribes the latter's insolence to this privation.[113] We are inevitably carried back to Rousseau's one and only terse statement on the subject in the memoirs: "My gondola was taken from me." He does not even say that the ambassador had three luxurious gilded ones, as we know from the *Venetian Despatches*.[114] The simplicity of his narration is remarkable from a literary point of view, whatever moral judgment we may be tempted to make about the pretensions of the two men. By contrast, Montaigu in his letter is undisciplined, indulging in extravagant accusations against the secretary,

[113] *C.C.*, II, 50. In spite of the ambassador's refusal to grant him a gondola in September, Rousseau was apparently happy, judging by two letters addressed to Montaigu, one of October 7, 1743, from Alary and another of October 25, 1743, from the chevalier (A. de Montaigu, *Démêlés*, p. 25). There are extracts from these letters in *C.C.*, I, 201–202. At the end of October, the secretary still had no gondola (*ibid.*, p. 202, letter from Rousseau to Le Blond, October 29, 1743). Yet, judging by a letter addressed to the count by his brother on November 19, 1743, the former must have acceded to the request by then (A. de Montaigu, *Démêlés*, p. 68 *n*1, who errs however in attributing the letter to the ambassador, as Mr. Leigh points out).

[114] *O.C.*, Pléiade, III, 1821–1822 *n*1 (to p. 1093).

much like those he made the following year against the consul, such as disloyalty, spying, insolence, and mediocre service for the duration of a year's engagement. He even intimates, with characteristic suspicion of the intellectual, that he could not trust his subordinate with the embassy ciphers.[115] He further accuses the young Rousseau of maliciously presenting letters for signature at the moment the post was leaving. Perhaps he did. Perhaps it *was* the post that was leaving, instead of the ambassador who, in the pages of *Les Confessions*, is impatient to be away on post days, leaving the secretary alone to relay to Naples the dramatic news of Austria's movements and save the day at Velletri. The count of course does not acknowledge any collaboration at all on the part of the secretary whom he seeks to discredit at court. He writes with such abandon that he makes us more sensitive than ever to the restraint of the autobiographer's story.

In his letter Montaigu further charges his secretary with resentment at the prospect of being excluded from the society of the Duke of Modena, who was expected to visit the palace but never did. The ambassador does not say why the young man was to be excluded, but since the latter was obviously informed of all state secrets, one can hardly assume that it was for diplomatic reasons. In any case, the incident, also carefully narrated in *Les Confessions*, was like the Veronese affair, a major cause of dissension in the embassy sometime about mid-February. Indeed, it must have occurred between January 1 and February 26, when the duke was in Venice for family reasons, and certainly not before January 20, when he was released from quarantine. Perhaps it took place even as late as February 22, when Montaigu was in touch with

[115] Derche, who supports Dufour to defend Rousseau against the accusation of smuggling, also exonerates him of the suspicion of espionage, recalling that Montaigu made the same accusation against others, including Le Blond, denounced as a spy in a letter of September 19, 1745 ("Autour du séjour de J.-J. Rousseau à Venise," pp. 136–138).

him for news of the army, the very day that Rousseau first began to think of returning to Paris apparently as a result of some major vexation.[116] Since the duke, who left for the Spanish front on February 26, was to owe his safety to the diplomatic advice received at Velletri in June, and therefore at least in some degree to the secretary's offices, the situation created by the count's pretentiousness is pregnant with dramatic irony, which is brought out by the memorialist's antitheses. Of course there are no such subtleties in the ambassador's letter, but his account of the incident basically accords with the one in *Les Confessions*. Yet there are no further grounds for comparison between them. In the work of art literal truth of circumstances is respected but transfigured into a visible reflection of the soul, its insatiable pride aggravated by an ever present and deep-rooted diffidence.

These spiritual responses are vaguely reflected in another act of rebellion of which Montaigu accuses his secretary in the same letter. This is the haughty refusal to take the public diligence to Padua, where the count was on holiday at his marble villa on the Brenta Riviera, the resort of wealthy patricians, situated between Venice and Padua.[117] The public water coach of Padua was notorious, as Rousseau must have known since he had taken it on his arrival the year before: the passengers in the normal course

[116] *O.C.*, Pléiade, III, 1117, 1142 contains references to Montaigu's connections with the duke, who was in quarantine until January 20. The latter's family was in Venice since his territory had been occupied by Charles-Emmanuel III of Sardinia in early June, 1742.

[117] Regarding the Brenta Riviera in the eighteenth century see Monnier, *Venise au XVIIIᵉ siècle*, p. 43; and Diehl, *Une République patricienne: Venise*, pp. 303–304. Courtois ("Chronologie critique," p. 43 *n*2) does not understand that the palace "at Padua" is in fact the holiday villa on the Brenta, a river linking Padua with Venice. A. de Montaigu (*Démêlés*, p. 70) mistakenly asserts that the palace on the Brenta is the house in Venice on the Canareggio canal watered by the Brenta river. This is strange since he knew of his ancestor's letter to Alary of August 15, 1744, where the ambassador, referring to his country house, implies that it was between Venice and Padua (*C.C.*, II, 51).

of life enacted scenes that might have belonged to some boisterous comedy or grotesque farce.[118] His refusal is therefore not very surprising. However, Montaigu in his letter implies that the secretary refused to take any means whatsoever to wait upon his orders at the country house.[119] This would belie *Les Confessions*, since the writer describes the villa as though he had seen it. He probably had, since in an extant contemporary letter, cited above, he proposes to join the ambassador there the following day and submit to him the Olivet report together with some embassy dispatches. But the matter is trivial. Disputes like this about the Paduan diligence find no place in the work of art, for they lack distinction and depth of meaning.

But another of the count's indictments resounds strangely in the mind and memory of the reader of *Les Confessions*. The ambassador declares in his letter to the court that he finally dismissed the secretary for engaging the second secretary to transcribe a memorial for the Venetian senate instead of doing it himself, on the pretext that the other man's hand was more beautiful than his own.[120] This action, which Montaigu does not present in any context, would be incomprehensible unless he himself had already employed de Binis or someone else to handle not private letters but official correspondence, which the punctilious and hypersensitive first secretary regarded not merely as his duty but as his special prerogative. Such, for example, was the copy of the Olivet report prepared for the Minister for the

[118] Monnier, *Venise au XVIIIe siècle*, pp. 49–50.

[119] Monglond accepts this allegation as one explanation of the quarrel between the two men ("Rousseau, secrétaire de M. de Montaigu," pp. 69–70 n57). Even the editors of the Pléiade edition of the works see no discrepancy between Montaigu's version of the breach and Rousseau's (*O.C.*, Pléiade, I, 1397–1398).

[120] Monglond accepts this statement too as made in Montaigu's version of the quarrel and separation ("Rousseau, secrétaire de M. de Montaigu," pp. 69–70 n57). For him, the refusal to go to Padua and the entrusting of the memorial to the second secretary, de Binis, explain the violent breach. Rousseau's departure is discussed below.

Navy and forwarded by Le Blond.[121] This alleged injustice figures in the memoirs just before the secretary's final withdrawal from the palace of the legation. No doubt readers of *Les Confessions* are meant to link the two events, the Olivet affair and Rousseau's retirement, and to see again in his zeal the real cause of his employer's alienation. This contention constitutes the real discrepancy between the autobiographer's version of the quarrel and the ambassador's. Yet, in a sense, the latter confirms the former, at least by implication. Montaigu unwittingly implies in his letter that he was painfully conscious of his intellectual inferiority to the secretary. This self-consciousness, which would have been enough to breed in his mind distrust and suspicion of the latter's zeal, appears in the final paragraph of his letter, where he complains of his subordinate's contempt for his faltering dictation and thus naïvely testifies against himself. Inadvertently he almost supports Rousseau's view of the real reason for the breach between them. In any case, throughout his letter, he touches upon and verifies in advance the literal veracity of many details incorporated into the gloomy pages of the Venetian story. His version of the crisis will be discussed below.

It will be seen from the foregoing analysis that the ambassador's letter to the court records allusively and enigmatically some of the younger man's resentment. Years later the same mood is still fresh in the soul of the memorialist, and it finds meaning only in his book. There we see how it arises from an acute, over-susceptible sense of dignity which springs in turn from a consciousness of inner worth and accomplishment but is pitifully vulnerable, wounded to the quick by exclusion from a ceremonial banquet or the privation of petty privileges. The hero of the memoirs exemplifies what the author of *Emile* calls "the mad vanity of youth that rebels against humiliation." The portrait taking shape in the seventh book is not

---

[121] See p. 71 above. The copy, like other extant copies, was made at the consulate and Le Blond undertook to have it sent to the Admiralty.

that of a man on display exhibited by an apologist who is concerned with his "public image" as we say nowadays. The contrast between the petty pride set forth here and the energy of soul depicted earlier recalls the praise of Plutarch cited above. In the Greek writer's biographies Rousseau admires just such contradictions and intimate traits that teach us to love nature or human truth and to know ourselves. Moralists who denounce the autobiographer as a man pay no small tribute to his ability as a portraitist. In the pages under discussion his classical simplicity of phrase and rigorous austerity of detail add clarity and power to the expression of moral confusion and spiritual weakness masquerading as pride. What we have called the leitmotiv of the book reappears in a renewal of the conflict between natural and social values, bringing havoc in its train for the individual who is ill prepared to cope with it.

A CRISIS

The scene in *Les Confessions* showing the last encounter of the principals in the Venetian story is tense with drama. The secretary is suddenly called into the presence of His Excellency. Montaigu is convulsed with rage, provoked by a letter from his brother, to whom Rousseau has appealed for his discharge and a successor after several similar and futile petitions made to the ambassador himself. When the count accuses his secretary of selling the embassy ciphers and is consequently derided on the grounds that no one in Venice is stupid enough to give a penny for them, he threatens to have the servants throw the young man from the window. The secretary gains control of the situation, bids his employer a grave farewell, and makes a dignified retreat, passing through the antechamber where attendants rise in homage as he leaves the palace never to return. Such is the well-known version of the affair.

This scene is based on an actual situation described in

contemporary correspondence, and the truth of the autobiographer's presentation may be partly understood by a
comparison with the letters. These include Montaigu's
above-mentioned letter to the court wherein the only
theme that remains to be discussed here is the situation in
question. The count's missive dwells at length upon the
circumstances of the last meeting between the two men on
August 6, 1744, nine days before it was written. The ambassador confesses to his fury culminating in a threat of
violence but says he had already discharged his secretary
for being arrogant about the memorial to the senate. He
does not say that he had located a new one a month before.
He attributes his rage to a dispute over certain deductions
he had made in the account and to which the young man
insolently objected. The account, by the way, is in the
Montaigu family collection in the Bibliothèque Nationale.[122] It shows that the deductions were for certain traveling expenses, notably the journey to Chambéry which
Rousseau had made in the vain hope of taking an overland
route; for excessive carriage charges levied by the embassy
on merchandise that he had ordered from Paris; and for a
sum which he owed to a merchant of Venice and which the
count, alleging that he had given caution, insisted upon
paying although, according to the *Venetian Despatches*, he
had debts enough of his own, and although, according to
the memoirs, Carrio too reimbursed the creditor. The
ambassador discusses some of the details of the account in
his letter. He does not say what incited him to summon his
secretary on August 6 and close the account at that time.
He does not say it was a letter from his brother. Nor does
he mention other details of the situation described in *Les
Confessions*, such as Rousseau's repeated requests to be
replaced or the accusation of selling the ciphers, although
elsewhere, in the same letter, he thrice hints vaguely at
distrust and suspicion of his secretary. This is all he says.

Yet this item of his letter helps to clarify the circum-

[122] *C.C.*, II, 275–278 (Appendix 54).

stances of Rousseau's dismissal in actual life. It confirms other contemporary evidence showing that the dismissal originated with Montaigu and, as we have already observed, was tentatively proposed in February, and more resolutely in June. However, even this evidence does not necessarily belie *Les Confessions*, since the secretary chose to take the first threat more earnestly than it was intended, as we have seen in his letters drafted in February and April, presumably for Alary and the chevalier. When the ambassador failed to act upon it—and this proves that he was much less serious about it than Rousseau—the latter conceivably raised the question himself in their subsequent relations with one another, just as he does in his April correspondence, probably because of an obvious incompatibility of character. Montaigu's other letters show that he located a new secretary toward the end of June. Rousseau received his discharge shortly after July 25, on which date he drafted messages of homage to possible Parisian patrons, perhaps in view of future dependence. He may have received it on July 31 if it was really occasioned, as the ambassador has said, by a dispute about a memorial to the senate, since a memorial was submitted by the embassy on that day. In any case, on August 1, he notified a correspondent that he had ceased to exercise the functions of embassy secretary. In fact the second secretary wrote the regular court dispatch the same day. The violent scene took place a week later. During the intervening period Rousseau was still residing at the embassy, handling some of the official correspondence and apparently training the second secretary to cope with his duties until the successor should arrive in Venice.[123] Historical documentation therefore

---

[123] For the above-cited letters of homage see *ibid.*, pp. 30–31. For the memorial of July 31 see Cérésole, *J.-J. Rousseau à Venise*, pp. 102–103. It relates to an attempt on the part of Montaigu to recover effects left in Venice by his predecessor. For the letter of August 1, addressed to François Régny, see *C.C.*, II, 37. On August 4 Rousseau wrote a letter for Montaigu to M. de Vertmont, private secretary to the French ambassador at Soleure, and another to a certain Mme de Montigny, though the latter may perhaps date a few days earlier: *ibid.*, pp. 34, 39.

verifies Montaigu's version of the sequence of events as related in his letter to the court. But we are still left wondering what induced him to call his secretary to account and terminate their relations so abruptly, especially since the second secretary was not qualified to fill the vacancy and assume powers originally delegated to the consul himself. Nor did the successor arrive to alleviate the situation until October.[124] By reason of this psychological gap in the letter it is unconvincing. It lacks the clarity and consistency of Rousseau's narration.

The real clue to an appreciation of the truth and artistry of the farewell scene as told in *Les Confessions* is to be sought elsewhere. Montaigu's story to the court is complemented by the secretary's private correspondence, clarifying our view of actuality that later becomes a source of art. Rarely does a writer describe in letters events that have just occurred and that are to furnish him with the elements of a major scene in a work of art a quarter of a century afterwards. I refer in particular to two missives which he wrote on August 8, the next day but one after the stormy encounter. One is addressed to Montaigu's correspondent, the Abbé Alary, and the other is the first of three so-called *Venetian Letters*, which Rousseau wrote personally to the head clerk in the Foreign Office to complain about his treatment at the hands of the ambassador and which Voltaire scandalously procured and partially published in 1766 in an effort to bring disgrace upon his rival.[125] As far as we know, none of these letters was honored with a reply.

[124] The archives show that from July 25 to October 17, 1744, Montaigu's letters, with very few exceptions, were written by de Binis. When the count wrote in his letter to Alary of August 15 that he tolerated Rousseau until he was sure of his present secretary, he must have been referring to the Abbé de Binis. Le Blond's indignation at being replaced by the second secretary is seen in a letter of October 10, 1774 (*ibid.*, p. 61).

[125] Regarding the fate of these letters see *O.C.*, Pléiade, I, 1402 *n*1 (to p. 324); and III, p. ccxlvii; and especially *C.C.*, II, 46, 63–64. Cf. *C.G.*, XVI, 200, letter from Rousseau to M. du Chauvet, January 5, 1767. Voltaire published fragments of the first two letters in *Notes sur la lettre de monsieur de Voltaire à monsieur Hume.*

The message to Alary is very different from the February draft expressing vague nostalgia for Paris. This new one, actually dispatched, is valuable because it shows that what produced the count's sudden decision to settle matters with his secretary was a letter from the chevalier. Rousseau tells Alary that he had confided his discontent in writing to His Excellency's brother, adding that the man might have made different use of the letter if he had merely consulted his own reason and sentiments.[126] The meaning is that whatever use he made of it clearly kindled Montaigu's hostility. Rousseau's appeal to the chevalier, like the latter's missive to the count, has disappeared and may have been quite unlike the April draft,[127] but the role of both lost letters in precipitating the catastrophe is implied in the secretary's definitive communication to the abbé in August.

In Rousseau's second letter referred to above and addressed to the Foreign Office, as in the one to Alary, the writer, having said that grievances were reciprocal, refrains from rehearsing his own, since it would distress him to mitigate them for the sake of verisimilitude. He simply implies that, on account of them, he had welcomed his employer's decision to relieve him of his post and to look for someone to replace him, although he had hoped that they would part in a dignified manner.[128] Thereupon he tells of being unexpectedly summoned into the ambassador's presence to find him in a rage, impatient to settle the account at once with his secretary. Rousseau does not explain here that the summons was motivated by the chevalier's missive, but the letter to Alary hints that this

[126] *C.C.*, II, 41–42.

[127] In writing Alary about the lost letter to the chevalier, Rousseau quotes from the April draft which may or may not be the letter mentioned in *Les Confessions*. Mr. Leigh thinks it is (*ibid.*, 1, 235–236).

[128] *Ibid.*, II, 43–45, and especially 43: "Les mecontentemens étoient réciproques, et il est aisé de juger que chaquun n'a reconnu que les siens pour légitimes; Monsieur l'Ambassadeur a enfin pris le parti de me congédier. Je comptois que la chose se passeroit avec ... honnêtteté ... "

was the case in actuality as well as in *Les Confessions*,
where all the "tangled threads" are wrought into a clear
design to give form to life and deepen its meaning. The
letter to the Foreign Office also tells of the threat of physical
violence that ensued, and discloses what induced it. The
cause was not the secretary's mockery of the accusation
about the ciphers, as we are informed in *Les Confessions*.
Later correspondence hints that this accusation was perhaps made about two months afterwards, although
Montaigu, who often took advantage of the younger man's
alien birth to taunt him with disloyalty, would conceivably
have repeated the charge at the moment of their definitive
breach. This is all the more likely since, on the day of the
secretary's departure from Venice, the count complained
to the Foreign Office that he had reason to suspect his
ciphers were known.[129] But these suspicions had nothing
at all to do with the threat of defenestration, as it has been
called. Rousseau's own letter of August 8 shows that matters reached that pass when he objected to certain deductions in the account, whether the objection was made
"respectfully," as he tells the Foreign Office, or "insolently," as his employer alleges.

Basically his letter confirms Montaigu's testimony about
the cause of near violence between them. It tells what
must have happened in actuality, and the author of *Les
Confessions* was undoubtedly fully aware of the facts.
Nevertheless, although he mentions the account four times
in the memoirs, where he calls it an "apothecary's bill,"
he deliberately refrains from doing so in the scene of the
crisis.[130] He omits reference to it, not to distort the facts,

---

[129] *Ibid.*, p. 62, letter from Rousseau to the Foreign Office, October 7, 1744,
conceivably written while he was en route to Paris, but perhaps composed by
the author twenty years later. Montaigu's letter to the Foreign Office, of
August 22, 1744, is given in *C.C.*, II, 65.

[130] *O.C.*, Pléiade, I, 309, where he describes the sordid conditions at the
embassy; 312, where he mentions the dinner with Le Blond; 324, where, on
his return journey to Paris, he verifies a detail of the account here called a
"mémoire d'Apothicaire"; and 326 where he acknowledges final payment made
in 1749.

nor even because he regarded money as lacking in grandeur and dignity for a theme of art, but because it was not morally what severed the association between the two men. Here we have a perfect illustration of Socrates' contention that "the actual falls short of the truth." To present the final rupture as a quarrel about financial matters would be essentially false and out of character. This is a case in which literal circumstantial truth would be morally and spiritually untrue. Events, which are intended to be raiment for the soul, would be nothing but a grotesque disguise to conceal it. There is however no real violation of factual veracity in the scene of *Les Confessions*. Similar scenes had certainly been enacted previously, for example in June when the secretary drafted a message of anguish presumably for Mari, and even earlier, in February, and again in April when he may have asked the count to act upon his word and relieve him. The scene in the book, like the dispatch to Naples, and perhaps the Veronese incident too, is undoubtedly a blending and a synthesis of a number of life experiences, which are treated with the historian of the soul's usual felicitous disregard for the sequence of events in the world of time and space. All these experiences are integrated, together with the discharge and the last violent encounter, into a single composite drama to express the young Rousseau's innermost being. He manifests a profound contempt for social order, which he regards as disorder, and an invincible conviction of his own intellectual superiority at the very moment of retreat. The result of these sentiments is an immense pride of spirit, momentarily prevailing over that innate languor and longing for solitude, which is born of moral frailty and diffidence and is as much a part of his nature as the present challenge to society and its inverted scale of values in the person of the count.

Some of the states of soul, portrayed in *Les Confessions* in the stormy leave-taking at the embassy, are reflected in other letters that Rousseau wrote at the time. For example on August 15, in the second of the *Venetian Letters* to the Foreign Office, as well as in the one discussed above, he is moved by a conviction of his own merits to appeal to the justice and mercy of the King. But he does so with little faith in his plea and little hope of redress for he is persuaded that social prejudice is set against the subordinate, even though he contends that Venetian public opinion openly favors him. He accuses the ambassador of having him pursued from house to house, of forbidding proprietors to afford him lodging, and of giving orders to have him beaten.[131] Finally he complains that his clothing is withheld at the palace. These details, which testify against the count and are therefore omitted in his letter to the court, are not included in *Les Confessions* either, even in a modified form, probably because they would impair the illusion of psychological truth and verisimilitude. Again we have occasion to observe that whenever any supposed apologetic end would conflict with his psychological purpose—and the two are in fact irreconcilable—he deliberately pursues the latter at the expense of the former. The historian of the soul, or, if we prefer, the introspective portraitist, gains at the expense of the man, and so does the *littérateur*. Our collation serves well to illustrate this important point. In the present case, a letter defining the circumstances surrounding the last scene at the embassy and the victim's psychological reactions brings us to realize once more the artistic moderation displayed in Rousseau's book to accentuate inner truth. Neither scene nor character is there disfigured. On the contrary, both are transfigured by the author's obvious restraint, by the elimination of sensational details, and by a powerful use of synthesis to achieve greater intensity for the expression of the spirit. There we see a man in his

---

[131] *C.C.*, II, 48–49; Montaigu may have resorted to the so-called "Braves" (hired bandits) which he recommended to Cattaneo to kidnap Barberina and which are defined in a dispatch as " ... espèces de gens ... dont on se sert pour des actions de vivacité quand les Princes l'ordonnent à leurs ministres." See *O.C.*, Pléiade, III, 1139, 1833 *n*1 (to p. 1139).

pride who paradoxically wins a victory and is obliged to withdraw at one and the same time and who will never let this experience fade from his mind and heart. Admittedly the same sentiments are reflected in both letters and memoirs. But in the letters the writer discourses upon injustice and social prejudice exemplified in melodramatic events, while in the work of art the same ideas are concretely portrayed in a tableau that gives an illusion of life itself. Yet there is an abyss between the diffuseness of life and letters too and the concentrated imagery of *Les Confessions*, where the two protagonists confront one another in a last monumental encounter, which is not only a struggle between the individual and society but also a struggle between the old order and the new. It is as if the young Rousseau has closed the door not merely upon the palace but upon the system of things for which it stands and has resolutely walked out into the world as the champion of another. The scene has all the gravity and fullness of meaning of an authentic crisis that is also a new departure already fashioning the future.

Reading this part of the master work without the correspondence, we might have been tempted to ask whether the author is really pursuing his avowed intention of reliving past emotions, or whether he is merely projecting present moods into the past and attributing them to the hero of the seventh book. We might have seen traces of misanthropic obsession, and wondered whether it was, or was not, an anachronism in the context. Reading the same pages in conjunction with the letters, we are brought to realize the psychological conformity of the story with real life and to wonder in amazement at its almost literal adherence to actual events. The latter are treated in the book as the cause or effect of emotions which are also recorded in the letters, but in a much less subtle and expressive form.

In the Venetian story, the hero's expulsion has a triumphant finale that is by no means the definitive finale but which contrasts in a magnificent crescendo with the sordid scenes that precede. Only these musical terms can really convey the spirit of the original text. He is straightway fêted by the consul Le Blond at a brilliant banquet attended by the most distinguished French residents of Venice. In this tableau, rather than in the previous one, and twice again in the ensuing pages, the author mentions the unsettled account. All the guests, apprised of his circumstances, open their purses in spontaneous sympathy for the impecunious young man and unanimously denounce the ambassador. This banquet is clearly an artistic pendant to the proposed dinner at the embassy for the Duke of Modena. The former secretary of France is also welcomed by the chancellor of the consulate, whose dwelling he is invited to share. He is even honored by the Venetian senate, which ignores a memorial from the count requesting his exile, and advises Le Blond that Rousseau may remain in Venice at his pleasure. In a word, he enjoys universal approval and esteem. Even foreign diplomats exchange courtesies with him. At last, financially assisted by the consul himself, he takes leave of the city of the lagoon and sets out on his journey northward. This whole sequence of pictures, symphonic in treatment, expresses the voice of public opinion resounding in his favor and responding to his own youthful indignation.

The pictorial drama contained in these pages of *Les Confessions* is a transmutation of actuality through the medium of artistic devices, conceived to bring out its symbolic meaning. We can illustrate this statement by an historical study of that same actuality which is the theme of another appeal supposedly made by Rousseau to the Foreign Office shortly after the events occurred and dated October 7 when he was already on his way to Paris. I say "supposedly" because there is strong evidence to prove that the writer did not merely rephrase the letter twenty years later as has previously been believed, but that he actually composed it only in 1763 to supplement the autobiography then under contemplation.[132] In any case, it recounts many of the above-mentioned circumstances incorporated into *Les Confessions*, and since it does so without transcending them it helps to bring out the literary merits of the book.

The letter mentions Montaigu's belated accusation about the ciphers, his memorial against his former secretary, and the Venetian senate's favorable decision conveyed in a message entrusted to Le Blond. It also cites other proofs of public esteem shown to the writer: the sympathy accorded him by the French population of Venice, the hospitality extended by the chancellor of the consulate, the generosity of everyone, especially the consul himself. Finally it refers to the unsettled account. Everything that is in *Les Confessions* is here too; everything except art— everything except the cumulative effect of the crescendo, gathering momentum as it rises to symbolize the resounding voice of public opinion, echoing his own turbulent emotions. The analogy of certain aspects of the writer's art with music, illustrated by the Pléiade editors, is amply justified by passages like these. The virtues of the memoirs and their musical tonalities are brought to our attention by a comparison with the correspondence, which lacks these qualities. The conclusion of the letter is that the testimony of all Venice to the writer's personal dignity and faithful service is his only defense against aggressiveness of rank in the person of the ambassador, who is allegedly quite lost to reason.

The archives of the Venetian inquisitors also report upon Montaigu's curious memorial against his former secretary, which, though actually presented on August 31 after the intended victim's departure for France, contrary to what we read in *Les Confessions*, was no doubt contemplated and discussed long before. Rousseau must therefore have been aware of it while he was still in Venice. This is why

---

[132] *C.C.*, II, 61–62 and explanatory notes on pp. 63–65.

the historian of the soul discusses it in that setting. In fact the petition it contained was delivered orally a week earlier, only two days after the secretary had left the city, although, as in the case of the accusation of smuggling, he was not named on the first occasion.[133] The council that received the memorial, and specifically the chairman Almoro Zustiniani, who may be the impresario of the Veronese affair, declined to bring the matter before the senate or even to make a reply, and this may explain why the archives apparently contain no trace of the document. Instead he called upon the state inquisitors to notify not the ambassador but the consul of Rousseau's departure on August 22. Le Blond, already informed since he had advanced funds for the journey, replied that he had been unable to offer advice, by reason of Montaigu's character, for of course he bore the man no affection and had previously been the victim of his disloyalty as he was later to be the victim of another of his amazing memorials.

Such are the matters of fact, but in themselves they are utterly formless in every sense of the word: formless because they are lacking in harmony and ordered arrangement; formless too because they are mere records instead of modes of being for the revelation of the spirit. Yet they hold for us the fascination of actual scenes that have furnished the raw material for a great painting or inspired a magnificent symphony. This is all the more so, as the pages they have prompted in the memoirs recreate the author's inner life at a moment of intoxication and crisis, when he flatters himself that public opinion at least is on his side, and that this is the side of justice and of truth. These illusions, together with that excitement or agitation of spirit which invariably attends a disturbing, even tragic event in life, overlay for the moment the deeper wound which inevitably makes itself ever more painfully felt.

[133] *C.G.*, I, 253–255. This is a French translation of an extract from the archives, dated September, 1744. Mr. Leigh gives the original Italian text (*C.C.*, II, 58–60). For the memorial against Le Blond mentioned below see Derche, "Autour du séjour de J.-J. Rousseau à Venise," pp. 150–151.

SCENES OF INTROVERSION

Before recounting in *Les Confessions* the adventures of his journey northwards, Rousseau interrupts his narrative at this point to devote some dozen pages to confidences of a more intimate nature than the previous ones. He offers no explanation for setting aside these souvenirs in a sort of supplement. But there is clearly a certain symbolism in the very framework of the Venetian reminiscences, a symbolism which is everywhere explicit, as we have already observed, for instance, in the orderly arrangement of the "heroic" deeds, gathered together, and matched against the mortifications and embassy disorders, without regard for chronology. In the present case the writer scrupulously separates the most highly subjective impressions of his story from the account of his stewardship that precedes. Perhaps he means to signify that the pleasures he relives in these pages are to be taken as an afterthought and nothing more in the life of the ardent young secretary of the house of France. Much more probably, these emotional experiences, which transmit the same spirit recognizable in all its manifestations, disclose some vital truths about the real meaning of the fateful year that is now drawing to an equally fateful end.

MUSIC AND THE SOUL

An important part of what we have called the supplement is devoted to the pleasures of music, which, together with other amusements such as dancing and, more rarely, games of chance, Rousseau shares with his friends.[134] The latter include the consul and his large family; the amiable and

---

[134] The balls are mentioned in the *Venetian Despatches*. Montaigu and Mari each held two balls without entrance fee like those given by the Venetian republic. Both men attended one of the latter on the last day of the carnival in St. John Chrysostom theater, where the illuminations were such as they had never before seen (*O.C.*, Pléiade, III, 1165). Further with regard to Rousseau's lighter moments in Venice, in the *Lettres écrites de la montagne*, he recalls amusing his friends with oracles and divination. He refers to this passage in the sixth book of *Les Confessions* (*ibid.*, I, 241).

witty Carrio or Carrion, secretary to the Spanish embassy,
whom he saw years later in Paris; a young Spanish student,
Altuna, whom he is soon to join in the French capital;
and a few Englishmen of intelligence and learning among
whom is undoubtedly Lord John's tutor mentioned in
Emile.[135] The reader is a witness as the youthful Swiss
conceives an enduring passion for Italian music. Rousseau
has not forgotten hearing an orchestra in Turin years
before, but in Venice it is mainly Italian song that takes
possession of his soul. He hears it for the first time on the
lips of gondoliers. Afterwards it so charms him at the
opera with its sweet harmonies and enchanting airs that
one evening at the theater, as he is roused from sleep by
the sound, he imagines himself in paradise. Even more
delightful to his ear is the music of the four houses of
charity, especially the Mendicanti, where he lingers to
listen to cloistered orphan girls, wards of the state, singing
at vespers in the chapel and accompanied by a great
orchestra but screened from public view. Meeting them
later at a collation, he is cruelly disillusioned by their
personal ugliness. To his astonishment, however, it is
transcended again thereafter by the beauty of soul poured
forth in their song. Moved by these revelations he engages
musicians to rehearse with him, not only Italian arias,
but orchestrial pieces from his own unfinished ballet, *Les
Muses galantes*, parts of which are also performed at the
most magnificent of all Venetian theaters, St. John
Chrysostom, owned by Grimani of Veronese fame. These
pages of *Les Confessions* fairly pulsate with intense feeling
as the writer, a quarter of a century later, travels back
over the years and from among the vague, shadowy
depths of the past allows the fitful light of impassioned
recollection to bring forth only the most deeply emotional

---

[135] For Carrio (n) see *ibid.*, pp. 304, 305, 313, 316, 318, 322, 508; for Altuna
see pp. 305, 313, 327–330, and see below; with regard to the Englishmen, one
of whom was no doubt Lord John's tutor, consult the fifth book of *Emile*
(*O.C.*, Hachette, II, 442).

moments: memories of a barcarolle, the first pure song to strike his ear; of music from the heavenly spheres and choirs of angels exquisitely sweet.

In this part of the autobiography the writer conveys the pure impressions of music, shorn of all imagery, which has been so effectively used until now. The change of method is clear enough in the text of the book itself where the only pictures that emerge are austere evocations of the listener, asleep in his loge or sharing a collation in an almshouse. The modification in form becomes still clearer by comparison with documents of an impersonal nature, originating in the same phase of life. Before considering contemporary evidence, it is enlightening to consult Rousseau's musical writings which contain autobiographical details relating to the same perceptions but deliberately excluded from the memoirs. For example, the most important of these works, the *Lettre sur la musique française*, which dates less than a decade after the Venetian sojourn and is a declaration of the superiority of Italian music over French, contains an engaging picture of a singer, who is probably Rousseau himself, in the midst of a company of friends in Venice. He succeeds in enchanting an Armenian with a badly sung aria of Galuppi but merely astonishes his hearer with a tolerably executed French monologue.[136] This tableau, which is so pleasantly appealing to the imagination, does not belong in *Les Confessions*, since it does not relate to the writer's own intimate impressions.

Even more valuable for an understanding of this aspect of the book is his *Dictionnaire de musique*, composed at the same time as the autobiography and dealing with the varieties of music mentioned therein, especially the barcarolles and opera, for, significantly enough, he alludes only briefly to the orphan choirs in the more objective publication. In the dictionary he recalls hearing in Venice the most beautiful of barcarolles, Tasso's *Jerusalem Delivered*, which the gondoliers on summer evenings used to sing by heart,

[136] *Ibid.*, VI, 178–179. Early in Book VIII of the memoirs, Rousseau sings Italian arias and barcarolles in Paris.

alternating from gondola to gondola and responding in turn.[137] This colorful image finds no place in the story of the writer's soul, as though he had intentionally eliminated picturesqueness in the pages on Venetian music. It is also remarkable that, in both dictionary and autobiography too, he speaks of the opera as if he saw in it no spectacle at all: he reduces it to pure melody that expresses all states of mind and modes of being, and seeks out the deepest recesses of the listener's heart.[138] Since this is essentially its function and its effect, he manifests both without having recourse to material forms that are so obtrusive in opera but of which he gives not a hint.

The same principle is most striking in his treatment of the unseen orphan choirs in *Les Confessions*. It is further demonstrable by a comparison of the text of the memoirs on this theme with an epistle on the same subject which the author composed in verse during the Venetian sojourn and dedicated to Monsieur Bordes of Lyons.[139] In this new but fragmentary poem addressed to his Lyonese friend, Rousseau, nominally Catholic for sixteen years and destined to remain so for another decade,[140] shows the splendor of the Mendicanti chapel during Holy Week. He comes upon the shrine bedecked with worldly luxury and pomp, marred only by the mysterious litanies and exorcisms of the monks. Religious devotion that has drawn him hither is promptly forgotten as his senses thrill to painted images, fragrant censers, an orphan's song, and the beauty of the worshippers. After forty days of Lent he sees the charming Venetian women, arrayed like the lilies of the field and offering to the Virgin vows of adora-

[137] *Ibid.*, p. 353. Cf. Monnier, *Venise au XVIIIe siècle*, p. 342. For Rousseau's predilection for Tasso, whom he quotes in the *Lettre sur la musique française*, in *La Nouvelle Héloise*, and in *Emile*, and whose story of Olindo and Sofronia he translated, see *O.C.*, Pléiade, I, 1385–1386 n6 (to p. 294).

[138] *O.C.*, Hachette, VII, 339, under "unité de mélodie."

[139] *O.C.*, Pléiade, II, 1144–1145; or *C.G.*, I, 141–142.

[140] Rousseau was theoretically Roman Catholic from April 22, 1728, to August 1, 1754.

tion that they long to receive from the race of men, transmuting sensuous ardor into mystical ecstasy. The author of *Les Confessions* has deliberately excluded this spectacle from his book, for both artistic and religious reasons. His religious objections to the scene are implied in the epistle of many years before. In those verses the reader, who is on familiar terms with the writer, easily sees through the veil of the future. Rousseau's Calvinist nature will reject the splendor of Catholicism in favor of that Lenten austerity for which he was not yet spiritually prepared but which was to become the very keynote of his life and thought. The scene in the chapel is clearly not the occasion of a religious experience for him. It does not offer him a real artistic experience either, and, upon this account too, he has barred it from his autobiography. His innermost being responds not to painted images, however much they may caress his senses, but solely to the orphan's song, which alone finds a place in the annals of the soul. He is most deeply sensitive to music, an art that best expresses the unseen, all the mysterious vicissitudes of the human spirit, rather than the shapes of the material world, and whose effects are equally invisible and un-fathomable. Faithful to the nature of that art he renders, in the pages of *Les Confessions*, only the ecstasy of musical impressions and nothing more.

These pages of the memoirs contain striking proof of Rousseau's skill in artistic transposition, the use of words without imagery to convey the effect of music upon him. The reverberations of song in his inner life are his whole preoccupation. Everything else is superfluous and unsatisfying. By comparison with the hidden world, which is a source of art and beauty, the objective world of matter leaves him disillusioned. This is why he finds more delight in the invisible choirs than in the opera, which offers in addition a pageant for the sense of sight so pitifully inadequate that he banishes it by closing his eyelids as he listens and then falls asleep in the loge. For the same reason, when he finally sees the orphan singers, they seem to him ugly and ill-favored. Other writers, his contemporaries, for example Charles de Brosses, who visited Venice hardly five years before, describe them as beautiful. They appeared in public engagements too, clad in white in the religious manner but wearing clusters of pomegranate flowers in their hair.[141] It is difficult to believe that forty Mendicanti orphans, whatever flaws marred their youth, were less comely than other girls of twenty. In *Les Confessions* they are ugly only in relation to the beauty of their voices, echoes of the spirit, for beauty must be clothed in life as humbly as truth itself. Beyond a doubt this is the writer's meaning, for the white-robed orphans become beautiful again in his fancy, by virtue of their song. In other words, the inner reality of grace and emotion finally overshadows and obscures the mediocrity of material actuality, and by its very intensity and depth imposes itself as true. It is this inner reality, sheer musical impressions divested of all picturesque forms, that the author of *Les Confessions* clearly wants to render, not only in the case of chapel choirs but in all those pages where he relives the first powerful impact of Italian music upon him, or rather within him. Just as the barcarolles are quite simply the first pure song to fall upon his ear, as the opera is for him a divine harmony that stirs his being to consciousness and nothing else, in like manner the orphan choirs are the essence of beauty itself that is the more exquisite for remaining invisible and frees the mind from earthly bonds.

Since Rousseau's autobiography is really a self-portrait, it excludes other arts to which he was almost insensitive.

[141] Charles de Brosses, *Lettres familières (écrites d'Italie en 1739 et 1740)*, I (Paris: Perrin, 1885), 193ff. There are five letters in which he speaks of Rosalba Carriera, Venetian palaces and painting, and the music of the forty cloistered orphans in each of the four houses of charity (the Pietà, Mendicanti, Incurabili, and Ospedaletto). Finally he sings the praises of Venetian courtesans, including a certain Julietta, who has been compared to the Zulietta of *Les Confessions*.

The plastic arts of sculpture and painting seem to have left him unmoved, even in Venice where masterpieces abound. Or if his sensuous nature did indeed answer to the sensuousness of Titian, for example, and Venetian Renaissance art, we search in vain for some trace of these "correspondences." The bright canvases of his Venetian contemporaries, then the greatest school of painters in the whole of Italy, most of whom were at the height of their careers at this time, seem to have made no impression on his mind and heart: neither Tiepolo's frescoed festivals of light, nor Rosalba's delicate portraits in pastel, nor Longhi's elegant interiors, nor Canaletto's or even Guardi's brilliant visions of the Ventian scene.[142] All these artists were adorning and enriching the city during Rousseau's sojourn, yet he does not even mention them in any of his works. Why does he ignore them, while he speaks with unconcealed delight of the contemporary Venetian composer Galuppi? How can we explain his indifference to painting, as opposed to his passion for music? In *Emile* he says that painters like Raphael and Il Albano to whom he is not indifferent are too remote from nature. But if we conclude from this statement that he is a man of direct sensation, attracted by nature alone, and that painting, as an art of imitation, distracts the attention from life and nature, which we see only through the artist's spiritual reactions,[143] what else does music do, or literature either for that matter? Music too is an art of imitation, even though formal rhythm is an important source of the pleasure it affords. However it does not normally attempt to represent the external forms of life and the world; it usually confines itself to conveying the inner being of man and creation. In fact Rousseau himself says that music paints visible things only indirectly, by

[142] Rosalba Carriera was sixty-nine years of age when Rousseau was in Venice; Tiepolo was fifty-four years old; Canaletto, forty-seven; Longhi, forty-two; and Guardi was Rousseau's age.

[143] This explanation is proposed by the editors of *O.C.*, Pléiade, I, 1398–1399 *n*2 (to p. 313).

arousing in the soul the same movements we experience beholding them.[144] This is the real reason he prefers it to the plastic arts. This is also why music moves his creative gifts in much the same way as literature. It may be objected that literature, like painting and sculpture, expresses external reality too. But the world of matter is less obtrusive and more transparent when represented in words, rather than in such media as stone or pigment, which appeal so insistently to the sense of sight; words, appealing directly to the mind, are a more subtle mode of expression. This is not equally true of all literature but it is eminently true of *Les Confessions*. The book also illustrates the idea of Socrates, who tells us that "language is more pliable than wax or any similar substance," including pigment. Throughout its pages, the author paints pictures in words, except when conveying his love for music.

Paradoxically, he seems to have been indifferent to architecture, which has the same limitations and the same powers as music, and which Schlegel even called "frozen music." Although elsewhere in his work Rousseau speaks with admiration of ancient classical ruins, such as the Pont du Gard, near Avignon, and the amphitheaters of Nîmes and Verona,[145] yet never once does he allude to Venetian Gothic and Renaissance palaces. The lovely House of Gold on the great lagoon seems not to have existed for him. He describes Montaigu's summer palace on the Brenta, richly inlaid with mosaics and adorned with fine marble columns and pilasters, but says not a word about

[144] See *Dictionnaire de musique*, article "Imitation" (*O.C.*, Hachette, VII, 140–141). In brief, Rousseau writes:
La peinture, qui n'offre point ses tableaux à l'imagination, mais au sens et à un seul sens, ne peint que les objets soumis à la vue. La musique sembleroit avoir les mêmes bornes par rapport à l'ouie; cependant elle peint tout, même les objets qui ne sont que visibles. ... Mais ... l'art du musicien ... ne représentera pas directement ces choses, mais il excitera dans l'ame les mêmes mouvemens qu'on eprouve en les voyant.
Of course Rousseau had no talent for the plastic arts as he had for music: see fifth book of *Les Confessions* in *O.C.*, Pléiade, I, 180.

[145] *Ibid.*, p. 256 (sixth book of *Les Confessions*).

the gleaming mosaics and marble splendor of Saint Mark's basilica or even the palace of the doges where he often appeared as the embassy envoy. Why? Because Montaigu's villa becomes a symbol of injustice and moral disorder, not because it was a source of aesthetic pleasure for the beholder, any more than Saint Mark's. In fact, the latter is used in *Emile* as an image of splendor, without secure foundations, to symbolize ostentatiously brilliant but ill-grounded encyclopedic learning, which is alien to his nature and violates his principles.[146] Rousseau's reactions always betray the same unfailing concern with his own inner being, which he apprehends rarely in the plastic arts but finds so fully expressed in Italian music and in his proper conception of literature.

Other phases of Venetian life seem hardly to have touched his consciousness. Even the natural graces of the city, whose gay frivolity inspired writers like de Brosses, Voltaire, and Goethe, and which later became a favorite theme of the melancholy romantics, failed to stir the sensibilities of the great precursor of nineteenth-century lyricism. His silence, which impressed us in the story of his arrival, remains unbroken to the very end. There is not a single Venetian landscape or seascape in the whole of his work, or letters either. His grave and austere Protestant nature seems alien to the blithe setting of the Venetian isles, to their nebulous enchantment of marble lacework and water; yet he was almost moved to write a supplement to his memoirs by the sight of the quiet, simple beauty of the Borromean Islands, which he saw on his return to France and thrice recalls in *Les Confessions*.

Not only was he indifferent to the city of the lagoon, but also to Venetian public life, which in the eighteenth century was renowned for the brilliance of its festivities. He refers only once in all his writings to a Venetian festival. In a footnote to *Emile* the value of state insignia and

[146] *O.C.*, Hachette, II, 95.

ceremonials is illustrated by the Ascension Day rituals in Venice, in which the doge, on board the bucentaur barge, cast a ring into the Adriatic to signify the marriage of the city and the sea.[147] In other words, the magnificent ceremony is merely used to exemplify a political idea. In the story of his soul Rousseau tells us nothing about the great feasts or even about the extravagant carnival that lasted half the year. His reserve is remarkable, since for six months of his sojourn the public squares were perpetually filled with throngs of merrymakers; masks and disguises sanctioned every license; the theaters and coffee shops, veritable centers of contemporary Venetian life, never closed their doors; and banquets, balls and fireworks turned night into day and day into night. All this the autobiographer passes over in silence, even though in one scene we catch a glimpse of him in mask and domino as he goes about his duties. His reticence is as eloquent as his most impassioned periods. The city and its life or the artists who embellished it could strike no chord in his nature that is powerful enough to resound in his memory or in his memoirs.

THE ZULIETTA PARABLE

Yet this is not entirely so. Before taking leave of Venice the writer makes confession of having tasted, however timidly, the fruits of voluptuousness, abounding in a city famed for its beautiful women. These confessions are not astonishing in a book so entitled. The reader is, in a sense, prepared for them. On the other hand, one is often surprised by careless little asides that cast a sudden and sinister gleam upon the moral fiber of a century, as frankly wanton as any other. For instance, in presenting his friends to us, Rousseau refers quite casually to their "mistresses." The word sometimes means "betrothed," as in the case of Miss Lucy in *Emile*,[148] but it also means "concubine," as in the case of

---

[147] See p. 11 *n*11, above.
[148] *O.C.*, Hachette, II, 443.

Bettina, who danced the ballet scenes from *Les Muses galantes* at a Venetian theater. Moreover, in the autobiography there is a tacit acceptance of the society of women as being quite normally of an intimate nature, without question of marriage. This is implied in remarks about the daughters of the French consul and the Prussian agent: out of respect for their fathers, his friends, Rousseau declines to pay court to them. The implication is that the act of homage he has in mind would be offensive to the friends, not because of any lofty moral principles on their part or on his but because of their paternal interest in the ladies. He has the skeptic's attitude toward chastity, for he takes pride in his record of continence during the Venetian engagement, of a brief eighteen months in *Les Confessions* and a still briefer fifteen months in actuality and hardly twelve in the city itself. These traits of contemporary manners, reflecting his own attitudes and desires, are an intrinsic part of the work, and bespeak a point of contact between him and eighteenth-century Venice, city of the Anadyomene no less than of Saint Mark. Even gentlewomen were as free as the air, and their love still freer. Moreover, the prestige enjoyed by courtesans and concubines was still a respected tradition. They combined wit and the most exquisite grace with a strange blending of voluptuousness and childish candor and ingenuousness.[149] These are the qualities that beguile even the grave and austere secretary of France.

The confessions of sensual indulgence relate to the end of Rousseau's residence in Venice. First we see him led by the scandalous Vitali to the chambers of the handsome Padoana, whose song is the only real favor his ducat affords him, since her embraces are little more than an occasion of fears, however groundless, for his health. Not long afterwards he meets the enchanting Zulietta. During a dinner on board ship, offered in gratitude by Captain Olivet to the young secretary, accompanied by his friend

[149] Monnier, *Venise au XVIIIᵉ siécle*, pp. 81ff.; Diehl, *Une République patricienne: Venise*, pp. 304ff.

Carrio, she suddenly alights from a gondola like an apparition: a charming, vivacious brunette of hardly more than twenty, with large, dark, almond-shaped eyes, and speaking the sweet accents of Italy. Willfully confusing Rousseau at first with some lost lover of the past, she takes him as her slave on condition that he be wholly hers or not at all. And so he is. He behaves like a man in a trance. He holds her fan, her sash, her veil; he dismisses the gondola at her behest and sits wherever he is bidden. As he and Carrio escort her after dinner to the island of Murano, he wonders at her careless indifference to money, her own much more than theirs. When they conduct her to her apartments in the evening, he admires the pride with which she explains that the pistols on her table safeguard the respect of her person. The next day he returns alone to her dwelling place and, in an unforgettable scene, discovers his soul completely. We are even told in the autobiography that this confession is the most illuminating of all. As he embraces "his" Zulietta, who, arrayed like a flower to enhance her charms and graces, is for him the awe-inspiring goddess of love and beauty herself, he is suddenly stricken by painful reflections and moved to tears. He tells us why. Won by her wit and warmth and radiance, he imagines princes as her slaves and kings at her feet; instead, she is is at the disposal of a common sailor. Perplexed, he concludes that there must surely be some secret flaw. He discovers one, the "téton borgne."[150] But, he reasons, this imperfection alone cannot possibly explain the tragic incongruity: surely the tiny blemish must be merely a sign of some monstrous natural vice, which alone could make her the social outcast she is. Zulietta, discomposed by his tears and doubts, coldly and disdainfully dismisses him, scornfully recommending that he renounce the ladies and devote himself to mathematics. Three days later, still striving in vain to reconcile her personal perfections with

[150] Malformation of the breast.

the indignity of her estate, he returns by appointment, only to find her gone from the city and to mourn her loss. This narrative is supplemented and complemented by that of the fair and gentle child, Anzoletta, offered for sale by her infamous mother to the secretary of Spain, who proposes to share her with his colleague of France. However their paternal affection for her would have led them to protect her innocence at the time of her nubility if Rousseau had not left Venice before his virtue could be put to the test to convince the skeptical reader.

These confessions are framed to heighten the story of Zulietta, which is in fact the concluding incident of the Venetian drama in the autobiography. Before consulting contemporary evidence upon the subject, it is indispensable to appreciate fully the text of *Les Confessions* as it stands, especially since, in this case, it has not attracted the attention it deserves. These pages exemplify the author's art at its best. The man who writes them is master of the most powerful resources of literature, and he exhausts them all. Everything is carefully calculated, and nothing is left to chance. The tale of Zulietta, five pages long in the Pléiade edition and longer than any other single incident in the book, is in striking contrast with the brief page given to the Padoana affair, which is its antipathetic prologue. The story finds an echo or response in the appended page about Anzoletta, where there is also an element of contrast with the principal narrative, especially in the feminine figures, between blonde and brunette, gentleness and impulsiveness. The situation involving Anzoletta, unfinished as it is, would not in itself make a forceful ending to the vitally important story of the Venetian sojourn but must be seen in relation to the preceding scenes.

These scenes, of which Zulietta is the heroine, are of rare literary beauty for the wealth and depth of portraiture they contain. Of all the people he knew in Venice, with the exception of the lightly sketched Anzoletta, Rousseau takes pains to make a moving portrait, physical as well as

moral, but certainly not objective, of Zulietta alone, although later he presents, somewhat more briefly, the young
Spanish student, Altuna, whom he cultivates again in
Paris. He does not even hint at the traits of Le Blond or
Carrio. But the evocation of Zulietta is one of the most
startling images in *Les Confessions*, and indeed in all literature. In the eyes of the writer, the single blemish cannot
justify her tragic role in life and the place to which society
has relegated her, *unless it betokens some great natural vice.*
We must observe that this vice is never revealed. Does it
even exist? Is this lovely creature really a monster, an outcast of nature, no less than of men and of love? If she is
not, then society stands condemned. And so it does. The
parable of Zulietta, for it is really a parable, is one of the
most terrible indictments of society in the whole of Rousseau's work. It is intended to proclaim once more his thirst
for justice and for truth. In the final analysis nothing can
reconcile nature's blessing and society's curse in the figure
of Zulietta, or even in the heavy heart of Zanetto, as she
calls him, for he is sorrowfully conscious that his weakness
makes him an accomplice of social injustice.[151] There is
something very compelling about this story. The Lady of
the Camelias, or her musical counterpart in *La Traviata*,
are not more disturbingly moving than Zulietta, who gives
perfect form to the tragedy of life, intensified for the narrator by the depth of his sympathy and by Zanetto's complicity. The pathos of her disappearance and the young
man's poignant sense of sadness and of loss when she
vanishes as suddenly as she first appeared contrast arrest-
ingly with the brilliant, even intoxicating, scene of the
dinner on board ship. For those who know how to "read
from all points of view at once" these contrasts are not
only an endless source of aesthetic delight, flattering the
taste and beguiling the imagination, but they also promote
a new awareness of the writer's meaning by bringing it

[151] See below where his complicity is discussed in the case of Thérèse Le
Vasseur. The same complicity embitters his happiness with mamma in Book VI.

into unusual relief and thus inviting reflection. We may even find ourselves wondering whether Zulietta's fate is partially told in the person of Anzoletta, whose lot was that of many others, bartered by their parents in early childhood through regular contracts recognized as legal or rather, in the Rousseauist vocabulary, betrayed by society.[152] Is this a clue to the mystery of the hauntingly beautiful Zulietta?

There are few contemporary documents relating to this episode of *Les Confessions*. Apart from de Brosses' letters of 1739, praising the beauty of a Venetian courtesan called Julietta,[153] we have three poems presumably composed by Rousseau in tribute to the Zulietta of actual life. They are inscribed on embassy papers and were kept in the Montaigu family archives before being transferred to the Bibliothèque Nationale. The subject of these rather indifferent verses appears only vaguely reminiscent of the apparition in the story of the soul, which is much more profoundly personal. In other words, the lady of the poems is as remote from "his" transfigured Zulietta of the memoirs as de Brosses' Julietta certainly is, and as the flesh and blood creature of historical fact probably was. In one of the pieces, hardly more than descriptive, the writer enumerates her charms: the graceful address, delicate frame, dazzling complexion, and winsome features, matchless wit, and utter sweetness. In another one too he is lavish in her praise, and yet it is as insipid as the first by comparison with the text of *Les Confessions*, for it is equally lacking in depth of feeling and sympathy in the full etymological sense of the term. The lady, like mamma in the memoirs, is the new Aspasia and, like the old who was renowned in antiquity as the friend of Socrates and wife of Pericles, is famed for the brilliance of her mind and of her person. Triumphantly she holds the universe in thrall. France, Spain, Italy, and

[152] For these contracts see Monnier, *Venise au XVIII° siècle*, pp. 364, 366.
[153] Critics usually compare Rousseau's text with de Brosses'.

Switzerland are slaves at her feet, so sweeping is her sway over the hearts of men.[154] This idea of her rightful sovereignty reappears in the love scene of *Les Confessions*, where, however, the young man suddenly penetrates beneath the surface to see the roles reversed and the sovereign herself in thraldom. Inspired by the same scene in a third contemporary poem, he abandons French altogether, takes refuge in another tongue, and speaks the language of Zulietta, in whom he sees the goddess of love and beauty as in *Les Confessions*. Disconcerted by his mockery, for so she interprets his tearful doubts, she stands at the window with head bowed and eyes downcast, the shadows of the palings falling upon her features, so that the sun of her beauty bursts into a thousand stars.[155] This is the only poem of the three where there is a trace, however faint, of the wistfulness of *Les Confessions*, a feeling that is immeasurably heightened in the story of the writer's inmost being, where it strikes a chord of deepest intimacy.

The profoundly personal quality of these pages of *Les Confessions* is deliberate and shows beyond a doubt that vastly more is implied than the romantic rehabilitation of the courtesan. The author himself warns us that the

---

[154] The text of these two poems is given in *O.C.*, Pléiade, II, 1145–1146, and in *C.G.*, I, 223. "France" in the second poem may or may not be Montaigu or his predecessor, the Count de Froullay, notorious for his romanesque adventures. The Julietta of whom Froullay was enamored, according to de Brosses, is identified by Monglond with Rousseau's Zulietta ("Rousseau, secrétaire de M. de Montaigu," p. 69). Jean Guéhenno doubts this; see his *Jean-Jacques*, I (Paris: Gallimard, 1962), 154. For mamma and Aspasia, see *O.C.*, Pléiade, I, 199.

[155] *C.G.*, I, 215. The Italian poem is not included in the Pléiade edition. Perhaps the editors feel that the authorship is too doubtful. The lines are inscribed in Rousseau's hand on the verso of the draft of a letter written by him on behalf of Montaigu and addressed to one of the latter's colleagues. It would be difficult to prove that Rousseau composed the poem. The most that can be said, on the grounds of certain linguistic errors, is that it is not likely to have been written by an Italian as it stands: e.g. "Tienea" (the reading "Trenca" given in *C.G.* is impossible) instead of "Tenea" in the fourth line; and "de' " instead of "da' " in the fifth line. Of course, these may be simple errors in transcription.

love scene in particular fully depicts his own nature. He does so in a passage unlike any other in the memoirs:

> If there is a circumstance in my life which portrays my nature well, it is that which I am going to relate. The forcefulness with which I recall at this moment the object of my book will bring me to despise the false delicacy which would prevent me from fulfilling it. Whoever you may be who wish to know a man, have the courage to read the following two or three pages, and you will become fully acquainted with J. J. Rousseau.[156]

This means that the autobiographer, who has shown various facets and phases of his temperament and feelings through an infinite variety of situations, now reveals himself completely in the experience of love. His method of using the theme of love to express a personal knowledge of life recalls that of modern fiction, derived from the Freudian doctrine that a man reveals himself in sensual passion. The method also reminds us of Rousseau's statement, made earlier in the seventh book in reference to Monsieur Parisot of Lyons and his lady Godfroi, that a man's true inclinations (and therefore presumably his attitude toward life) are best shown by the nature of his attachments.[157] The idea is symbolically set forth in Valère, Rousseau's Narcissus, whose love is quite literally the perfect image of himself. The theme is far more cleverly handled in *Les Confessions*, where, in the light of the writer's own statements,

[156] *O.C.*, Pléiade, I, 320:
S'il est une circonstance de ma vie qui peigne bien mon naturel, c'est celle que je vais raconter. La force avec laquelle je me rappelle en ce moment l'objet de mon livre me fera mépriser ici la fausse bienseance qui m'empêcheroit de le remplir. Qui que vous soyez qui voulez connoitre un homme, osez lire les deux ou trois pages qui suivent vous allez connoitre à plein J. J. Rousseau.
Of course some people are convinced that he is referring to sexual frigidity; e.g. Maxime Nemo, *L'Homme nouveau Jean-Jacques Rousseau* (Paris: La Colombe, [1957]), pp. 130–135. Even if this were true, it would not invalidate my interpretation of this episode.

[157] *O.C.*, Pléiade, I, 281, and the author's note. The text reads: "Rien ne montre mieux les vrais penchans d'un homme que l'espèce de ses attachemens. Quand on avoit vu la douce Godefroi, on connoissoit le bon Parisot." Cf. p. 142.

the love scenes and situations must be taken as allegorical portrayals of character and soul to deepen our knowledge of the man and his art.

What then do the scenes with Zulietta serve to symbolize? Perhaps the young Rousseau's spiritual inadequacy as he takes refuge in the senses from the demands of actuality, but especially his moral disquietude. These disclosures are made as much in Zulietta's person as in Zanetto's reactions. He manifests himself in and through her, and in this way the writer uses her, as he does everyone else, to tell about himself in the past. We see this when she first appears upon the ship, and the enchanted young man obeys her slightest wish or whim as though he were under a spell. He is her word made flesh, and she the spirit pervading him with life, like Emile "when the soul of Sophie seems to animate him."[158] Zulietta's command that Zanetto be wholly hers or not at all finds an echo in his own temperament shown in a reflection, occurring toward the end of the book, that for him there is no middle term between the whole and nothing.[159] Her sentiments are his. Her indifference to money is his own. How carefully the writer refrains from mentioning payment in reference to her, he who makes a point of the matter in the story of the Padoana, and Anzoletta too, where financial gain is the main issue.[160] Moreover, Zulietta's demand for respect corresponds not only to the young Rousseau's awe in her presence but also to the demands of his own pride for

[158] Zanetto and Zulietta are reminiscent of Emile and Sophie. Here is Emile falling in love: "Il ne parle plus, il ne répond plus, il ne voit que Sophie, il n'entend que Sophie. Si elle dit un mot, il ouvre la bouche; si elle baisse les yeux, il les baisse; s'il la voit soupirer, il soupire; c'est l'âme de Sophie qui paraît l'animer." Finally Sophie takes possession of him, tells him what to do, commands him as her slave (O.C., Hachette, II, 387, 396).

[159] O.C., Pléiade, I, 332. He is referring to Mme de Warens' promiscuous affections. Cf. p. 522 (Book X) where, speaking of his friendship with M. and Mme de Luxembourg, he writes: "J'ai toujours été tout ou rien." Cf. p. 422.

[160] Rousseau did not make payment to Zulietta (ibid., p. 287). He says that he paid for sensual gratification only once in his life, which must be on the occasion of his visit to La Padoana.

deference to his person and his place. This claim and not money produced the storms in the embassy. For it must be remembered that his love for Zulietta is a sequel of the Olivet affair and therefore belongs to the period of his disgrace. In actual life it dated from about July 26, when the affair was settled. He was still at the legation, as the three poems scribbled on embassy papers prove, although he had perhaps but not necessarily been replaced at his post. His plight brought into play certain traits in his character, such as the need for total commitment, indifference to money, and the tyranny of pride which the writer quite naturally sees exteriorized in the person of Zulietta.

In the love scene of the autobiography a sense of the ruthlessness of life is suddenly borne upon the hero, now that the brief moment of triumph and illusion is almost over and is expiring with the excitement of the banquet with Le Blond and his friends. This event precedes the Zulietta episode in the book, even though the dinner party that inspired it actually occurred after Rousseau's meeting with the Venetian courtesan. The sequence of events in the book is not chronological but psychological and artistic. The author deliberately inverts their order to conclude this part of his story with a tragic picture instead of a triumphant one, a fact that has not been hitherto appreciated but which is nevertheless extremely important. This pathetic picture represents forcefully and concretely a much deeper level of consciousness in the young man than the precarious exultation of the dinner with the consul. Zanetto, weeping over Zulietta, feels united with her in a common destiny, for her life, which becomes for him the symbol of our human condition, is also meant to be a symbol of his own. Her brilliance and degradation are akin to his natural genius, which had lately burst into light with the inspiration of *Les Muses galantes* in Paris and had then been exploited and degraded by society. In his own eyes, what else has he been doing but prostituting himself, selling his talents to Montaigu for the performance of trivial tasks, as he was later to sell them to others, the Duke de Richelieu, Voltaire and Rameau, Madame Dupin and Francueil? Nor has he gained anything thereby. The outcast in the Zulietta story is himself.

The writer of *Les Confessions*, from his vantage point in time, conceives this moving drama as synthetizing his own social dilemma in those far-off days, and the conflicting moods of his troubled spirit. For him, the young Rousseau's humiliation can be neither explained nor justified by the assumption of "some monstrous natural vice." Yet in the parable of Zulietta, he confesses to a frailty that was only occasionally apparent in the proud scenes at the embassy. This does not mean that he accepts responsibility. In the person of Zulietta he tells us that society vitiates the individual and fosters his weakness to degrade him. In this way it makes him an accomplice of its prejudices and iniquities, in which Zulietta participates as much as Zanetto. The tears he sheds over her are shed for his own fate, which he equates with that of mankind. It was precisely this analogy that awakened from its long sleep the genius of the pilgrim of Vincennes here foreshadowed in Zanetto and his love. He identifies himself and humanity with her, and so does the autobiographer, much as Rousseau the novelist identifies himself with Julie, as I have illustrated in a previous study. The comparison is not inappropriate. The name of Zulietta is immortalized in that of his famous heroine and in the title of one of his greatest books, for "Zulietta" is the Venetian diminutive of "Julie," as "Zanetto" is of "Jean."[161] The author of *Les Confessions*, who might have taken to himself Flaubert's well-known dictum in the form "Julie is myself," now sees himself in the deeply human Zulietta. This explains the tone of urgency in the narrative. Beyond a doubt, Rousseau portrays himself completely in this tableau which, no less

[161] In Book IX, describing the dreams whence *Julie* emerged, he recalls "the bewitching Zulietta whom my heart cannot forget."

than the others and even more, permits him to eternize in living memory "a man and his sincere love of justice and of truth," a love which the Venetian adventure has failed to requite.When at the beginning of the Zulietta story he promises to make us fully acquainted with J.-J. Rousseau, he does not seek to lead us astray by falsely pretending to offer a clue to his character, as some readers have suspected. Nor does he, as still others have supposed, mysteriously conceal himself under the pretext of revealing himself.[162] On the contrary, we recognize him unmistakably in this parable, not only as he was in 1744 but as he was to become in his celebrated discourses, and in the masterpieces that are like milestones marking the course of his journey through time. The essential themes of all his writing are best treated here, in the crowning work of his life: the incompatibility between the man of nature and the social man, the impairment and demoralization of the one by the other, accompanied by a shift of moral liability, that in some curious way allows nature's graces, in spite of their complicity, to remain essentially intact as the object of society's disgrace. Not even in the *Discours* have these paradoxical ideas been more passionately or imaginatively treated than in *Les Confessions*, which culminates twenty-five years of artistic discipline. Rousseau the writer, no less than the man, stands before us in these scenes of the Venetian story, scenes richly fulfilling the pledge implied in the words: "It is the story of my soul that I have promised. . . . "

The whole supplement of the Venetian engagement, as told in *Les Confessions*, is as prophetic of the future as the experience it consummates and whose most hidden shades of meaning are mirrored in translucent images. The ardent meditations upon music are a warning of the potent reality

---

[162] These theories are advanced respectively by the Pléiade editors (I, 1401–1402 *n*1 [to p. 321] and Guéhenno (*Jean-Jacques*, I, 154–155). The latter sees in the Zulietta story a mere device to follow the fashion of the day and introduce a licentious trait into the memoirs. He therefore marvels at the solemnity with which Rousseau promises to reveal himself completely in the tale.

of Rousseau's inner life, which in a moment of intoxication can exclude all else and bend the world of matter to its will. This inner life finds a mode of allegorical expression in the apologue of Zulietta and Zanetto, where the individual, struggling against the forces of arbitrary social judgments, admits his own moral disarray and yet is sensible of the latent but very real powers that were ultimately to play no small part in molding the destiny of modern Europe. Whether we approve of that mold or not has absolutely nothing to do with the skill of the artist to express the potency and vulnerability of an undeniably significant figure.

FINAL TABLEAUX

As the memorialist resumes the story of his travels to Paris in quest of retribution—for he tells us about his plea made to the Foreign Office from Venice—he shows once again that he is not simply recording his movements through the world of space and time. The recollections of this journey on the overland route through Northern Italy and Switzerland are as subjective and symbolic as those of the much misunderstood voyage to Venice which they serve to counterpoise. While the solitary wayfarer, drawn to Venice almost in spite of himself, is the outward token of an invincible aspiration to solitude that quite blinds him to the wonders of Provence and Italy, the embittered outcast, on his way back to Paris, portrays an ardent desire for justice and nothing more. He takes his course through Lombardy and the lovely Italian lake district, where he admittedly has interesting adventures and is touched by the spectacle of the Borromean Islands in Lake Maggiore, especially Isola Bella. However, the writer of *Les Confessions* refrains from describing these things as one would normally do in the chronicle of an itinerary, since he is recording the annals of the soul where the object is to render states or movements of mind and heart. He does not use imagery simply for the sake of picturesqueness. He dismisses the Alps in an incredibly laconic phrase: "I crossed the Saint Plomb!" In other words, the traveler took the "St. Plomb" (Simplon) road that he had thought of taking the year before, though the auto-biographer does not explain this or comment further. He hardly mentions Sion, the capital of the Valais, in the heart of country that inspired the most eloquent pages in *Julie*. The hero of the memoirs passes blindfold, as it were, through the most magnificent landscape, for the author excludes everything that is not significant to convey a disconsolate spirit and the cruel inner reality of an actual or imagined injustice. It matters little whether or not the young Rousseau was on this occasion warmly greeted in life, as he is in the book, by the French agent personally in Geneva, as he assuredly was at Sion and as he had been in his native city seven years earlier. The newly appointed agent at Sion at once sent news of the visitor to Montaigu, who in replies of September 12 and October 10 sought to discredit his former secretary. He did so by saying that Rousseau had been forced to leave Venice and the states of the republic "for good reason," by insinuatingly inquiring about his proposed course from Sion, and by calling him an adventurer who had been careful not to reveal the rest of his "adventure."[163] In the autobiography the "adven-turer" is simply a man in search of justice and of truth, clutching at the least promise of comfort or the shadow of a promise.

The most meaningful incidents of his travels are the two that the writer brings into high relief: only two, as in

[163] For his visit to M. de Chaignon, the French agent at Sion, see Courtois, "Chronologie critique," p. 47 *n*6. For Montaigu's letters see Souchon, *Corre-spondance diplomatique*, p. 99, and *C.C.*, II, 55–56, 65–66. For the visit to the French resident in Geneva see Courtois, "Chronologie critique," p. 47 *n*6; and François Mugnier, *Madame de Warens et J.-J. Rousseau: étude historique et critique* (Paris: Calmann-Lévy, 1891), pp. 153 *n*1, 219 *n*2. Apparently Rousseau was greeted at Geneva, not by the French agent personally, as he had been in 1737, but by the chaplain and secretary. For the visit of 1737, see *C.C.*,I, 45, 47.

the case of the journey southward. In them he visualizes
the disillusioned idealist as the victim of society, which has
robbed him of his honor and of the laborer's hire. These
incidents are the last reunion with his father Isaac at
Nyon, and a visit to Lyons. The harm to his reputation
is shown in a sense of humiliation which almost makes him
renounce in shame the meeting at Nyon. His mortification
is further underlined by his tribute to a friend who over-
comes this sentiment for the sake of others more pleasing
to the human heart by bringing father and son together
for the last time. The joy that ensues only accentuates,
by its sudden and brief intensity, the pervading gloom of
these pages of *Les Confessions* and deepens the reader's
insight into the young man's dismay. There is a fine contrast between the highly subjective scene of filial and
paternal love, and the intentional and almost forced ob-
jectivity of the second incident illustrating another injustice to which he is exposed, the withholding of funds
that belong to him.

He goes to Lyons to verify the weight of a box for which
carriage charges from Paris to Venice were deducted from
Montaigu's account—the famous apothecary's bill mentioned above—at an enormous rate of payment out of all
proportion to the contents of the shipment. This incident
is founded in historical fact and we have already referred to
the deduction in question. The box contained merchandise
which Rousseau, in a letter from Venice dated November
23, 1743, had asked Madame de Montaigu to forward by
sea, that is from Le Havre together with her own effects.
Since, in making the request, he had suggested that another
rather large item for the count be sent overland to Lyons
by coach, and then dispatched to Marseilles and Genoa,
she must have decided to do the same with the box, for
she was uncertain when her belongings would be shipped.
Judging by the contents, a vest, some cuffs, stockings,
linen, and a few other clothes, the box in question could
hardly have been heavier than the one in the memoirs

which weighs forty-five pounds and which doubtless refers
to the secretary's one and only shipment recorded in
historical documents.[164] In the book, the visit to Lyons is
of an abstract, mathematical aridity that reduces equity
to its traditional symbols, the scale and balance, "emblems
of the Lord's own justice." The narrator is clearly intent
upon setting aside respect of persons and all human considerations, for the traveler appears to have no thought
for the friends who, only two years before, sent him aus-
piciously on his way to Paris. At this moment in time they
no longer exist for him, or so it seems. Does he avoid them
for fear that, if they were to see him dishonored and unpaid,
they would favor society's judgment against the personal
qualities they once professed to admire? I think not.
Probably Rousseau actually did see them, as he saw many
things and many people, for he had a number of experiences that the artist fails to record. The latter simply
disengages from a welter of incidents the two that, in
conjunction with one another, give singular expressiveness
to a sense of injustice and desolation of soul.

In *Les Confessions*, the Venetian sojourn lasts eighteen
months, as the author says twice. In actuality Rousseau
was back in Paris by October 11, 1744, exactly fifteen
months after he had left, almost twelve of which he spent
in Venice itself. In contemporary letters, calculating the

[164] Regarding the contents of the famous box, see *ibid.*, pp. 212–213, 224;
and *C.G.*, I, 271, letter from Rousseau to Mme de Montaigu and two letters to
Roguin. The latter are dated February 7, 1744, and July 9, 1745. A. de Montaigu (*Démêlés*, p. 178) tries to show that there were two boxes, one sent by
sea and the other by land, and that Rousseau is intentionally confusing them
in an effort to charge the ambassador with fraud. The Pléiade editors reject
this explanation (I, 1403 *n*9 [to p. 324]); Mr. Leigh accepts it (*C.C.*, I, 214,
and II, 55, 86) for the following reasons, upon which I comment in parentheses:
(1) Rousseau had asked that the shipment be sent by sea, that is from Le
Havre, instead of through Lyons (but there is no evidence that it *was*); (2)
Mr. Leigh feels that the box must have been heavier than the memorialist
admits (but forty-five pounds seems reasonable enough judging by the contents); (3) several shipments must have been made (but there is no evidence of
more than one).

length of his engagement, he always includes the time spent in traveling. For example in the first of the *Venetian Letters*, dated August, 1744, he says he had been in Montaigu's service for fourteen months. Perhaps the author of *Les Confessions* meant to do likewise and forgetfully added the three months twice. Either the historian of the soul ignores time altogether, as in the Veronese and Naples stories, where no one would suspect that three and then eight months respectively elapse, or else, when he does take the trouble to compute time, he uses his own measure, as in the case of the duration of his absence from Paris in Montaigu's service.

In the memoirs the young man's return to the French capital only widens the rift between the soul and life, between natural self-respect and social abasement, which is the burden of the seventh book. By universal accord he is a victim of the ambassador's folly and cruel iniquity. But, being a foreigner, he has no right to national protection, and so his pleas to the Foreign Office are ignored. In this passage, where the memorialist puts his finger on the real reason for the government's failure to act, the bitterness of Montaigu's former secretary is intensified by that of the author of *Les Confessions*, who had already given to France the flower of his genius. Besides, as a mere secretary, the young Rousseau is sacrified to so-called right order, which, we are persuaded, has nothing to do with truth or justice either. This principle is manifested by Madame de Beuzenwal and the Jesuit friend who had recommended him to her good graces for both of them withdraw their patronage. The same principle reappears, but without the artistic antithesis between public sympathy and apathy, in two contemporary letters attributed to Rousseau and supposedly written shortly after his return to Paris. One, which is surely not authentic but conveys some of the spirit of the memoirs, is directed to Madame de Beuzenwal and is a bitterly ironical attack on rank that exempts a man from dignity, nobleness of purpose, honor, and integrity.[165] The other, the last of the *Venetian Letters* to the Foreign Office, dated from Paris, October 11, 1744, is a plea in self-defense of far richer and more genuine feeling even though it too fell upon deaf ears. The ambassador's apparent injustice and violence, in return for a perhaps over-zealous devotion to his service, have bewildered and unnerved the writer, who, as he had also complained in the second letter two months earlier, is defamed merely because he is the subordinate even though he can prove his rights in matters of honor and honorarium too.[166] Here we are witnessing the evolution of ideas that are ever more forcefully interpreted in literary works of the future, and especially in the memoirs. To realize this, and to appreciate the fact, is not to accept the ideas or even to reject them, but simply to relate various versions of them and to find their perfect formulation in *Les Confessions*.

The last pages of the Venetian story in the autobiography are inspired by events in Venice after Rousseau's departure and by his later contact with Montaigu in Paris. In the book, the ambassador almost at once shows his indiscretions to the world through his relations with his household, especially the newly appointed secretary, who robs him ruthlessly and is finally arrested and imprisoned. These sordid facts have their counterparts in history, and this is quite undeniable. The new secretary was the notorious Henry, who was a real "adventurer" and not an imaginary one like the visitor to Sion. His mediocre talents are shown

---

[165] *C.C.*, II, 376–377. Cf. *O.C.*, Pléiade, I, 1404 *n*1 (to p. 326). For the origin of this letter see *C.G.*, I, *n*1, and *C.C.*, I, 7.

[166] *C.C.*, II, 66–68. In later letters, too, Rousseau makes similar complaints; e.g. on p. 256 he writes thus to Mme de Warens, February 25, 1745: " ... je me plains de mon cheval d'Ambassadeur, on me plaint, on m'estime et l'on ne me rend pas d'autre justice: Ce n'est pas que je n'espére m'en vanger un jour en lui faisant voir, non seulement que je vaux mieux, mais que je suis plus estimé que lui." This is the thought in his mind when he completes *Les Muses galantes*; see p. 163 below. The letter to "mamma" is close to the text of the memoirs but the idea of a spurious social order is absent.

in the deterioration in the style of embassy dispatches. Engaged before Rousseau's discharge upon the recommendation of the count's Parisian banker, Jean-Pierre Kolly, as we have seen, he was entrusted with the direction of the palace of France and turned out to be something of a banker himself for he seized the opportunity to defraud his employer until he was at last convicted of embezzlement and smuggling.[167] His sway at the legation actually lasted three years and not just one as in the case of the new secretary in the Venetian story, where the author has in this case attenuated the ambassador's lack of discernment.

Other incredible reports circulated about Montaigu's relations with his dependents in actual life. For example, his enemy Le Blond tells of a closure of the embassy brought about in 1749 by a fierce quarrel between the count and two servants whom he had dismissed. When they complained of their wages he flew into a rage and beat them with his cane while they retaliated with insults and stoning.[168] Accounts like this are far less restrained than the story in *Les Confessions*, where the embassy scandals finally give rise to Montaigu's recall. This interpretation of events was impugned by historians like Cérésole eighty years ago, since the government did not recall the ambassador until May, 1749, when, after having asked for temporary leave of absence, he was summoned to relinquish his post.[169]

[167] For Henry's escapades see Faugère, "Jean-Jacques Rousseau à Venise," p. 1076; A. de Montaigu, *Démêlés*, pp. 46, 82–86; and Derche, "Autour du séjour de J.-J. Rousseau à Venise," pp. 161–169, where there is a careful study of this affair which led to the ambassador's ultimate downfall.

[168] Letter from Le Blond to the Foreign Office, September 13, 1749, cited by Derche, "Autour du séjour de J.-J. Rousseau à Venise," pp. 154–155, and in *O.C.*, Pléiade, III, 1843–1844 *n*1 (to p. 1198). See also note in *C.C.*, I, 188.

[169] Cérésole, *J.-J. Rousseau à Venise*, p. 108. The "researchers" of the next sentence are: Faugère, "Jean-Jacques Rousseau à Venise," p. 824; A. de Montaigu, *Démêlés*, pp. 92–93; Souchon, *Correspondance diplomatique*, pp. 416, 525–535; Derche, "Autour du séjour de J.-J. Rousseau à Venise," pp. 169–173; Monglond, "Rousseau, secrétaire de M. de Montaigu," p. 49; *O.C.*, Pléiade, I, 1404 *n*5 (to p. 326); III, 1810 *n*1 (to p. 1052); and *C.C.*, I, 188. Derche and Monglond definitively established the fact that the recall was an act of disfavor.

But half a century later the same interpretation was confirmed, and researchers established beyond a doubt that his recall was in fact an act of disfavor, as *Les Confessions* suggests. He pleaded against the order in June but was told not to delay his departure beyond August, when the consul, Le Blond, would relieve him until a successor could be found. It has been said that the consul, who was in Paris at the time, contributed to Montaigu's downfall, but the latter's own escapades testify against him more powerfully than anyone, including Rousseau, for whom the ambassador is clearly not an individual at all, but the symbol of an unjust society.

In the count's case, term of office was no sign of the approval of his superiors, any more than it was for his predecessor. Froullay held the post for a decade despite the fact that, after a period of reputable service, he was completely discredited and even incapacited during the last three years and was notorious for his scandalous escapades, including the seduction of the patrician Maria de Riva within the sanctuary of her convent.[170] In the same way, Montaigu's undeniable incompetence did not prevent the impoverished French government from retaining him in a relatively inactive embassy, instead of appointing a more qualified person, and pensioning the count for his thirty-seven years' military service, as it was finally obliged to do.[171] Historical research shows that he was miscast in the role he tried vainly to play. He betrayed himself from the moment he assumed his mission. As we have already observed, he was reproached for the form of his dispatches and for disrespect to the King before Rousseau arrived in Venice. After the young man left, the soldier-diplomat was reproved for giving the French court unwarranted assurances of Venetian neutrality, as well as for the form of a memorial to the Venetian

---

[170] Of course the corruption that existed even in monasteries is notorious; Monnier and Diehl both speak of it. See also *O.C.*, Pléiade, III, 1820 *n*1 (to p. 1087).

[171] A. de Montaigu, *Démêlés*, p. 95 *n*3, and *C.C.*, I, 188.

senate and of court dispatches too. He was even recalled in 1746. But it was scarcely possible to replace him without compensating him. The astonishing fact is that he received no emoluments until 1749, whereupon he was given a successor.[172] When the government first proposed to relieve him of his post, he was quick to remind it of its obligations toward him, and this, rather than friendly intervention on his behalf, is no doubt the real reason why the matter was pursued no further at that time. The count's dispatches are full of pleas for money, even during Rousseau's secretaryship. The government's indebtedness is not even mentioned in Les Confessions, where the settlement of the account between the two men, upon the occasion of Montaigu's definitive recall, concludes their mutual relations.

Some early critics censured the writer for failing to say that the ambassador himself had not previously been paid.[173] Yet this omission hardly constitutes a violation of moral truth, since Montaigu, who never once acknowledged the younger man's services as secretary of the embassy, might at least have been expected to draw upon his own personal income in order to pay his private secretary's modest salary, if such was Rousseau's official position or title. Everything concurs to prove that the count was a man of means: his private life reflected in the inquisitorial files, the opulent splendor of his summer villa extravagantly remodeled in the French style, and the vast sums of which he was despoiled by Rousseau's successor, probably amount-

---

[172] Montaigu received a quarter's salary before leaving for his post but after he arrived in Venice he received nothing. The Venetian Despatches are full of requests for money: O.C., Pléiade, III, 1079, 1108, 1117–1118, 1131, 1133–1134, 1145, 1170, 1186, 1193, 1209, 1212, 1228. For example, on May 14, 1746, when he was first recalled, Montaigu wrote thus to the Foreign Office: "Je suis tout prest de partir quand il plaira a Sa Majeste, mais il faut absolument pour que je sorte d'icy que vous ayez la bonté de me faire payer tous mes appointements qui ne sçauraient payer toutes les dettes que j'ay contracté à Venise. ... "

[173] Two examples are Ritter and Seilliere.

ing to more than twenty thousand francs.[174] Yet it is true
that he did not compensate his subordinate until he himself was finally recalled, paid, and retired all at once. If
we acknowledge this, we do so not to convict or exonerate
anyone but simply to know the role of truth, or rather
factual truths, in the autobiography and the treatment
they receive in that book. The author, in incorporating
them into the story of his soul, does not do violence to
them or disfigure them in any way. In these passages, he
gives proof of the same moderation observable in his
account of the earlier embassy scandals. He records a few,
but not all, of the unhappy and often incredible adventures
that might have testified against his former employer. He
could have said much more in his own defense, as historians have amply demonstrated. Again he sacrifices
material that would have been valuable to an apologist,
and he does so for the sake of his psychological purpose.
His omissions, which distort nothing, neither external fact
nor inner truth, serve to safeguard the clarity, simplicity,
and integrity of both.

But we must look beyond events to grasp the truth of the
memoirs, a truth intimately bound to the art of the writer.
Rousseau respects events, it is true, but he molds them to
impart his spiritual message, and thus he transcends them.
This message, which is nothing else but his own inner
response to life, implies an indictment, not of a man, not
even of Montaigu, but of society, whose arbitrary, abstract
principles have less to do with reality than the myths of
the "Contract." Unfortunately the count lent himself to
the unsympathetic part he plays in the book, as the embodiment of a hostile world. His defects are contrasted
with society's awe of rank and wealth in his person, to
which the secretary is represented as being complacently

---

[174] The calculation is Mr. Leigh's; see *C.C.*, II, 54. One might add his willing-
ness to pay a year's rent to free himself from a three-year lease of the Querini
palace after residing there for only five months: *O.C.*, Pléiade, III, 1121–1122,
1828 *n*1 (to p. 1122); and Cérêsole, *J.-J. Rousseau à Venise*, pp. 64–65.

sacrificed, in spite of the latter's part in the holocaust. Artistic discipline, far from concealing, most effectively reveals the flame of indignation kindled in Rousseau's youthful soul and still flickering ominously through the writer's words many years later. The young man sees an immense and ever widening gulf between nature's gifts and fortune's favors, and this discrepancy is only adding fuel to the fire of his wrath. His rebellious spirit is storing up resentment against the day of retribution which would surely dawn, as dawn it did, and judgments were reversed, long before the memorialist took up his pen. For example in 1761 Rousseau had occasion to decline a new post in the diplomatic service offered by the Duke de Choiseul, then Minister of Foreign Affairs.[175] The offer came too late. Besides, the next year in the writer's life ushered in a long period of exile, persecution and misanthropic obsession that lasted until death. This is why recognition never healed the scars of distrust in human society that are visible in all his works, from the *Discours* to the *Dialogues*.

The Venetian story, concluding as it began by a vague communication with the count in the setting of Paris, is an excellent example of the sustained artistry of Rousseau's composition in *Les Confessions*. There is a remarkable completeness in this reconstitution of fifteen critical months in his life, wherein he arouses, reawakens, revives, and actually relives the visions, aspirations, emotions, and pschological impressions of his youth. All his passions and prejudices are set before us. He uses the world of sense to translate them into a variety of pictures that blend harmoniously into the portrait of a man in search of "justice and truth." We can hardly fail to see this, whatever moral judgments we may have formed about the writer as a man, or the image he transmits. Opposite this image there stands another figure, intended as the very personification of injustice and ignorance, of moral and intellectual disorder,

[175] Rousseau tells us this in the eleventh book of *Les Confessions* (*O.C.*, Pléiade, I, 553).

who embodies at the same time the glorification of high birth and wealth. This figure is the Montaigu of *Les Confessions*. From a purely factual point of view he bears a close resemblance to his model in life, and there is little difference between them. But, artistically, there is a vast gulf separating the two. This new avatar of social prejudice and tyranny, created by the writer, is infinitely more significant and monumental than the man of flesh, whose eccentricities are none the less scrupulously respected. But the figure in the book is enlarged and expanded by a most skillful and powerful contrast with the younger man into a great symbol of society, whose mandate he holds and with which the unprivileged individual, who is yet projected as a privileged soul, struggles in an epic encounter. Rousseau, grappling with society in the person of its official emissary, is Jacob wrestling with the angel again to win a blessing. Only this time his adversary turns out to be the Adversary, the fallen angel of light transformed into an angel of darkness. And so Jacob in the person of Jean-Jacques, son of a latter-day Isaac, wrestles in vain and obtains only a curse. This analogy serves to illustrate the spirit of the epic tale and to bring into relief Rousseau's ideas on the relations of the individual to the social environment. We are made to feel that the protagonist cannot hold his own or prevail against a society fallen from primitive grace to its present state of defilement, mainly because he is vitiated, instead of being superelevated, by it. But the weaknesses of his opponent, unfaithful even to its minions, are shown in the fate of its figurehead, the count. If a kingdom divided against itself is doomed to fall, then the old order, or rather social disorder, cannot prevail forever. The young Rousseau is an optimist and the memorialist espouses his conviction that an orderly society must emerge in the end. It alone, in his eyes, can redeem the individual, just as social disorder is for him responsible for the fall. The idea haunts his mind and adds the force of passion to his quest as he resumes the struggle on the Parisian scene.

III

Confessions
of the Epilogue

The seventh book of *Les Confessions* is a triptych, with the Venetian story as the central panel. The pattern of events at the end forms an artistic pendant to the year preceding the embassy appointment. There is a similar sequence of situations: fresh efforts to win fame and fortune in Paris, a renewal of musical aspirations in the completion of *Les Muses galantes* corresponding to the defense of ciphered music in the earlier period, new appeals to wealthy patrons of the arts, then more intimate confessions and recollections of friends, especially Diderot, already presented in the opening pages. Rousseau has intentionally extended his story in the last part to include a range of experience full enough to stand in counterpoise to the first. These two analogous narratives frame the Venetian story perfectly with their echoing responses of theme and character. They are well matched in length, even though the one represents but a single year and the other five times as much. The historian of the soul marks the years not by their number but by their weight. The spiritual evolution of those five dreary years in Paris scarcely outweighs by its fruits that of the Parisian debuts and is measured accordingly in the autobiography. The symmetry of the two panels is accentuated by the parallelism of existence in the French capital before and after the Venetian drama. Both devices, symmetry and parallelism, contribute to produce a weary impression of the monotonous repetition of life. Once more art comes to the aid of the spirit to make the reader share the writer's burdensome sense of his "sad and slow career."[1]

As he begins to retrace his steps in life after the Venetian disaster, the author of *Les Confessions* formulates the moral of the story. He writes:

> The justice and futility of my complaints left in my soul a germ of indignation against our foolish civil institutions whereby the real public welfare and true justice are always sacrificed to some apparent order, in reality destructive of all order, that does nothing but add the sanction of public authority to the oppression of the weak and the iniquity of the strong.[2]

This passage recalls the thirst for justice and for truth illustrated throughout the seventh book and continually frustrated by the cleavage between social and natural, that is, true values. It also defines again society's moral liability for the consequences of the anomaly: the oppression of the weak by the strong who are armed with the prestige of wealth and high birth. That responsibility, which was very subtly implied in the prologue and clearly stated in the Venetian story, becomes more and more accentuated in the epilogue to prepare us for the forthcoming rebellion. More than anything else the above-cited text says explicitly and bluntly what the writer has already said figuratively and artistically everywhere in the book, namely that the violent explosion a few years later was an inevitable result of the past and particularly of the Venetian

---

[1] See *L'Allée de Silvie* in *O.C.*, Pléiade, II, 1146, line 8.

[2] *Ibid.*, I, 327:

La justice et l'inutilité de mes plaintes me laissérent dans l'ame un germe d'indignation contre nos sotes institutions civiles où le vrai bien et la véritable justice sont toujours sacrifiés à je ne sais quel ordre apparent, destructif en effet de tout ordre, et qui ne fait qu'ajouter la sanction de l'autorité publique à l'oppression du foible et à l'iniquite du fort.

affair. If we have until now entertained any doubts at all about the value of that affair to the writer, this sentence hardly leaves us the possibility of denying it in good faith, unless we reject his own candid testimony. Of course we are always free to do so, but we should hardly be justified in the present case, since his statement is convincingly illustrated in impressive scenes and confirmed by a large body of evidence, including contemporary documents like the *Venetian Letters*.

THE ALTUNA-THÉRÈSE PARADOX

Before he relives the tedious years the memorialist contrasts the disillusionment of actuality with a vision of perfection that is the very source and object of all his restless longing. What he now calls his "love of justice and of beauty" is embodied in a sublime portrait of the "virtuous Altuna" of the Venetian story. The young Rousseau dwells with him on the fashionable Saint-Honoré street shortly after the return to Paris and until the following spring. This portrait, like Zulietta's, and Montaigu's too by way of contrast, becomes part of the slowly evolving self-portrait of *Les Confessions*. The picture is full of symbolism and charged with meaning. Even the name, which in the book differs from the Spanish original, has symbolic implications. This Altuna, created by the author, is not Manuel Ignacio like the man of flesh and blood that was his model in life, but Ignacio Emmanuel de Altuna. If this is an error, as the historians tell us, it is a happy one.[3] On the other hand it may well be an indication of artistic dispositions in the writer who gradually broadens the scope of ideas suggested by the names. The given names proclaim the

---

[3] For historical research on the young Rousseau's Spanish friend see Ritter, "Jean-Jacques Rousseau (Notes diverses) III. Don Manuel-Ignacio Altuna," *Annales de la Société Jean-Jacques Rousseau*, III (1907), 190–191. See also XXII (1933), 244–245 of the *Annales*. There is also a note in *C.G.*, V, 373; see also errata in *C.G.*, VI, 384. The most important information now available is given in *O.C.*, Pléiade, I, 1405 n1 (to p. 328), and *C.C.*, II, 77.

Spanish Catholic: Ignacio; who is truly Christian: Emmanuel, "the God who is with us." The surname is too close to the Spanish "altura" meaning loftiness or summit, even the height of heaven itself, for the reader not to establish a psychological link, which is also a source of aesthetic pleasure. The portrait in *Les Confessions* is a tribute to all the virtues of mind and heart and soul. The young student's unswerving pursuit of learning is the goal of Rousseau himself for whom, we are told, the arts divorced from knowledge can never satisfy a noble nature. In this ideal Altuna of his choice, the writer astonishes us by honoring charity, chastity, and the sanctity of marriage, without a trace of his usual skepticism;[4] he extols angelic piety, miraculously reconciled with tolerance for the faith of others or their faithlessness. At last he depicts the tall, fair form, temple of a lofty spirit. Every detail suggests an ideal, one which he obviously finds unattainable in what he considers a disorderly society, but for which he affects to yearn all the more ardently. With this elusive phantom of his dreams, the hero of the book builds castles in Spain to replace those at the Charmettes, evoked in the opening pages but now vanished with the chatelaine, "mamma,"[5] and plans to retire to a remote estate beyond the Pyrenees, there to dwell in a perfect world of his own imagining. Events separate him forever from the *alter ego* of his desires. The writer concludes helplessly that the innocent intentions of the good are seldom or never accomplished. This means that the good are those with good but often unfulfilled intentions, and by this standard the indolent Rousseau counts himself among their number. His best intentions and the professed object of his quest in life are incarnate in Altuna of *Les Confessions*.

[4] The same idealism is to be found in *Emile,* where the youth's first and only love is Sophie, while, for her part, Sophie seeks a lover who will be a life-long master. Their marriage is therefore envisaged as an indissoluble bond (*O.C.,* Hachette, II, 375–376, 447).

[5] *O.C.,* Pléiade, I, 279–280.

The form that emerges from these pages of the autobiography is completely and very subjectively transfigured.
It is not merely transcribed from life, for it bears only a
vague resemblance to the historical model glimpsed in
contemporary letters. In truth, there is an abyss between
them, and the dissimilarity can hardly be explained by any
but artistic and psychological motives on the part of the
writer, certainly not by those of an apologist or by a de-
fective memory, which would have robbed the portrait of
intensity. Rather, if we compare the portrait in the book
with available documentation upon its origins in actuality,
we see once again what happens to the latter when absorbed
into the artist's world. For example, in a letter that Rousseau wrote to Madame de Warens on February 25, 1745,
only a few months after his return to Paris, he speaks
warmly enough of the "good and generous" Spanish friend
whose Parisian abode he is sharing for a time but whose
invitation to make a new life together in Spain he has no
serious thought of accepting.[6] The letter writer's expressed
plan for the present is to remain in society, to prove his
worth and win esteem in defiance of the ambassador, but
he fondly caresses his old illusion of ending his days with
"mamma." It is she who, so he alleges, still represents,
however unconvincingly, his persistent inclination to withdraw. This view is reinforced by the absence of correspondence with the young Spaniard, even though there is a dearth
in Rousseau's letters at the time of their association.[7] There

[6] *C.C.*, II, 74. The writer says: "Ce bon et généreux ami est un gentilhomme
Espagnol asses à son aise, qui me presse d'accepter un azile dans sa maison,
pour y philosopher ensemble le reste de nos jours. Quelque conformite de gouts
et de sentimens qui me lie à lui, je ne le prens point au mot, et je vous laisse à
deviner pourquoi?" Although he was staying with Altuna when this letter
was written, he apparently did not do so immediately upon his return to Paris,
since in the last of the *Venetian Letters*, dated October 11, he gave his address
as the Hôtel d'Orléans near the Palais Royal.

[7] The period in Rousseau's adult life for which the correspondence furnishes
fewest letters is 1746–1749. We have one letter by him or addressed to him
between December 11, 1745, and June 30, 1748, or, if the latter is apocryphal,
August 26, 1748. It is to Mme de Warens, significantly enough, and is dated
December 17, 1747.

are no letters at all from Altuna, and there is only one addressed by Rousseau to his friend. It is dated June 30, 1748, three years after their separation in Paris, and its authenticity has been questioned.[8] It refers regretfully to their common hopes for the future as something unrealizable, partly because the man to whom the letter is addressed is bigoted and intolerant, and the very opposite of the liberal-minded figure in the memoirs.

It makes no matter what the friendship was in actuality. In the work of art, the author uses it to express in imagery an intense and oft-recurring mood, the temptation to turn his back upon the world. He has already conveyed this mood in the story of his removal from Chambéry for the first engagement with society, and again in the pages upon his journey to Venice for the second encounter. Now, as he faces the future again in retrospect, his friend is transformed into a beatific vision of justice and order, of intellectual and spiritual discipline that beckons the distraught and demoralized individual to abandon a corrupt society and take refuge in a nostalgic dream of happiness embodying the desire for the good life in blessed seclusion. The Altuna of *Les Confessions* belongs to ivory towers or mirages that take shape in desert solitudes, far from the haunts of men. There the new Alceste longs to abide, he who would love all men and live with them, if only they were perfect. But, alas, they are no more perfect than the man who meekly relegates his most noble desires to the

[8] *C.G.*, I, 282–284; V, 373; VI, 384. See also *C.C.*, II, 377–378. The authenticity of the letter is defended by Julio de Urquijo in *Los Amigos del Pais* (San Sebastian: Impronta de la Diputacion de Giupuzcoa, 1929), pp. 7–17. It is also defended by L. J. Courtois in *Annales de la Société Jean-Jacques Rousseau*, XXII (1933), 244–245. Affirmative evidence is: (1) Altuna was in Azcoitia when the letter was written; (2) the writer sends good wishes for Altuna's forthcoming marriage which took place eleven months later; (3) there are similarities between the letter and that of August 26, 1748, from Rousseau to Mme de Warens. As Mr. Leight points out, this evidence merely shows that the possibility of the letter's authenticity cannot be excluded. However he considers it apocryphal (*C.C.*, II, 378–379). Altuna is named in an earlier letter from Rousseau to M. Duplessis at Nantes, September 14, 1745 (*ibid.*, pp. 87–88).

realm of what might have been. And so the sublime creature of his fancy vanishes beyond the bounds of France, beyond the Pyrenees to the empyrean, never to emerge into the world of things.

In the pages of his book the ideal is immediately contrasted with the sorry facts of reality. The autobiographer takes leave of Altuna and their dreams of life together to make confession of the young Rousseau's liaison with the illiterate servant, Thérèse Le Vasseur, with whom he actually did live for the rest of his life, and this will explain his later conviction that a man who thinks should not take to wife a woman who does not.[9] Only many years later did he marry her in a formal ceremony and, even then, he did so by way of a mere declaration made in the presence of witnesses. He was, incidentally, ten years older than Thérèse, who was the same age as Altuna. If, in *Les Confessions*, Altuna gives visible form to an obsession all the more enticing after the Venetian tragedy, Thérèse mirrors pathetically the desolation of actuality, attributed directly to the former secretary's disenchantment. At the beginning and end of the sordid story,[10] we are insistently reminded of his blighted ambitions in the diplomatic service, ambitions born of social circumstances and killed by the same means. It is as though the writer would convince himself and us that this liaison, like the affair with Zulietta, is an excusable attempt to find compensation in the sentiments of the heart for the enforced renunciation of a brilliant future. Again he would show the tragic consequences of

[9] *O.C.*, Hachette, II, 380 (*Emile*, V). For historical research on Thérèse Le Vasseur see *O. C.*, Pléiade, I, 1406–1407. For Rousseau's misgivings, see p. 421.

[10] *O.C.*, Pléiade, I, 329: before telling the story he contemplates the disadvantages of dependence upon others: "Ayant vu renverser dès leur naissance les projets d'ambition que l'occasion m'avoit fait former, rebuté de rentrer dans la carrière que j'avois si bien commencée, et dont neanmoins je venois d'etre expulsé ... " After the confession, p. 331, he writes: "Il me falloit à la place de l'ambition éteinte un sentiment vif qui remplit mon coeur." In the same paragraph he adds: "Il falloit que la douceur de la vie privée et domestique me dedomageât du sort brillant auquel je renonçois. Quand j'étois absolument seul mon coeur étoit vide, mais il n'en falloit qu'un pour le remplir." Cf. p. 413.

social injustice. The tableau is a masterly one, and cleverly, or insidiously as a moralist would say, presents the embittered young man as a victim, not of his weakness, which is so skillfully revealed to us, but of the social conditions to which that weakness is ascribed. Deprived of Altuna's companionship sometime about March, 1745, he returns to the left bank hotel of the period before the Venetian engagement. There he befriends the ignorant laundress and finds consolation in her, he who only two years before had objected to dining with Madame de Beuzenwal's servants. This astonishing and reciprocal affection has its origin in his defense of the girl against the indecency and brutality of their social environment. Once more society is held responsible and stands condemned, while the individual is acquitted upon the grounds of extenuating circumstances, in spite of his obvious involvement. The writer excuses his hero while accusing him. Indeed there follows an avowal of personal guilt, but it is conveyed most subtly, or from a moral viewpoint, evasively. It is Thérèse who makes confession of a previous "fault," imputed to her ignorance and the art of a seducer. Since this is precisely her present plight, the autobiographer again implicates society to exonerate the real seducer in these scenes of *Les Confessions* by contending characteristically that in Paris virginity can hardly be expected at twenty. This is the man who has just been vaunting the chastity of Altuna, but of course here he is depicting another world altogether. As a last resort to justify the young transgressor, he proffers the plea of past education: did not Madame de Warens create the void in his heart, a void all the vaster now that the lamp of his hopes is quenched in darkness? Again the writer points an accusing finger at society. Clearly he means to relieve the individual of responsibility by tracing the origins of this strange attachment to social disorder and the Venetian catastrophe, and he would enlist the sympathy or complicity of his readers by persuading them to do the same.

Yet in these very pages he remains a consummate artist true to his purpose. The literary contrast between Thérèse and Altuna is artistically admirable. It is also a valuable chapter in the story of the soul. It betrays extraordinary lucidity on Rousseau's part, not about other people but about himself and the conflict within him between the dream and life, between aspirations to purity on the one hand and the compromise of existence upon the other. If Altuna is his most noble self, the one that God or nature made, Thérèse is the creature fashioned by men, as the writer of *Emile* would say. The memorialist undeniably portrays in her, moral or immoral dispositions that answer to those of his youth at this moment in time, and that consequently betray his own inner life in the past rather than hers. Again he sees himself in the nature of his attachments.[11] Not unlike Narcissus, he contemplates himself, as he once was, in the object of his affections and manifests himself in and through her, as he had done in Zulietta. But what an immense gulf there is between the dazzling Zulietta and the pallid form of Thérèse! If in the one we saw an image of genius debased by society, in the other we see a man bereft of his genius by the same agent which has left a very ordinary mortal in its train. The sad figure of the servant in the book is meant to be a faithful reflection of the young Rousseau's spontaneous reaction to disgrace, of his inadequacy in the face of social rejection, and his complacent submission to the sordidness of life in a wretched setting. Her eyes with their remarkable animation resemble his own,[12] and his nature matches hers as they are

[11] See p. 135 *n*157, above. Rousseau admits in a note that there are exceptions but adds that in referring to these exceptions he does not intend any injurious application to his wife. He says that she is more ignorant (bornée) and more easily deceived than he had believed but insists that her pure, excellent character, quite exempt from malice, is worthy of all his esteem.

[12] The reader is reminded of Narcisse (Valère) in Rousseau's comedy who, falling in love with a portrait of himself arrayed as a woman, admires the eyes especially which, he observes in the third scene, resemble his own. He says to the servant Frontin: "Voilà d'honneur la plus jolie figure que j'aie vue de ma vie. Quels yeux, Frontin! ... je crois qu'ils ressemblent aux miens" (*O.C.,* Pléiade, II, 984).

both depicted: sensitive, timid, self-conscious, quite unprepared to cope with the injustice of life and its brutality. Exactly as in the Zulietta scenes he is the seducer and the seduced, the betrayer and the betrayed, abased by the archfiend society to its own level of abasement and then implicated in its guilt. This liaison, as eternized in *Les Confessions*, is a powerful manifestation of his own moral frailty and indolence in the wake of the Venetian tragedy, which leads him to retreat without a struggle, not only from the ideals framed in the person of Altuna but from objective reality too, and then to take refuge in the nether world of the senses and sensations. The last Venetian experiences in the master work anticipate this capitulation of the individual to equivocal social or anti-social pressures, implying a denunciation of modern society and a vindication of its supposed dupes. Just as he was led to the Padoana by Vitali, as Zulietta was brought to him by Olivet, and as Anzoletta was discovered and proposed to him by Carrio, so he and Thérèse are represented as helplessly thrown together by an evil society.[13] In all these scenes he gradually assumes the martyr's role. Each one of them plainly shows the sentimental infirmity of the youth who succumbs and of the writer who, like a father confessor, absolves him but whose absolution does not make the confession less lucid and frank. What is less obvious, perhaps by reason of its utter perfection of form, is that this portrayal of moral weakness is proof of rare artistic strength. From the carefully delineated conflict between the soul and life there gradually emerges the true shape of the soul, expressing itself pallidly in the life of a man but intensely in the work of his genius. This is particularly true of the Altuna-Thérèse paradox, which is the very crux of Rousseau's inner drama, presented here in the heart of *Les Confessions*.

[13] Rousseau finally concluded that the only defense against his moral vulnerability was to retreat to a much simpler society than the one in the midst of which he had become involved in guilt, an idea connected with the thesis of *La Morale sensitive* planned at the Hermitage (*ibid.*, I, 409).

THE AUTOBIOGRAPHER'S EPILOGUE

In the last pages of the seventh book Montaigu's victim rouses himself once more from his lethargy to challenge society to a new engagement, corresponding harmoniously with that of the inventor of ciphered music three years earlier. His creative gifts are suddenly stirred to new life by the power of musical inspiration fostered in Venice. In the summer of 1745 he completes the ballet, *Les Muses galantes*, begun before his appointment to the diplomatic service. Thus he antagonizes Rameau, who had, as we have seen, detected the real flaw in the cipher system. The eminent master's supposed jealousy of the young dilettante is used to externalize, in a single set of images, not only proof of the latter's natural talent but also evidence of society's reluctance to accept it and hostility toward the artist. In the image sequence Rameau discredits *Les Muses galantes* and, through his powerful patrons, intrigues to prevent it from being given at Versailles. He also discredits its author's work on *Les Fêtes de Ramire*, an opera of Voltaire and Rameau adapted by Rousseau to a fresh theme at the Duke de Richelieu's request, and with Voltaire's written approval.[14] The great musician is shown revising the new adaptation and then suppressing his own name on the program of the public performance rather than include Rousseau's. Although historical research tells us that Rousseau's overture to *Les Fêtes de Ramire* was not retained as he believed, his work on the opera was fairly extensive, judging by the payment he was intended to

[14] For Voltaire's letter of approval, dated December 15, 1745, and transcribed in Book VII of *Les Confessions*, see *ibid.*, I, 335–336. He excuses the flaws in his work on the grounds that it was done in a wink, although in fact it took him ten ten months; see p. 1410 *n*1 (to p. 335). Cf. *C.C.*, II, 94–95, as well as 92–93, containing Rousseau's request for permission dated December 11. The two men probably met just once, some five years later in Mme de Graffigny's salon; see Edmond Bruwaert, "Madame de Graffigny et Jean-Jacques Rousseau," *Revue hebdomadaire*, VIII (August 30, 1924), 567–592.

receive but never did.[15] Was it to conceal this work and to avoid acknowledging his collaboration with illustrious contemporaries that all three author's names were, by an unprecedented measure, omitted from the program of the December, 1745, performance, even that of the proverbially vain Voltaire? The author of *Les Confessions* thought the latter was named. This error is probably not proof that the autobiographer's misanthropy is poisoning the fruits of the emotional memory, or that the same obsession is already present in the young composer.

In contemporary correspondence Rousseau records his real vexations, at least those to which *Les Muses galantes* gave rise. Probably he was moved to resume the work partly through a desire, expressed by Altuna's guest in the February message to "mamma," to vindicate himself against the ambassador by proving that he was both more estimable and more esteemed than his former employer. He was also counting upon the ballet to relieve his extreme financial distress. Upon completing it on July 9, 1745, he wrote to Monsieur Roguin, a friend in Paris. In the letter he says that since he has had no response from Montaigu, presumably to written appeals no longer extant or to those sent to the Foreign Office, his only resource against poverty is this work, born of an afflicted, melancholy spirit. Yet he dreads the struggle to win recognition for it. In fact he is so weary of the society of men that only the law of honor can detain him among them until his debts are paid.[16] Two months later in another letter, addressed to an acquaintance in Nantes, he testifies to his dismay and consternation when he is cheated of all his hopes through Rameau's opposition to the ballet. The famous man's animosity and brutality are manifest in accusations of

---

[15] For the overture see Ritter, "Les Fêtes de Ramire," *Annales de la Société Jean-Jacques Rousseau*, I (1905), 246–259. Regarding the payment proposed for Rousseau see Charles Malherbe, *Oeuvres complètes de J.-Ph. Rameau* (Paris: Durand, 1906), pp. xxix–xlvi.

[16] *C.C.*, II, 84–85.

plagiary directed against Rousseau's work and also in various intrigues to prevent performances of it from being given at Paris and Versailles. A passage in the letter reads:

> Do you know that my ballet is finished, that I had to have it performed at Madame de la Popelinière's (Rameau's patroness), that Rameau was there? That my music put him in a bad mood, that he declares it is too good to be mine . . . and that, instead of his zealous partisan as I have always been, I shall find myself the victim of his brutality if no one intervenes . . . I should long since have been free of all this if my ballet had been given at Versailles, as was proposed: but again I found Rameau in my way, and he would also like to stop it from being given in Paris; I have never seen such intrigue and animosity in all my life. My head spins . . . I take courage just the same; the fury of my enemies has shown me my strength.[17]

The turbulent emotions, so convincingly rendered in the correspondence, are revived in *Les Confessions*, where however the writer develops more concretely the idea of the last sentence quoted above. In the book Rameau's jealousy is used to prefigure the younger man's creative powers and to persuade us that in their birth they could arouse the envy of the bulwark of French music but could win the artist no grateful remembrance in the minds of men.

Les Muses galantes is little more than a pledge of the future, as its author knew. This is one reason why he withdrew it from the Paris opera after a dress rehearsal, another reason being the opposition of his adversaries, particularly Rameau, who ten years later even asserted that it had been rejected by the theater. Yet the score of the Hesiod act, which is the only one to survive, does hold promise, in spite of its mediocrity.[18] Moreover even Voltaire, in his previously cited letter, remarks upon the rare combination of the gifts of music and verse in a single artist.

---

[17] *Ibid.*, pp. 87–88. For this quarrel see G. Cucuel, *La Pouplinière et la musique de chambre au XVIIIᵉ siècle* (Paris: Fichbacher, 1913), pp. 118–125.

[18] The promise was fulfilled in his opera of 1752, *Le Devin du village*.

If, as Rameau suspiciously observed,[19] the Italian arias in the work were superior to the French music, the reason is to be sought not in plagiary on the composer's part but in his marked preference for the music of Italy, still resounding in his ear so shortly after the Venetian experience. The poetic themes of the libretto, briefly recorded in the memoirs just before the departure for Venice, cast even more light upon his inclinations after his return and reflect the liaison with Thérèse.[20] They may be studied in the original text preserved in its entirety at Neuchâtel. The composer says quite freely in the lyrics that happiness in love may take the place of fame and greatness and even inspire the lover with the divine gift of music, won not by servile effort but by sovereign grace abounding in a pure and a tender heart. This tribute to the power of feeling is meant, not simply as a justification of the liaison, although it is that too, but rather as a reply to Rameau's attack on his untutored talents, for Rousseau was an autodidactic in music as in every sphere he entered. Another answer to criticism is to be found in his later musical writings. But the reply in *Les Confessions* is the most artistic of all. There Rameau himself becomes a symbol of his pretended victim's natural creative powers and their repudiation by the social order.

This third encounter with society is no happier than the other two, and in the autobiography the sequel is disaster, especially after a futile attempt to stage *Narcisse*. The young man entirely relinquishes the epic struggle against social decrees without even thinking yet of challenging them. He takes refuge again in the same "timidity, weak-

[19] Rameau's judgment and the statement that the work had been rejected by the Paris opera are to be found in *Erreurs sur la musique dans l'Encyclopédie* (Paris: S. Jorry, 1755), p. 41.

[20] Since the libretto refers to the liaison, and since the memorialist first discusses the work before the Venetian story, we might wonder whether the liaison dates originally from the demoralizing period following the failure of his system of ciphered music. Yet the date 1745 seems to have greater historical support: *O.C.*, Pléiade, I, 1406 *n*2 (to p. 330), and also p. cv.

ness and indolence" which he had deplored when he was first moved to compose the ballet, just before leaving for Venice. Again he suffers illness, poverty, and the subjection of his natural talents to tyrannical social demands, which are depicted as virtually suppressing the individual. Presumably some time in 1745 he accepts an appointment as secretary to Madame Dupin, her husband, and her stepson, Dupin de Francueil, to serve their intellectual ambitions at the expense of his own. Thereupon we are carried back to the dreary days of their mutual association before the Venetian tragedy.[21] The dull procession of events laboriously resumes its slow progress. Rousseau removes to the right bank to be close to his patrons and allows his life to be quite absorbed in theirs. In three years he produces only two trivial literary compositions, excluding the play *Les Prisonniers de guerre*, which he finishes at this time but which dates mostly from the glorious Venetian days. The autobiographer refers to it at this stage in his memoirs, but does so in a footnote, probably because the theme of the piece is not related to the spiritual character of the period of its completion. It hardly blends with the tone of lassitude which is the keynote of his reminiscences in these pages.

The other two works mentioned briefly in the same pages are a comedy and a poem. They help to reconstruct a little known phase in the contemporary history of the writer's inner life. Both were composed at the Dupin country home, the castle of Chenonceaux, which once belonged to Francis I and also to Diane de Poitiers. Rousseau spent the summer there in 1746 and 1747 performing chemistry experiments in Francueil's laboratory

---

[21] For the literary and scientific work that Rousseau did for Mme Dupin and Francueil see *O.C.*, Pléiade, I, 1413–1414 *nn*1 and 3 (to p. 342). At least a year before this period and probably almost immediately upon his return to Paris from Venice, while he was with Altuna, he had been pursuing his experiments in chemistry: *C.C.*, II, 74–75. The *Institutions chymiques* that resulted was published in the *Annales de la Société Jean-Jacques Rousseau*, XII (1918–1919), 1–164; XIII (1920–1921), 1–178. It was drawn up later.

and preparing the *Institutions chimiques*, ignored in the autobiography. The comedy, *L'Engagement téméraire*, dates from the autumn of 1747. It reflects the formal pattern of life in the Dupin household and also the author's readings of Marivaux, Molière, and Racine. More especially, it lays bare his spiritual dilemma at the time of composition, since his state of soul is portrayed in the person of a young lover, Dorante. Again the experience of love is used to express that of life. As a test of his devotion Dorante agrees to renounce briefly the right to manifest his sentiments. This pact is not more "temerarious" than the playwright's own "engagement," set forth in *Les Confessions*, to surrender his intellectual aspirations and place himself at the disposal of his patrons. The play is valuable as contemporary evidence of Rousseau's moods in real life. So is the poem, *L'Allée de Sylvie*, which dates exactly a year before the play,[22] and is more personal. Yet it says nothing that we may not read in the libretto of *Les Muses galantes*. It shows the writer seeking solace for his "sad and slow career" in the pleasures of the heart, which he rationalizes and defends to include them in his view of virtue and wisdom. Together the poem and the play provide a commentary on the state of mind of the Dupin secretary in real life.

These two compositions help to fill in an historical gap created by lack of correspondence at this time. We have only one letter written by Rousseau in a period of two and one half years, between December 11, 1745, and June 30 or more probably August 26, 1748. It is addressed to Madame de Warens in December, 1747, and is ominously uninformative about the writer who, so he says, desists from arousing compassion by a recital of his distress. The letter of the following August contains an illuminating passage. It reads: "I am always hoping that this period will not last forever. I wish I had some safe way of opening my heart to you about my real situation. I have the greatest

[22] For the text of the play and poem see *O.C.*, Pléiade, II, 875–931, 1146–1149. Cf. I, 1414 *nn*5 and 6 (to p. 342).

need of your advice. I exhaust my mind and my strength in efforts to behave wisely in these difficult circumstances and, if possible, to rise above this state of ignominy and poverty."[23] These shreds of evidence appear as odd pieces of our historical picture puzzle which remains incomplete and enigmatic to the very end. In fact contemporary documents do little more than foreshadow vaguely the picture of utter passivity and spiritual quiescence that appears in the text of *Les Confessions*.

Surely no more striking admission of moral chaos has ever been made than the one Rousseau makes in the book. The picture is consummated by a tragic story of children born out of wedlock and entrusted to the public hostel in both 1746 and 1748. But again the writer absolves his hero. More than twenty years after the event he traces this "fatal conduct" of his youth to the influence of acquaintances, that is to the social environment. We see the indolent dreamer meekly join the throng of "respectable people in society whose maxims bear a strong resemblance to those of knaves," but who are socially approved none the less. I quote here from *La Lettre à d'Alembert*, because Rousseau's bitterly ironical words in that piece bring out the meaning of a much misunderstood and frequently disputed passage of *Les Confessions* in the present context, which is similarly but more subtly ironical. Readers of this passage, overlooking the irony altogether, conclude that the autobiographer is being flippant to defend himself by alleging that honest people would condone such conduct as he describes.[24] The conclusion might seem justified by his allusion at this point to Francueil's conjugal infidelity and liaison with Madame d'Epinay, which might be taken as an example of analogous if not identical conduct. But in actual fact Rousseau is castigating

---

[23] *C.C.*, II, 101–102 and 108–109.

[24] See, for example, Guéhenno, *Jean-Jacques*, I, 185–186; and the editors of *O.C.*, Pléiade, I, 1416–1417. For the quotation from *La Lettre à d'Alembert* see *O.C.*, Hachette, I, 203.

his favorite scapegoat, society. All these confessions imply a new indictment of social disorder with a view to exonerating the protagonist and presenting him as a victim of the environment. From a literary point of view the corresponding disorder of the individual's life, which is none the less clearly delineated for the shift of responsibility to others, serves to portray the thraldom of the spirit and its inability to react or resist.

Yet his submission is deceptive and precarious. This is shown in his renewed relations with literary circles, including Condillac and especially Diderot. Together with Diderot he plans a periodical, *Le Persifleur*, to be composed alternately by the two friends. The first issue, sketched by Rousseau, has survived and is animated by an independence of spirit suggesting the he is about to shake off the yoke.[25] In the journal he undertakes to criticize new publications with impartiality declaring that, although like most men he combines wisdom with folly, his greatest folly is the desire to consult only reason and tell nothing but the truth. There is somewhat of a challenge in these words.

The text of *Les Confessions* gives other evidence of imminent rebellion. Early in 1749 Diderot provides the young composer with an opportunity to make another foray into the field of music, inviting him to write the articles on music for the great encyclopedia. In life the young Rousseau pours forth his enthusiasm for this new venture in a triumphant letter to Madame de Warens, dated January 27 of the same year.[26] This letter, which is all the more striking by comparison with the other of six months before telling only of illness, poverty, and degradation, contains a passage reminiscent of the autobiography at the beginning of the seventh book. The letter writer, like the memorialist, compares himself with Athenian captives who, after the defeat of Nicias at Syracuse, won their livelihood

[25] *O.C.*, Pléiade, I, 1103–1112 (text).

[26] *C.C.*, II, 112–113. For the letter to Mme Dupin mentioned below see pp. 115–116.

among their enemies by reciting songs, and in a similar
way he hopes to subdue his adversaries with encyclopedia
articles. If the articles were intended to be a new reply to
Rameau, they hardly betray the fact in their present form,
since they were edited and mitigated by Diderot's colleague
d'Alembert and consequently show none of the high
spirits reflected in the eloquence of the previously cited
message to "mamma." In a letter addressed to Madame
Dupin four months later he seems more submissive again
and even contemplates a position as counselor to the young
Chenonceaux, who was soon to be married. But by the
time the marriage took place Rousseau was already committed to his true vocation, and the "fire" with which he
felt "kindled" could no longer be controlled. The author of
Les Confessions would make us aware of this at the conclusion of the book we are discussing. There he conveys a
sense of excitement and impatience by the increasingly
rapid pace of the narrative, which contrasts sharply with
the painfully slow gait so tastefully adopted in the beginning. The feeling of agitation reaches a climax when
Diderot is suddenly imprisoned at Vincennes as a result of
his provocative pen in the *Lettre sur les aveugles* and in
earlier equally defiant pieces, beginning with the *Pensées
philosophiques* some three years before. His friend's
exultation turns to despair as the tragic story comes to an
abrupt end. Hostile society, ominously present in the pry-
ing eyes and listening walls of the opening pages, and again
in the failure of the young Rousseau's Parisian debuts,
prevails anew. The very distortions of this vision of life are
skillfully used to accentuate the sharpness of focus that
distinguishes the self-portrait.

All these situations of *Les Confessions* give lucid form to
Rousseau's youthful spirit, baffled by the inconsistency
between his innate powers and his failure to find an outlet
for them in life. Primed by years of experience, he pleads
ardently for justice and truth, which he sees violated in the
person of Diderot. He even writes a letter to Madame de

Pompadour which, by the way, has never come to light, begging her to procure the philosopher's release or have the writer imprisoned with him. In the annals of the soul, the hero's anguish has more meaning than a simple sign of friendship, however devoted. His friend's situation is not intrinsically very different from that of the happy hermit of the lazaret who had contentedly established himself for a quarantine as he might have done for a lifetime.[27] But the implications are as dissimilar as his own responses. Diderot becomes for him the symbol of natural genius in bonds fashioned by the archenemy, society. Rousseau, uniting himself with the prisoner in mind and heart and soul, is, at least in his own eyes, a bondsman of the same master. As usual, the event is impressively used in the autobiography to echo his personal prejudices and feelings. The passion for liberty, bursting forth in the violence of his protests, recalls the fine freedom of earlier days, when Diderot first befriended a young man recently come to Paris in the fond hope of startling the world with a new system of musical notation.

[27] *O.C.*, Pléiade, I, 296: " ... comme un nouveau Robinson je me mis à m'arranger pour mes vingt-un jours comme j'aurois fait pour toute ma vie."

IV

Conclusion

Rousseau's turbulent reaction to Diderot's imprisonment leaves the reader of *Les Confessions* with the distinct impression that the Venetian drama, which fostered in the soul of the protagonist a fierce indignation against existing social institutions and a consuming desire for what he calls justice, is still a living force in his inner life. Yet five years have elapsed since that tragic experience which seemed fatal to the man no less than to the artist, preceded as it was by the unhappy Parisian debuts of the musical theorist and followed by the equally unhappy debuts of the aspiring composer. The memorialist represents the early effects of all these failures in the young man's capitulation to degrading social pressures which abase, suppress, and almost efface the individual enslaved to pretentious patrons. For a time it seems as if the "snowy" years have quite enveloped the Venetian disaster in a shroud of oblivion. Nothing could be further from the truth. Once all its potency had been fully felt and realized, it had to become firmly embedded in the subconscious and completely absorbed in the soul and in time before the real fruits could take root and grow and come to the birth. This is precisely what the aftermath, recorded in the seventh book of *Les Confessions*, is intended to disclose. The reader is thereby prepared for the abundant harvest that the future was to bring forth and to which the memorialist himself refers in other books of his work.

The study of all ramifications of Rousseau's Venetian experience is a vast area of scholarship that has yet to be explored. This essay deals with only one of them. However barren the affair seemed at the moment when he left the city of the doges empty-handed and unhonored if not disgraced, and however barren it apparently remained for years, yet in the end it proved on the contrary to be one of the most powerful generative forces in his life, productive of personal enrichment as well as honor and fame. In a position of prominence, his timid, introspective nature was temporarily drawn into contact with the world of men and things. The Venetian affair became for him a fruitful source of ideas, aspirations, sentiments, and images upon which he drew freely for the great works that abundantly endowed both himself and posterity and won him a place among the immortals. This is indicated in my introduction where I recreate the memorialist's point of view as he set about writing his story. In truth, the fecundity of that memorable year in the diplomatic service did not come to an end with Rousseau's life but is still giving proof of the most exuberant vitality in the history of literature and of thought. If that year sowed the seeds of the future for him, it did the same for us too, since it contained in germ some of the most essential ingredients of modern occidental civilization, embodied in works like *Du Contrat social.*

TRUTH

Not the least among the fruits of the Venetian adventure is the one that is the theme of this essay, the book of *Les Confessions*, where the story is magnificently told. Our collation of the text with contemporary evidence has shown that the author fully realizes his professed intentions. He promised us not his apology but his portrait: the likeness of a man in all the truth of nature, and particularly his inner being. Our analysis of one of the most controversial parts of the whole autobiography has

revealed that, although the seventh book has always been
judged as apologetics, it has little value as such. This is
partly because of Rousseau's deliberate reticence in
handling the most sensational material at his disposal.
But it is mainly because of his success as a psychologist
and introspective portraitist who entrusts himself un-
reservedly and even imprudently to his readers. Quite
frankly looking at the world through his own temperament,
through his personal passions and pride and prejudices, he
records not merely events but their causes or effects within
him and his feelings about them. Morever he presents them
with utter fidelity. Our collation confirms the veracity
of his confidences. It does so in two ways. In the first
place, it shows that the modifications of objective reality
in the book falsify neither the soul nor events or any
aspect of factual experience as these are known to us
in contemporary documents. Secondly, it shows that these
modifications are not arbitrary but have been imposed upon
the writer by the literary form of his work.[1] He warns us
about them himself, but his warnings have until now been
ignored. He tells us openly that he uses events and his
whole apprehension of life, including things and beings,
to give artistic form to psychological truth and to incarnate
in a series of pictures a succession of psychic states characteristic of himself in the past and relived in the present.
All his images serve a purpose and they all serve the same
purpose. In each one of them he uses his adventures and
companions "to acquaint us fully with J.-J. Rousseau."
Thus the great situations and characters of the book give
diaphanous form to his own shifting moods and frame of
mind or heart, until all encounters of every kind become
an integral part of the self-portrait.

  We have observed that retouching is most noticeable
in his use of other people to incarnate various facets of
his own life and personality. Some of these blend smoothly

----

[1] I have discussed these matters in my article, "In Defense of Literature,"
to appear shortly in *Studi Francesi*.

into the self-portrait, while others are used as elements of contrast to betoken a hostile society and its effects upon the protagonist. For example, the ambassador is magnified into a symbol of social injustice, while Rameau and Mesdames de Beuzenwal and Dupin represent the tyranny of arbitrary social decrees. On the other hand, the sympathetic figures, each personifying some aspect of the writer's character, merge quite naturally into the many-sided and composite "portrait of the artist as a young man," for he is persuaded that everyone's true inclinations are shown in the nature of his attachments. These sympathetic characters are Zulietta, Altuna, Thérèse, and Diderot. In them he contemplates a reflection of himself with which he is as enchanted as Narcissus, significantly the theme of his first literary work, as we have remarked. This narcissism remains characteristic of him. He sees his future vocation and martyrdom in Diderot, the rejection of his genius in Zulietta, and in Thérèse the man whose genius has apparently deserted him and left him a prey to his weakness on the morrow of the Venetian catastrophe. Our analysis shows that these portraits are not historically and objectively true, any more than our own view of life and men can be entirely impersonal and impassive; much less so, since Rousseau does not have the pretension of presenting anyone else but himself, and he has given us fair warning more than once. The creatures of flesh and blood have undergone a certain transubstantiation and are intensified and deftly adapted to his theme to which they lend themselves perfectly, echoing his own tastes and inclinations.

To justify himself, he has the precedent of all great artists, whatever media they employ, including his Venetian and French contemporaries, who have left us such a rich legacy of plastic images and whose integrity we should hardly think of questioning, although they too portray the world reflected through their own temperaments. Consider the freedom of Guardi, for instance. What art lover in Venice has not stood entranced before his "San Giorgio" in the Venetian academy and then walked away into the dazzling light to search out the artist's viewpoint and gaze across at the tiny island in the sun? Only the most prosaic among us would reproach the artist for that trans-figuration of the actual by the magic alchemy of art and accuse him of lying to us on the canvas. Do we not rather delight in the privilege of being admitted into the artist's world, of participating in his creative vision and responding to it? This is what we must do in the case of all art, if it is true that the artist's function, whether he is a writer, painter, or musician, is to give new sight to the blind, to open the ears of the deaf, and to unseal the lips of the dumb. If we are willfully deaf-mute and blind, if we refuse to see, to heed, and to respond, then we can hardly be enlightened. In other words, in studying the imagery and eloquence of Rousseau's literary work we must be prepared for, and welcome, a transmutation of actuality conceived to in-carnate spiritual truth, such as he announces quite bluntly in the Zulietta scenes. Once we understand that he is not transcribing the facts of existence but is giving symbolic form to the life of the soul as he proposed, then we also realize that he has achieved his object in *Les Confessions*. The problems of art and truth are inseparable.

ART

We may now conclude that art for Rousseau is, as he says in one of our epigraphs, a means for the manifestation of truth in the classical sense. It is therefore not surprising that the quality of his book which our collation has most frequently brought to light is its realism, external as well as internal. But it is surprising that there are so few discrep-ancies between a work of art and the records of its source material in life. After all, the two bodies of writings deal primarily with a different order of things, the one circum-stantial and the other psychological. They have a completely dissimilar object and employ quite divergent modes of expression, the book being a literary and artistic transposition of the historical fact. We find ourselves wondering how it is that, in a creative work existing in its own right, quite apart from the incidents inspiring it, the author has not distorted actuality in order to communicate his personal view of life in a suitable, harmonious form. How has he succeeded in giving us an imaginative vision of events and in transforming them to suit his purpose without deforming them? How has he contrived to enhance historical truth and to throw it into relief through the resources of his art without ever sacrificing it? The solution of these questions is to be sought in the peculiar quality of his imagination, and also in the specific modes of artistic composition that he uses to impose form upon the stream of existence. Both methods must be clear to us if we are to understand how he reconciles artistic intentions with the pursuit of reality, as we have seen him do over and over again, throughout the Venetian story.

The historical authenticity of a book depends more upon the imagination than upon other artistic processes. If the writer gives free play to his creative imagination and power of invention, then the historical validity of his work might be dubious except as evidence of his romanticism. If, on the other hand, he engages the intuitive imagination, then far from distorting facts and events he extorts from them all their fullness of meaning without substantially altering them except to organize, synthetize, simplify, or even transpose them in the interests of spiritual truth and aesthetic harmony. Which form of imagination does Rousseau adopt in *Les Confessions*? His theme is admittedly romantic in conception, and his inspiration is partly so. Like the great romantics he uses the sentimental memory to recapture situations that serve as a point of departure for his work, with the result that the greatest scenes are the most deeply emotional moments in life. Nevertheless his method is not entirely romantic, as our collation has proved. In exploring these emotional crises and presenting them to the reader, he curbs his imagination and has recourse to intuition and the most penetrating and ruthless introspection to discover the truth within himself and to reveal it in the ordinary things of life. This can be verified even in the most dramatic scenes, like the love scene with Zulietta with its almost cynically realistic overtones. He spares neither his vanity nor pride, dignity nor modesty. In fact, morally speaking his shamelessness is shocking and unsavory, at the same time as it is essential to the examination of conscience he proposes. This is why the dictum of *Emile* that "the lies of modesty are worth more than truth" could not be applied by the autobiographer. The latter shows the same love for what is true whether it makes him look ridiculous or heroic, virtuous or vicious. This is so in spite of all his alibis, repudiations, and excuses. The fact that he absolves himself at the expense of society and is convinced that confession of his faults is better than innocence itself does not make the confession any the less searching and genuine. His predilection for truth was fostered first by Plutarch and possibly also by his Calvinist conscience and by his varied religious experience. But probably it was also an intrinsic part of his nature, inducing him to expose his soul, with all its taints and blemishes, to the eyes of the whole world. Whatever its origin, his intellectualized method leads him to unfold not merely the impassioned impulse that was the mainspring of his inspiration but his whole personality and innermost being as well: *intus, et in cute* (inside and beneath the skin), as he says in the epigraph of *Les Confessions*. Furthermore, though he promises to reveal no man but himself, as usual he gives much more than he promises. He goes far beyond the eccentricities of his own individuality and, without exposing any other individual, he plumbs such depths within himself that he reaches the universal and eternal traits of human nature. In other words, his disciplined imagination transforms his romantic theme into a classical one, whose truth transcends both time and place. The same faculty safeguards in addition the historical integrity of his work.

The historical authenticity of *Les Confessions* is not marred either by the writer's need to impose form upon the phenomena of existence for the sake of achieving orderly arrangement, proportion, balance, and harmonious design. Again our collation has brought this out in a remarkable way. In the seventh book, for instance, we have seen him use such contrivances as rhythmic alternation of themes, paradox and parallelism, symmetry, antithesis and artistic synthesis, without significantly altering the facts and circumstances that are transposed from life. There is, we have observed, alternation between the dreamer's aspiration to solitude and the active man's desire for social prestige, and again between ambition and submission; there is paradox inherent in the position of an alien in the French diplomatic service; there is parallelism and contrast too between the "heroic" Venetian scenes and ensuing mortifications; there is antithesis between the ambassador and his secretary; there are at least two, and perhaps even three, fine examples of artistic synthesis, that is, the fusing of a host of actual events into a single composite one, for instance in the message to Naples, possibly in the Veronese story, and certainly in the farewell scene at the palace of the legation. In the same farewell scene the matter of the account has been eliminated and then transposed into other contexts, so that the last scene at the embassy might not be falsified psychologically. These devices, designed to satisfy the demands of art and inner reality, have been exhaustively illustrated in our analysis and explain the minor discrepancies between the memoirs and objective documents. They are found in all art of every period, including classical and romantic. Strangely enough, Rousseau's peculiar mode of applying them is classical rather than romantic, and that is why they do not affect the historical validity of his narrative. For example, his use of antithesis, paradox, and parallelism is utterly simple and natural. The reader must stop and reflect in order to become aware of it at all. It is therefore not in the least studied, self-conscious, or exaggerated, as in the case of romantic writers. The same may be said of his symbolic use of persons, situations, and especially love scenes to lay bare his soul. Although he does not present them objectively, he never forcibly projects his moods into them, but rather quite naturally sees in the persons or things depicted the causes or effects of his moods, which are consequently evoked by them. Thus visible forms in the book correspond perfectly to the truth he has promised to divulge, a truth so deeply subjective that it finally becomes human in its range and realism. Once he has expressed it, he says no more.

The economy, or rather austerity, of his narration is singularly observable in the Venetian story and brought to our attention by a comparison with archives. He might have included a great many startling tales that history has brought to light. Instead he has mitigated the embassy scandals in his account of them. If, as we strongly suspect, he has done so for the sake of psychological verisimilitude, the advantages are far from being exclusively psychological. They are artistic too. The imagery is saved from ostentation. In fact, throughout *Les Confessions*, it remains unobtrusive and discreetly employed, showing rare self-control on the part of the writer. This artistic mastery and literary discipline often serve to discover the moral anarchy of the man which is all the more striking for that. Consequently, spiritual being, either well ordered or in a state of disarray, is not in the least overshadowed by superfluous or sensational details. Rather it is completely or, if you prefer, immodestly disclosed in the great moments of the writer's life, which are also those of our "human condition," even if we are unwilling to admit it.

Rousseau's success in reconciling art and inner truth, and in respecting the objective facts of history too, is therefore fully demonstrated in our study of art and truth in the Venetian story. Like the great classics, and especially Plutarch, he has taken his material from life without essentially altering it to fulfill his avowed intention, which is to manifest a man to the world in a work of enduring artistic and spiritual significance. Although the man is himself and the initial purpose is therefore romantic, if a real romantic had written the story, any resemblance it might have borne to the circumstances inspiring it would have been purely coincidental. As it is, the story is very close to history.

Yet the circumstantial validity of the narrative does not determine or explain the essential truth and beauty of the work, or unveil the secrets of the writer's prestige. Nor does the relative truth or falsehood of his ideas, which are often mere platitudes or brilliant restatements of contemporary prejudices. The real virtue of his work consists in his use of ideas, events, and personalities for the perfect portrayal of life in himself and in humanity, of states of soul that are totally and eternally true. From a series of tableaux there gradually evolves an authentic picture of himself of such compelling truth and absolute conviction that he has become more familiar to us than any other modern writer and is known to the world by his Christian name, like Dante and the great artists of the past. This is not merely because he solicits our complicity in his work, for every true artist does that. It is because he is intimately known to us. It is also because, so exhaustively and relentlessly does he probe into his spirit that he even probes into our own and reveals us to ourselves. His nature is ours, whether we recognize it and like it or not. He reveals what every man conceals carefully, not only from others but even from his own consciousness. By Rousseau we gain a fuller knowledge of ourselves and of mankind "and grow wise at the expense of the dead."

But the satisfaction he provides is not only spiritual and intellectual. It is also literary and aesthetic and comes from a classical correspondence between his vision of character and its cloak of imagery, its embodiment in persons, places, and events. Once we become conscious of the universal truth of the book and the perfect choice of forms to envelop that truth, their utter suitability to perform their predetermined function, then we begin to realize the beauty of the work. We do so even if the truth it conveys be distasteful and unflattering in itself, for the beauty of art and literature does not depend upon beauty of subject, except for those who lack maturity of judgment. In the same way, we may respond to a portrait of that other great precursor among autobiographers, Rembrandt, and find it true and beautiful, even though the sitter be ugly and no more true or false than the rest of us. It is the brilliance of the portraiture that holds us spellbound as we muse, and leaves us richer for the musing: the consummate artistry with which the human spirit is clothed in visible form and given life and animation, so that its most abstract modes of being appear as living shapes for our pleasure and enlightenment. To experience this we need not be enamored of the artist as a man, any more than Boileau was enamored of monsters when he wrote the opening lines of the greatest canto of his *Art poétique*. There he says that any serpent or ugly monster may delight the eye in the imitations of art, for the pleasing craftsmanship of a refined and sensitive brush —he might have said pen—can make the most hideous things attractive or charming, and therefore beautiful.[2] The same may be said of the flaws and faults of men as depicted in the great works of portraiture.

It is not inappropriate to quote the *Art poétique* here. We have seen that Rousseau's expressed literary profession of faith is classical. At the end of the fourth book of *Emile*,

---

[2] Boileau, *Art poétique*, Chant III, vss. 1–4:

Il n'est point de serpent ni de monstre odieux,
Qui, par l'art imité, ne puisse plaire aux yeux:
D'un pinceau délicat l'artifice agréable
Du plus affreux objet fait un objet aimable.

Rousseau read Boileau at the Charmettes in 1736; see *C.C.*, I, 38.

the writer, full of admiration for Plutarch and the ancients, declares that the judgments of taste, which are really a function of common sense, can be cultivated only by the study of nature and of truth. The external aspects of both in *Les Confessions* are in fact flawless reflections of the soul, and this is precisely what critics have failed to see in the past. Rousseau's artistic realism and depth of psychology, which are unique in the eighteenth century, are clearly part of the legacy of classicism. This bequest is visible at once in his clear, simple, natural utterance, and in his controlled use of the traditional resources of art to enhance the eminently human substance of his work. He combines the universal truth and formal simplicity of the classics, of whom he is the heir, with the intimately personal themes and emotional inspiration of the romantics, whom he foreshadows,[3] so that the great conflict of two opposing ideologies and art forms is centered in his person, in his thought, and in his work. The impact is most powerfully felt in this book, where the theme is quite frankly the object of Pascal's anathema, the self. But the writer soothes his classical literary conscience by his reverence for the truth, as he humbles himself before it and then pursues it through the mysterious domain of the soul. The perfect likeness he captures and fixes faithfully for all eternity is the portrait bust that survives the city where it took its form. And the city? It is Geneva, and Paris, and others too, but it is also Venezia.

[3] It is significant that, in other books of *Les Confessions* where Rousseau draws attention to his creative (romantic) imagination, either in life or literary work, he always makes a lucid distinction between the "ideal" world and the "real" world: see, for example, Books IV and IX (*O.C.*, Pléiade, I, 159–160; 427–428).

Selected Bibliography*

PRIMARY SOURCES

Archives of French residents in Italy and other parts of Europe from which a few documents have been published, e.g., archives of the French consulate in Venice studied by Cérésole, *q.v.*, and letters from Rousseau to the Count de Castellane, French ambassador to Constantinople published by Monglond, *q.v.*, and Bernard Gagnebin, v. P.-P. Plan, *Table de la Correspondance générale de J.-J. Rousseau avec une introduction et des lettres inédites* (Geneva: E. Droz, 1953).

Archives du ministère des affaires étrangères à Paris. Correspondance politique de Venise. Vols. 205, 206, 207. Correspondance politique de Vienne. Vol. 238.

Archives nationales (Fonds Marine). Dépêches du ministère de la Marine.

Archivio di stato di Venezia. Collegio. Esposizioni principi, Filza no 129.

———. Senato (segreta). Corti. Filza no 261, 262.

Encyclopédie, ou dictionnaire raisonné des sciences des arts et des métiers par une société de gens de lettres. Mis en ordre et publié par M. Diderot; et quant à la partie mathématique par M. d'Alembert. 36 vols. 3rd ed. Geneva: Pellet, 1778–1779.

Jean-Jacques Rousseau à Venise (1743–1744) raconté par lui-même. Paris: Maurice Glomeau, 1920.

Rousseau, J.-J. *Correspondance complète.* Edited by R. A. Leigh. Vols. I, II. Geneva: Institut et Musée Voltaire, 1965.

———. *Correspondance générale.* Edited by T. Dufour. 20 vols. Paris: Armand Colin, 1924–1934.

———. "Institutions chymiques." Published and annotated by Maurice Gautier. *Annales de la Société Jean-Jacques Rousseau,* XII (1918–1919), 1–164; XIII (1920–1921), 1–178.

---

* This bibliography does not include general studies of Rousseau's life and work even though they may touch upon the historical facts of his sojourn in Venice and may therefore be mentioned in footnotes.

———. *Oeuvres complètes*. 13 vols. Paris: Hachette, 1885–1898.

———. *Oeuvres complètes*. (Bibliothèque de la Pléiade.) Vols. I, II, III. Paris: Gallimard, 1959–1964.

CRITICAL STUDIES

MONOGRAPHS

Baschet, Armand. *Les Archives de Venise*. Histoire de la Chancellerie secrète. Le Sénat, le Cabinet des ministres, le Conseil des Dix et les Inquisiteurs d'Etat dans leurs rapports avec la France, Paris, 1870.

Bertaut, Jules. *L'Italie vue par les français*. Paris: Librairie des *Annales Jean-Jacques Rousseau* [1913].

Broome, J. H. *Rousseau: A Study of his Thought*. London: Edward Arnold Ltd., 1963.

De Brosses, Charles. *Lettres familières (écrites d'Italie en 1739 et 1740)*. 2 vols. Paris: Perrin, 1885.

Buchner, Margaret Louise. *A Contribution to the Study of the Descriptive Technique of Jean-Jacques Rousseau*. Baltimore: The Johns Hopkins Press. London: Oxford University Press, 1937.

Cérésole, Victor, and De Saussure, Théodore. *J.-J. Rousseau à Venise, 1743–1744 (Notes et documents recueillis par Victor Cérésole ... , publiés par Théodore de Saussure)*. Geneva and Paris, 1885.

Comisso, G. *Les Agents secrets de Venise au XVIIIe siècle* (1705–1797). Translated by L. Leluc. Paris: Bernard Grasset, 1944.

Culcasi, Carlo. *Gli influssi italiani nell'opera di G. G. Rousseau*. Rome: Società editrice Dante Alighieri [1907].

Diehl, Charles. *Une République patricienne: Venise*. Paris: Flammarion, 1935.

Duhamel, Georges. *Les Confessions sans pénitence, suivi de trois autres entretiens: Rousseau, Montesquieu, Descartes, Pascal*. Paris: Plon, 1945.

Duparc, M. Pierre. *Recueil des instructions données aux ambassadeurs et ministres de France, XXVI (Venise)*. Paris: Editions du Centre National de la Recherche Scientifique (Gap, impr. de L. Jean), 1958.

Eigeldinger, Marc. *Jean-Jacques Rousseau et la réalité de l'imaginaire*. Neuchâtel: La Baconnière [1962].

Faguet, Emile. *Rousseau artiste*. Paris: Société française d'Imprimerie et de Librairie, n.d. [le bicentenaire].

Firpo, Luigi. *Rousseau in Italia*. Turin: E. di filosofia, 1963.

François, Alexis. *Nouvelles informations sur le séjour de J.-J. Rousseau à Venise en 1743–1744*. (Unpublished study of 1920, the results of which have been utilized by Jean-Daniel Candaux, editor of the *Dépêches de Venise*, in *O.C.*, Pléiade, III [1964].)

Grimsley, Ronald. *Jean-Jacques Rousseau, A Study in Self-Awareness*. Cardiff: University of Wales Press, 1961.

Grosclaude, P. *Jean-Jacques Rousseau à Lyon*. Lyons: Rey, 1933.

Guéhenno, Jean. *Jean-Jacques*. (Part I: *En marge des Confessions*.) 2 vols. Paris: Gallimard, 1962.

Guyot, Charly. *Plaidoyer pour Thérèse Levasseur*. Neuchâtel: Ides et Calendes [1962].

Hazlitt, William Carew. *The Venetian Republic, Its Rise, Its Growth and Its Fall, 421–1797*. (Vol. II: 1423–1797.) 2 vols. London: Black, 1900.

Jansen, Albert. *Jean-Jacques Rousseau als musiker*. Berlin: Reimer, 1884.

Lathon, Lucien. *Jean-Jacques Rousseau et le Valais*. Lauzanne, 1953.

Maurois, André. *L'Art d'écrire*. (Contains about fifteen pages on J.-J. Rousseau.)

Mignon, Maurice. *Les Affinités intellectuelles de l'Italie et de la France*. (Section on *Jean-Jacques Rousseau et l'Italie*.) Paris: Hachette, 1923.

Monnier, Philippe. *Venise au XVIIIᵉ siècle*. Paris: Perrin, 1907.

De Montaigu, Auguste. *Démêlés du comte de Montaigu, ambassadeur à Venise, et de son secrétaire Jean-Jacques Rousseau (1743–1744)*. Paris: Plon, 1904.

Mugnier, François. *Madame de Warens et J.-J. Rousseau: étude historique et critique*. Paris: Calmann-Lévy, 1891.

Nourrison, Paul. *J.-J. Rousseau et Robinson Crusoe*. Paris: Spes, 1931.

Peyre, Henri. *Literature and Sincerity*. New Haven and London: Yale University Press, 1963.

Plan, Pierre-Paul. *Table de la correspondance générale de J.-J. Rousseau avec une introduction et des lettres inédites*. Geneva: Bernard Gagnebin, E. Droz, 1953.

De Saint-Pierre, J. H. Bernardin. *La vie et les ouvrages de Jean-Jacques Rousseau*. Edited by Maurice Souriau. Paris: Cornély, 1907.

De Saussure, Hermine. *Rousseau et les manuscrits des Confessions*. Paris: E. de Boccard, 1958.

Souchon, Joseph. *Correspondance diplomatique du Comte de Montaigu, ambassadeur à Venise (1743–1749)*. Paris: Plon, 1915.

Tiersot, Julien. *J.-J. Rousseau*. (Les Maîtres de la Musique.) Paris: Alcan, 1920.

De Urquijo, Julio. *Menendez Pelayo y los Caballeritos de Azcoitia*. San Sebastian: Imprenta de Martin y Mena, 1925.

———. *Los Amigos del Pais*. Vol. I. San Sebastian: Imprenta de la Diputacion de Giupzcoa, 1929. (Reprinted from the *Revista internacional de los Estudios vascos*.)

Vaussard, Maurice. *La Vie quotidienne en Italie au XVIIIe siècle*. Paris: Hachette, 1959.

Voltaire. *Oeuvres complètes*. XXVI, 29–35 (*Lettre de monsieur de Voltaire à monsieur Hume* and *Notes sur la lettre de monsieur de Voltaire à monsieur Hume*). Paris: Garnier, 1877–1885.

Wilkinson, Spenser. *The Defence of Piedmont 1724–1748. A Prelude to the Study of Napoleon*. Oxford: Oxford University Press, 1924.

Wilmotte, Maurice. *Etudes critiques sur la tradition littéraire en France*. I, 215 (section on "Jean-Jacques Rousseau et les origines du romantisme") (Paris: H. Champion, 1909).

ARTICLES

Bruwaert, Edmond. "Madame de Graffigny et Jean-Jacques Rousseau," *Revue hebdomadaire*, VIII (August 30, 1924), 567–592.

Candaux, Jean-Daniel. "Jean-Jacques Rousseau à Gênes et à Venise. Quelques documents nouveaux," *Studi Francesi*, VIII (May–August, 1964), 250–254.

———. "J.-J. Rousseau au secours des prisonniers de guerre," *Journal de Genève*, May 10, 1963, p. 8.

Courtois, L. J. "Considérations sur la chronologie de la vie et des oeuvres de Jean-Jacques Rousseau," *Bulletin de l'Institut national genevois*, XLV (1922), 143–172.

————. "Chronologie critique de la vie et des oeuvres de Jean-Jacques Rousseau," *Annales de la Société Jean-Jacques Rousseau*, XV (1923), 1–240.

————. "Compte rendu de Julio de Urquijo, *Los Amigos del Pais*," *Annales de la Société Jean-Jacques Rousseau*, XXII (1933), 244–245.

————. "Notes de chronologie rousseauiste," *Mélanges d'histoire littéraire et de philologie offerts à Bernard Bouvier*. Geneva: Editions Sonor, 1920, pp. 117–123.

Derche, Roland. "Autour du séjour de J.-J. Rousseau à Venise. La politique et le caractère du Comte de Montaigu, ambassadeur à Venise de 1743–1749," *Annales de l'Université de Grenoble* (Nouvelle Série), Section Lettres-Droit, I (1924), 131–176.

Dufour, Théophile. "Compte rendu de Auguste de Montaigu, *Démêlés ... ,*" *Annales de la Société Jean-Jacques Rousseau*, I (1905), 305.

Ellis, M. B. "In Defense of Literature," *Studi Francesi* (in press).

Faugère, Prosper. "Jean-Jacques Rousseau à Venise," *Le Correspondant*, CLI (June 10, 1888), 813–833; (June 25, 1888), 1061–1076.

De Feytaud, Jacques. "Variations: De Montaigne à Proust," *Bulletin de la Société des Amis de Montaigne*, No. 31, pp. 20–32.

Gribble, Francis. "Rousseau at Venice," *The Fortnightly Review*, LXXXIV (New Series, July–December, 1908), 318–326.

Leclerc, Hélène. "Jean-Jacques Rousseau (1712–1778): La musique et le théâtre," *Revue d'histoire du théâtre*, XV, 160–165.

Monglond, André. "Rousseau, secrétaire de M. de Montaigu, ambassadeur de France à Venise, documents inédits," *Annales de la Société Jean-Jacques Rousseau*, XXIV (1935), 39–78.

————. "Lettres inédites de l'abbé de Bernis, ambassadeur à Venise, au comte Des Alleurs, ambassadeur à Constantinople," *Revue d'histoire diplomatique*, LII (1938), 353–376.

Montigny, Maurice. "Jean-Jacques Rousseau secrétaire d'ambassade," *Revue des études historiques*, XCV (January–March, 1929), 419–434.

Outrey, Amédée. "Un épisode de la querelle de Voltaire et de Jean-Jacques Rousseau: La publication des 'Lettres de Venise,' " *Revue d'histoire diplomatique*, LXIV (1950), 3–36.

Pendley, R. L. "Rousseau's *Epître à M. Bordes:* an unpublished variant," *Romanic Review*, XLII (December, 1961), 256–260.

Plan, Pierre-Paul. "J.-J. Rousseau à Venise (4 septembre 1743–22 août 1744). Documents inédits," *Mercure de France*, CLXVII (November 1, 1923), 577–606.

Pritchett, V. S. "Intermingling of the real and the dream in Rousseau's *Confessions*," *New Statesman and Nation*, XLVI (July 11, 1953), 50–51.

Ritter, Eugène. "Nouvelles recherches sur les *Confessions* et la correspondance de J. J. Rousseau," *Zeitschrift für neufranzosische Sprache und Literatur*, Band II, Heft 3. Opole: Franck, 1880, pp. 305–344.

————. "Les Fêtes de Ramire," *Annales de la Société Jean-Jacques Rousseau*, I (1905), 246–259. (Publication from MS of the original work in the Bibliothèque Nationale; see also *O.C.*, Pléiade, II, 1084–1091.)

————. "Jean-Jacques Rousseau (Notes diverses) III. Don Manuel-Ignacio Altuna," *Annales de la Société Jean-Jacques Rousseau*, III (1907), 175–221 (especially 190–191 on Don Manuel-Ignacio Altuna).

————. "Jean-Jacques Rousseau. Notes et recherches," *Annales de la Société Jean-Jacques Rousseau*, XI (1916–1917), 1–235 (especially 30–57: Part VI entitled "La Seconde Partie des *Confessions*".)

Saint-Marc-Girardin. "Du séjour de J.-J. Rousseau à Venise," *Journal des Débats*, January 22, 1862, pp. 3–4.

Starobinski, Jean. "Jean-Jacques Rousseau et les pouvoirs de l'imaginaire," *Revue internationale de philosophie*, XIV, 43–67.

Taylor, E. "Rousseau's Conception of Music," *Music and Letters*, XXX (July, 1949), 231–242.

Temmer, M. J. "Art and love in the Confessions of Jean-Jacques Rousseau," *Publications of the Modern Language Association of America*, LXXIII (June, 1958), 215–220.

Voisine, Jacques. "Quelques personnages secondaires des *Confessions*," *Revue des sciences humaines*, No. CX, pp. 221–237.

Index

Actuality: Rousseau's attitude toward, 19–21; illustration of his attitude, *passim. See also* Truth

Aesthetic pleasure: value of, x, xi, 23, 132, 155, 182–183

Aesthetics: concept in *Emile*, 15, 182–183. *See also* Art

Alary, Abbé Pierre-Joseph: Rousseau's letter (February 22, 1744), 65, 66, 94; Montaigu's letter (August 15, 1744), 100–107, 108–110; Rousseau's letter (August 8, 1744), 110–111

Albano (Francesco Albani), 125

Alceste (character in *Le Misanthrope* by Molière) and Rousseau, 27, 59, 157

Alembert, Jean Le Rond d', 168, 170

Allegory: in the Venetian story, 33; in "The Zulietta Parable," 132, 135–137. *See also* Symbolism

Alternation of themes. *See* Antithesis; Contrast; Symmetry

Altuna, Manuel Ignacio: his studies, 15*n*; Rousseau's friendship for, 120, 132; portrait of, 154–158; mentioned, 163, 166*n*, 175

Analogy: use of, 89–91. *See also* Symmetry

Annecy, 37

Antithesis: of individual and society, 26; in "The Rousseau-Montaigu Antithesis," 34, 48, 49; in the "Anticlimax," 89, 91; mentioned, 179, 180

Anzoletta, 131, 133, 136, 161

Apologetics: role of, x, 2, 3, 22, 156, 173; and psychology, 91, 114; sacrificed, 99, 100, 107

Apothecary's bill, 108, 112 and *n*, 117, 142

Architecture: Rousseau's attitude to, 126–127

Art. *See* Aesthetic pleasure; Aesthetics; Allegory; Alternation of themes; Analogy; Antithesis; Artistic transposition; Arts; Classicism; Composite scenes; Contrast; Creativity; Crescendo; Detail; Discipline; Drama; Imagery; Imagination; Irony; Lyricism; Melodrama; Method; Parable; Paradox; Parallelism; Personification; Picturesqueness; Poetic license; Realism; Restraint; Romanticism; Selection; Sensationalism; Simplicity; Symbolism; Symmetry; Synthesis

Art and truth: theme of this study, 4–5, 7; "Problems of Art and Truth," 14–24

Artistic transposition, 28, 123

Arts: evil effects of, 10; must not be divorced from truth, 15; basis of Rousseau's French "patriotism," 58; plastic arts and Rousseau, 125–126 and *n*144. *See also* Architecture; Music; Painting

Ascension Day: in Venice, 128 and *n*

Asceticism, vii

191

Aspasia: Zulietta and Mme de Warens compared with, 133, 134*n*
Austrian Succession, War of, 38, 49, 58, 64, 77–87

Barberina Campanini (ballerina): 63*n*, 63–64, 65, 66, 67
Barcarolles, 120, 121 and *n*, 122, 124
Barjac (valet de chambre of the Cardinal de Fleury), 34, 35 and *n*
Beuzenwal, Baroness de (née Catherine Bielinska): Rousseau meets, 29; role of, 30, 31, 175; withdraws patronage, 144
Binis, Abbé de: his position, 48; copies Olivet memorial, 69, 70*n*; interim secretary, 109–110 and *n*; mentioned, 105
Biography: and historical fact, 1; of Rousseau in Venice, 5; Rousseau's ideas on, 17–18; in Plutarch, 107; mentioned, vii. *See also* Plutarch
Boileau-Despréaux: and Rousseau, 182 and *n*
Bordes, Charles: epistles to, 27, 122
Borromeans, 127, 140
Bourbons: debt to Jean-Jacques, 77–87; and Erizzo, 97; mentioned, 88, 90
Brenta: Montaigu's villa, 90, 104 and *n*, 126, 127
Broglie, Marchioness de (daughter of the Baroness de Beuzenwal), 29

Calvinism: in Rousseau, 123, 178
Canaletto, Antonio: ignored by Rousseau, 125 and *n*
Carlo of the Maltese Cross (Montaigu's "gentleman"), 89, 92, 93*n*, 94*n*
Carnival: and Rousseau, 59, 68 and *n*; in Venice, 68*n*, 128
Carriera, Rosalba. *See* Rosalba
Carrio(n), François-Xavier de (secretary to Spanish ambassador): Rousseau's friendship for, 120, 132; meets Zulietta, 130; and Anzoletta, 131, 161

Casanova, Jacopo: compared with Rousseau, 59, 92, 100
Castellane, Michel-Ange, Count de (ambassador to Constantinople): Rousseau's letters to, 84 and *n*
Cattaneo, Giovanni di (Prussian agent in Venice): and Barberina, 63, 64; his daughter, 129
Cattolica, 82
Chambéry: Rousseau's journey from, 25; Follau dismissed there, 35; Rousseau's visit to, 37 and *n*, 38, 108
Charles VII (of the Two Sicilies), 82
Charmettes: idyll of, 4; Rousseau leaves, 26; Rousseau visits, 37; mentioned, 155
Chemistry: and Rousseau, 166 and *n*, 167
Chenonceaux, castle of: Rousseau's sojourn at, 166
Chenonceaux, Dupin de: Rousseau's tutorship of, 30; his marriage, 170
Choiseul, Etienne-François, Duke de: his offer to Rousseau, 150 and *n*
Chronology: in *Les Confessions*, 87, 119, 137. *See also* Time
Ciphers: Rousseau's use of: 42 and *n*, 43, 52 and *n*; Montaigu's avoidance of, 42, 43; Montaigu's suspicions about, 103 and *n*, 107, 112, 117
Classicism: of Rousseau's literary doctrine, 15, 182–183; in hairdresser story, 77; in account of scandals, 92; of expression, 99–100, 107, 179; of imagination, 178–179; conclusion, 183. *See also* Discipline; Imagination; Realism; Restraint; Simplicity; Truth
Composite scenes: in "The Veronese Theme," 67; in the "War Story," 85; in "Crisis," 113–114; mentioned, 179. *See also* Synthesis
Condillac, Abbé Etienne Bonnot, de: friendship with Rousseau, 169
Constantinople (Istanbul), 50, 84
Contrast: in "The Rousseau-Montaigu Antithesis," 33–57, 151; between heroism and pettiness,

Contrast: (cont.)
107; in "The Zulietta Parable," 132; in "The Altuna-Thérèse Paradox," 160–161. See also Antithesis
Creativity in Les Confessions, 19–20, 21. See also Art
Crescendo: in banquet scene, 115–116, 117

Dante Alighieri, 25, 81
Dénouement: in "The Veronese Theme," 62–65; in "Anticlimax," 87ff.
Detail: Rousseau's treatment of, 100–107
Diderot, Denis: Rousseau's friendship with, 28, 29, 169; symbolism in Rousseau's presentation of, 171, 172, 175
Discipline, artistic: in "Art or Apologetics?" 100; in "The Ambassador's Letter," 100–102; in "A Crisis," 114; in Thérèse scenes, 161; mentioned, 150, 180
Doge, 11n, 62, 67
Doges' palace, 127
Dorante: in Les Prisonniers de guerre, 58; in L'Engagement téméraire, 167
Drama: in "The Olivet Theme," 74; in "War Story," 77, 87; in "Crisis," 107, 113; in banquet scene, 116; in "The Zulietta Parable," 138
Duhamel, Georges, 16
Dupin, Claude, 30
Dupin, Mme (née Louise-Marie-Madeleine de Fontaine): Rousseau meets, 29; role of, 30, 31, 138, 175; employs Rousseau, 166 and n, 167; Rousseau's letter (May 22, 1749), 170

Embassy secretary. See Secretary to the embassy
Emile: in Emile et Sophie, 18 and n; and the "Contract," 31
Emile and Sophie: their counterparts in Venice, 11 and n

Epinay, Mme Louise-Florence-Pétronille Lalive d', x, 78n, 168
Erizzo, Nicolò (Andrea): Montaigu's counsellor, 52n, 53, 56; on diplomatic immunity, 93 and n, 96 and n; maligned by Montaigu, 97 and n

Flaubert, Gustave, 138
Follau: Rousseau's predecessor in Montaigu's service, 34, 35
Francueil, Charles-Louis, Dupin de: Rousseau's connection with, 30 and n, 138; employs Rousseau, 166 and n; and Mme d'Epinay, 168
Frari Convent (Venice), 92
Frederick II (of Prussia): and Barberina, 63, 64
Froullay, Charles-François, Count de (Montaigu's predecessor and father of Mme de Créqui), 46n, 134n, 147

Gages, José Buenaventura Thierry Du Mont, Count de (Spanish commander), 78, 79, 79n, 81, 82
Galuppi, Baldassare (Venetian composer), 121, 125
Geneva, 25, 141 and n, 183
Genoa: Rousseau's quarantine at, 39
Gesvres, François-Joachim-Bernard Potier, Duke de, 60, 61n
Goethe, 127
Gondola: in "The Veronese Theme," 59; in "The Olivet Theme," 68, 70; Rousseau deprived of, 90, 102
Graffigny, Mme de: and meeting of Rousseau and Voltaire, 162n
Grimani, Girolamo: report on diplomatic privileges, 93
Grimani, Michele (Venetian impresario): in "The Veronese Theme," 60, 61, 62, 66; and Les Muses galantes, 67, 120
Grimani, Pietro (doge), 62, 67
Guardi, Francesco, 125 and n, 175–176

Henry: engaged by Montaigu, 108, 109, 110; succeeds Rousseau, 145–146 and n

History: not always impartial, 3; of Rousseau in Venice, 6; Rousseau's ideas on, 17 and *n*; memoirs as, 24

Hôpital, Paul-François, Marquis Galluccio de l' (ambassador to Naples): in "War Story," 77–87

Idealism: of Altuna portrait, 154–158

Imagery: in Rousseau's works, viii–ix; in the Venetian story, 12; and Rousseau's method in the memoirs, 21–23; in the presentation of Montaigu, 36, 44–45, 48, 49, 56, 113, 115, 149–151; in the account of the journey to Venice, 36–40; in "The Veronese Theme," 67; in "The Olivet Theme," 74; in "A Matter of Justice," 77; in "War Story," 86–87; in the account of the Modena incident, 104; in "A Crisis," 113, 115; in the account of the return journey to Paris, 140–143; in the Altuna portrait, 157; conclusion on the purpose of, 174; quality of, 180, 182

Imagination: quality of, 67–68, 74, 92, 99, 100, 177–179

Inquisition (Venetian): 9, 55 and *n*, 57; spy reports, 92 and *n*, 93 and *n*, 96, 101; reply to Montaigu's memorial against Rousseau, 117

Irony, 104, 168

Jacob (Bible): and Jean-Jacques, 151

John, Lord: in *Emile*, 11 and *n*, 120*n*

Jonville, François Chaillon de (French Minister at Genoa), 40 and *n*

Julie: and Zulietta, 10–11, 138

Justice: representations of the search for, 25–26, 31, 75, 88, 140, 142–143, 144–145, 150, 153 and *n*, 157

Kolly, Jean-Pierre (banker), 146

Lazaret: Rousseau's quarantine in, 39, 40, 171

Le Blond, Jean: replaced by Rousseau, 45, 50; royal secretary for the

Italian language, 46*n*, 46–47; his dissensions with Montaigu, 47 and *n*; timidity of, 57; and Olivet affair, 70 and *n*, 71, 106; and embassy household, 95 and *n*; Rousseau's letter (October 29, 1743), 102*n*; accused by Montaigu of espionage, 103; replaced by de Binis, 110*n*; in banquet scene, 116, 137; receives reply to Montaigu's memorial against Rousseau, 117, 118 and *n*; Rousseau's friendship with, 119; daughters of, 129; reports on embassy scandals, 146 and *n*; relieves Montaigu, 147; mentioned, 112*n*, 132

Le Vasseur, Thérèse: 132*n*; symbolic portrait of, 158–161, 175

Lies: confused with art, 20. *See also* Art

Lista, 92 and *n*, 94*n*

Lobkowitz, Jean-Georges-Christian, Prince (Austrian commander): 78–79, 81; his offensive, 82 and *n*

Lombardy, 82

Longhena, Baldassare (architect of the Querini palace and Santa Maria della Salute church in Venice), 41

Longhi, Pietro, 125 and *n*

Love, theme of: in "The Zulietta Parable," 128–140; in portrait of Thérèse, 158–161; in *L'Engagement téméraire*, 167

Lucy, Miss (in *Emile*), 11, 128

Luxembourg, Charles-François-Frédéric de Montmorency-Luxembourg, Duke de, 136*n*

Luxembourg, Madeleine-Angélique de, 136*n*

Lyons: Rousseau visits en route to Paris, 26–27; en route to Venice, 37 and *n*, 38; on return from Paris, 142–143

Lyricism: lacking?, 41; in "The Veronese Theme," 68; mentioned, 127

Mackensie, James Stuart: and Barberina, 63, 64

v

Mari, Don Estéban Mari Centurion, Marquis (Spanish ambassador): Montaigu's colleague, 49, 53, 54 and *nn*, 55*n*; their friendship, 57, 93*n*; and Barberina, 64; Rousseau's appeal to, 83, 113; his love of gaming, 101 and *n*

Marivaux, Pierre de: retouches *Narcisse*, 29; Rousseau's reading of, 167

Marseilles: Rousseau embarks there, 37*n*, 39

Mediterranean: Rousseau crosses, 37

Melodrama: excluded from memoirs, 115. *See also* Sensationalism

Memorials (to Venetian senate): written and transcribed by Rousseau, 51–52; Montaigu's memorial of January 2, 1744, 54; senate's replies, 55 and *n*; requesting theatre loges (September 9, 1743), 46 and *n*, 60; regarding Olivet (July 7, 1744), 69; against smuggling (June 5, 1744), 98; regarding diplomatic immunity (June 8, 1744), 98–99; regarding Froullay's effects (July 31, 1744), 105, 109 and *n*; Montaigu's against Rousseau (August 31, 1744), 116, 117

Memory (in Rousseau as autobiographer): lapses of?, 2, 156; quality of, 21–23

Mendicanti orphans, 120, 121, 122, 123, 124 and *n*

Metaphor. *See* Allegory; Imagery; Symbolsm

Metastasio, Pietro-Buonaventura, 10

Method, artistic, 21–23. *See also* Art

Modena, Duke of: at Velletri, 79; his proposed visit to Montaigu, 90, 100, 103–104, 116

Molière: Rousseau's reading of, 167. *See also* Alceste

Money: as a theme of art, 113; Rousseau's indifference to, 136 and *n*

Montaigne, Michel de: universality of, 15; his predilection for Plutarch, 17; compared with Rousseau, 18

Montaigu, Chevalier de: persuades Rousseau to go to Venice, 34; Rousseau's appeal to him on April 30, 1744, 66 and *n*, 94; in Venice, 76; victim of lawsuit, 76–77; role in Rousseau's dismissal, 108, 111–112

Montaigu, Mme de (wife of Count de Montaigu): Rousseau's letter of November 23, 1743, 46 and *n*, 61–62, 142; arrives in Venice, October, 1744, 76

Montaigu, Pierre-François, Count de: connections with Barjac, 34; engages Rousseau, 34; Rousseau's portrait of, 36; their early relations, 42–45; his avoidance of ciphers and faltering dictation, 42, 52–53, 106; his relations with Le Blond, 46–47 and 47*n*; his influence on Rousseau, 48, 67, 68; his peculiarities in correspondence, 53; his naïveté and lack of diplomacy, 54–56 and *nn*; his "rage" and "blindness," 56 and *n*: his role in the Veronese affair, 59, 62; invites Barberina, 63–64; dissensions over Veronese affair?, 65–66, 67; his role in the Olivet affair, 71, 72–73; Rousseau's letter to him, 72; dissensions over Olivet affair, 73 and *n*; receives letters regarding the hairdresser's note, 75–77; his absence on Saturdays, 77; dissensions over the Naples affair?, 83–84; signs dispatches to court, 83–84; engages Henry, 83, 108, 109, 110; his hostility to Rousseau, 88, 91; engages Vitali, 89, 92; his villa, 72–73, 90, 126–127; excludes Rousseau from proposed banquet, 90, 103; and gaming, 93; and diplomatic immunity, 93, 96–99; accuses former secretary of smuggling, 94 and *n*; his attitudes toward smugglers, 95 and *n*; blames Le Blond for disorders, 95; his ambiguous dispatches, 96–97; discredits Erizzo, 97 and *n*; his letter

Montaigu, (cont.)
  to Alary, 100–107, 108–110; discharges Rousseau, 107–110; his account with Rousseau, 108, 112 and *n*, 117, 142; submits memorial against Rousseau, 117–118 and *n*; discredits Rousseau, 141; discredits himself, 145–149. *See also* Imagery; Symbolism
Mont Cenis: road, 37–38
Moralist: Rousseau as, vii, viii
Morality: not the theme of this study, 6; mentioned, 102–107, 159, 178
Music: influence on Rousseau, 10, 119–128; of language and style, 22, 23, 115–116, 117; ciphered, 26, 28, 30, 171; Rousseau as composer of, 30, 162–165 and *nn*

Naples: correspondence with, 50; in "War Story," 78–86
Napoleon Bonaparte: in Venice, 54
Narcissus: theme in Rousseau, 14, 135, 160 and *n*, 175
Neutrality of Venice, 49, 54 and *nn*

Olivet, Captain: in "The Olivet Theme," 68–74; introduces Zulietta, 129, 137, 161; mentioned, 87, 100, 105–106
Opera: 120, 121, 122, 123, 124; Rousseau's, 164*n*

Padoana, 129, 131, 136 and *n*, 161
Painting: Rousseau's attitude toward, 125, 126
Parable: in "The Zulietta Parable," 128–140
Paradox: in Rousseau's nature, 25–26, 87; as a leitmotiv, 26; of Rousseau's position, 48; mentioned, 179, 180. *See also* Antithesis
Parallelism: in "Anticlimax," 89–91; of prologue and epilogue, 152–153; mentioned, 179, 180
Paris: Rousseau's journey there from Savoy, 25, 26, 37, 143; his débuts there, 28–32; his departure from

Paris for Venice, 36; his return to Paris, 143; mentioned, 183
Parisot, Gabriel: Rousseau's epistle to, 27, 29; and Godfroi, 135 and *n*, 160 and *n*
Pascal, Blaise, 183
Patizel, Jean-Charles (vice-consul): in "The Olivet Theme," 69, 70; credited with Olivet report and inquiry, 71, 90; his role in both, 72, 73, 116, 117
Pericles: and Aspasia, 133
Persecution mania: origins in Rousseau, 9 and *n*; in autobiographer, 23, 163, 170; in hero of autobiography?, 115, 163
Personification: in prologue, 31; in Montaigu, 36, 44–45, 48, 49, 56, 113, 115, 149, 151; in "The Altuna-Thérèse Paradox," 154–161; in the epilogue, 164–165; mentioned, 175. *See also* Altuna; Diderot; Montaigu; Thérèse; Zulietta
Petrarch (Francesco Petrarca), 10
Piati, Count: dismissed for smuggling, 89, 95 and *n*, 96*n*
Picturesqueness: use of, 23; sacrificed in pages on music, 121–122, 123, 124. *See also* Imagery; Method
Piedmont, 38, 82
Pio, Prince (Austrian ambassador), 44 and *n*
Plastic arts: and Rousseau, 125–126, 126*n*. *See also* Arts
Plutarch: Rousseau's model and ideal, 17, 100, 107, 178, 181, 183; Plutarch's object, 18; his classical ideal, 100
Poems composed by Rousseau, 133–134
Poetic license: in Rousseau, 19
Police action: at embassy, 93, 94, 95 and *n*, 96, 97, 98–99
Political ideas (of Rousseau): origins in Venice, 11, 153, 173
Pompadour, Jeanne-Antoinette Le Normand d'Etiolles, Marchioness de: Rousseau's lost letter to, 170–171

Portraiture: in Rousseau's memoirs, 15–16, 19, 23–24, 42, 107, 124, 174, 175; takes precedence over apologetics, 114, 149, 173; Rousseau's success in, 173–176; Rousseau's compared with Rembrandt's, 182. *See also* Altuna; Imagery; Montaigu; Thérèse; Zulietta

Positivism: and literature, 2–4, 16–21, 23–24, 84–85

Poveglia (Poveggia), 69 and *n*, 72

Proust, Marcel: compared with Rousseau, 21

Purpose: of Rousseau in his memoirs, 14–24 *passim*

Racine, Jean: Rousseau's reading of, 167

Rameau, Jean-Philippe (French composer): his objection to ciphered music, 28; mentioned, 138; attitude toward Rousseau, 162–165; his role in Rousseau's memoirs, 162–165, 175; Rousseau's reply to, 170

Raphael Sanzio: Rousseau's appreciation of, 125

Realism, in Rousseau's art, 14–24; in treatment of embassy scandals, 99–100; in "The Zulietta Parable," 128–140; mentioned, 176, 178, 183. *See also* Classicism; Discipline; Restraint; Truth

Rembrandt van Rijn: compared with Rousseau, 182

Restraint: in Rousseau's account of embassy scandals, 92–94, 95, 99–100; quality of Rousseau's narration brought out by comparison with Montaigu's letter, 102–103; illustrated in crisis, 114; in sequel, 149

Richelieu, Duke de (Marshall of France): and *Les Fêtes de Ramire*, 162; mentioned, 138

Ridotto (Venetian casino), 101 and *n*

Rimini, 82

Robinson Crusoe: the new, 39

Roguin, Daniel: Rousseau's letter of February 7, 1744, 65 and *n*; his letter of December 9, 1745, 163

Romagna, 82

Romanticism: in "The Veronese Theme," 68; Rousseau a precursor of, 127; and treatment of the courtesan, 134; in Rousseau's theme, 177–179, 181; mentioned, 183 and *n*. *See also* Imagination; Lyricism

Rosalba Carriera, 124*n*, 126 and *n*

Rousseau, Isaac (Jean-Jacques' father): letter to, 50*n*; in Nyon, 142; mentioned, 151

Saint Mark's Basilica, 127

Saint Mark's Square, 40

St. Petersburg (Leningrad), 50–51

Salary: Rousseau's and Montaigu's, 35 and *n*; Rousseau not paid, 89–90, 101, 116, 142, 148–149; Montaigu not paid, 148–149

Salavin (character in Duhamel's novels): compared with Rousseau, 16

Santa Maria della Salute Church (Venice), 41

Savoy: Rousseau leaves, 25; his journey from Savoy to Paris, 26, 37; Rousseau visits, 38; Rousseau's studies there, 50 and *n*

Scandals (at embassy): 89–99, 145–149; mitigated by Rousseau, 99–100, 149, 180

Sculpture: Rousseau's attitude toward, 125, 126

Secretary to embassy: Rousseau's position, 45–49, 45*n*, 46*nn*, 148

Selection (in narration): in "War Story," 80–86

Self-justification. *See* Apologetics

Self-portrait. *See* Narcissus; Portraiture

Senate (Venetian): communication with, 47, 51 and *n*; its servility, 54–55. *See also* Memorials

Sensationalism: avoided by Rousseau, 100, 114, 174, 180. *See also* Melodrama

Simplicity (of narration): in "A Matter of Justice," 77; brought out by a comparison with Montaigu's letter, 100–107. *See also* Classicism

Simplon: route to Italy, 38, 141

Sion (capital of Valais): Rousseau visits, 141 and *n*, 145

Slavonians: in Olivet affair, 69, 70*n*

Smuggling: Follau (Rousseau's predecessor) dismissed for, 35; Rousseau accused of, 94 and *n*, 118; at embassy, 95–99 and *nn*; Henry (Rousseau's successor) arrested for, 146

Society: conflict with individual, 26, 36, 58, 91, 107, 115, 151, 159–161, 162–166, 169; symbolic representation of, 31, 44–45, 113; role in "The Zulietta Parable, 128–140. *See also* Imagery; Symbolism

Socrates: as quoted in Book V of Plato's *Republic*, 113; as quoted in Book IX of Plato's *Republic*, 126; and Aspasia, 133

Sophie (character in *Emile*): and Miss Lucy, 11 and *n*; compared with Zulietta, 136 and *n*; idealism of, 155*n*

Spies: in Venice, 9, 50; in "War Story," 77–87; and embassy scandals, 92–93 and *nn*, 94*n*, 101; in Montaigu's service, 95

Symbolism: in Rousseau's method, 21–24, 180; in his account of the journey to Paris, 26–27; in the story of his débuts, 31; in his portrait of Montaigu, 36, 44–45, 49, 56, 113, 147, 149–150, 151, 175; in his account of the journey to Venice, 36–40; in "The Rousseau-Montaigu Antithesis," 49; in his portrayal of the desire for justice, 74–77, 142–143; in the crisis, 114–115; in the scene of Le Blond's banquet, 116, 117; in the framework of the Venetian story, 119; in "The Zulietta Parable," 128–140; in the account of the return journey to Paris, 140–143; in "The

Altuna–Thérèse Paradox," 154–161; in the image of Diderot, 171; mentioned, 174–175

Symmetry: in Book VII, 25, 152–153, 162, 179

Synthesis (in composite scenes): in "The Veronese Theme," 67; in "War Story," 85–86; in the crisis, 113; mentioned, 179. *See also* Composite scenes

Tasso, Torquato, 10, 121–122 and *n*

Taste, xi, 67, 183. *See also* Aesthetic pleasure

Technique. *See* Art; Method

Theatre: Rousseau's love of, 59; in "The Veronese Theme," 59–68; and *Les Muses galantes*, 67, 120, 164; Rousseau deprived of loge, 89

Tiepolo, Giovanni Battista (Giambattista): ignored by Rousseau, 125 and *n*

Time: in *Les Confessions*, 25, 152; in "The Veronese Theme" and "War Story," 65, 86; in the crisis, 113; and the duration of the Venetian engagement, 143–144

Titian (Tiziano Vecellio): ignored by Rousseau, 125

Transposition. *See* Artistic transposition

Truth: and Rousseauist criticism, x; and this study, 1–8; distinctions of psychological, spiritual, or moral truth, philiosophical truth, and circumstantial truth, 14–24; illustrated in "Prologue," 24–32; in "The Venetian Story," 33–151; in the "Epilogue," 152–171 *passim*; conclusions on, 173–176

Turin: Rousseau's journey from Annecy, 37; embassy correspondence with, 50; Rousseau's studies there, 50 and *n*; Rousseau's sojourn there, 120

Tuscany: 82

Valère (Rousseau's Narcissus), 135. *See also* Narcissus

Velletri: Austrian reverses at, 79, 81, 83; Rousseau's role at, 79–87, 103, 104

Veracity. *See* Truth

Verisimilitude: in "The Veronese Theme," 68; Rousseau sacrifices sensationalism for, 99–100, 114

Veronese, Anne-Marie-Coralline, 59, 61, 63, 66–67

Veronese, Charles-Antonine (actor): 59, 60, 62; and Barberina, 64–65, 66

Versailles: dispatches, 50–56, 81–83, 97–99; Rameau stops Rousseau's opera from being performed there, 162, 164

Vienna: correspondence with, 50; secret bulletins from, 54, 56, 78, 79, 79*n*, 83; orders Lobkowitz to advance, 82

Vincennes: vision of, 7–8, 138, 153–154; Diderot imprisioned there, 170

Vitali, Domenico ("gentleman" in Montaigu's service), 89, 92, 93*n*, 161

Warens, Mme de (née Françoise-Louise de La Tour): Rousseau leaves her, 26, 27; he goes to visit her, 37 and *n*, his letter of October 5, 1743, 41 and *n*; his letter of February 25, 1745, 145*n*, 156 and *n*, 163; lost to Rousseau, 155; his letter of December 17, 1747, 156*n*, 167; his letter of August 26, 1748, 156*n*, 157*n*, 167–168; his letter of January 27, 1749, 169; mentioned, 20*n*, 46, 136*n*

Zanetto (Jean-Jacques in "The Zulietta Parable"), 128–140

Zulietta: and Vincennes, 7, 138; and Julie, 10–11, 138; and de Brosses, 124*n*; symbolism of, 128–140; compared with Thérèse, 158, 160; realism in Rousseau's presentation of, 178; mentioned, 175

Zustiniani (Venetian impresario), 59–68

Zustiniani, Almoro: refuses to take action on Montaigu's memorial against Rousseau, 118

Rousseau's Venetian Story:

An Essay upon Art and Truth in *Les Confessions*

by Madeleine B. Ellis

designer: Edward King
typesetter: Baltimore Type and Composition Corporation
typefaces: Binny (text) and Deepdene (display)
printer: The Maple Press Co.
paper: Warren's Olde Style Wove
binder: Moore & Co., Inc.
cover material: Columbia Lynbrook Vellum

Lightning Source UK Ltd.
Milton Keynes UK
UKHW021035030120
356267UK00010B/827/P

9 781421 434476